Michael C. Thomsett
Stock Market Math

Michael C. Thomsett
Stock Market Math

Essential Formulas for Selecting
and Managing Stock and Risk

ISBN 978-1-5015-1581-1
e-ISBN (PDF) 978-1-5015-0742-7
e-ISBN (EPUB) 978-1-5015-0736-6

Library of Congress Cataloging-in-Publication Data
A CIP catalog record for this book has been applied for at the Library of Congress.

Bibliographic information published by the Deutsche Nationalbibliothek
The Deutsche Nationalbibliothek lists this publication in the Deutsche Nationalbibliografie;
detailed bibliographic data are available on the Internet at http://dnb.dnb.de.

© 2017 Michael C. Thomsett
Published by Walter de Gruyter Inc., Boston/Berlin
Printing and binding: CPI books GmbH, Leck
♾ Printed on acid-free paper
Printed in Germany

www.degruyter.com

Advance Praise

I am thankful Michael Thomsett was able to bring clarity and context to investment performance measurement. It's a foreign language to so many but vital to our ability to save and retire. A great read for anyone interested in the markets.

–Jakob Rohn, Co-founder,
WorkN and Board Member, Delta Data

Michael Thomsett has done it again—simple, practical and actionable advice for anyone seeking to understand how the stock market works while limiting downside risk. An essential encyclopedia of market knowledge presented with simplicity. A "must read" reference for anyone interested in the stock market.

–Gary Lynch, CEO & Founder,
The Risk Project, LLC

Score another winner for Michael Thomsett! In *Stock Market Math* the education guru is back, big time—providing us with the blueprints for success. With a writing style that is at once comprehensive, yet easy to understand, Thomsett's trademark ability to "make the complex simple" is on full display. Filled with wisdom, Thomsett's book tackles concepts that will appeal to investors at every level. Beginners will enjoy his breakdown of investment building blocks, while seasoned pros will appreciate his deeper dive into the material. Yet all will take something away from Thomsett's book—and that something is the ability to take higher and more consistent profits out of the stock market.

–Michael Stoppa, Author,
The Options Alchemist

Contents

Introduction

Investing requires mastery of certain mathematical tasks and calculations. However, knowing the formula is not enough; you also need to be able to understand and therefore express that formula in terms enabling you to quantify risk. This book is designed for that purpose.

Who this Book is For

This book is designed for a spectrum of investors, from novices to seasoned professionals. Its purpose is to summarize in a single text the limited number of calculations everyone needs to be a better-informed investor. This involves three broad areas where calculations need to be made. First is the *basic investment calculation* involving your portfolio, the computation of yield and return you need to make in order to judge your success. Because you hold investments for varying amounts of time, it is essential to develop a method of uniformity, so that your calculations are truly comparable and consistent. Second is the range of *calculations used by corporations* in computing their profitability, cash flow, and use of capital. As an investor, you need to understand these calculations so that you will be able to track corporate reporting and outcome of operations. Third is a broad range of *stock analysis* which is the means for picking one company over another. This occurs in two separate ways: fundamental analysis and technical analysis. The fundamentals are the financial reports and the study of them, and technical analysis involves a study of a stock's price trends.

This book is set up to break down the many calculations every investor needs into logical chapters, and to present this information in context. Most people will agree that investment success is more likely to occur when your information is sound. Not only do you need solid information to know when or if to buy or sell; you also need to utilize intelligent formulas and tests in order to make informed judgments.

Why Things Seem Harder than They Are

There are many different ways of calculating "profit" or "yield" or "return." No singular answer can be applied in every case, since these terms have different meanings. For example, a business net *profit* and a dividend *yield* are quite different than an investment's *return* on capital. The definition for each is separate and distinct.

Figuring out the mathematical aspects of investing money does not have to be difficult or confusing. It is made so by: (a) the variation between and unnecessary complexity of statements you receive from brokerage firms and mutual funds; (b) the cross-use of terms meaning approximately the same thing; and (c) the often-misleading claims made in ads about the kinds of rates you can expect to earn (or would have earned if only you had invested five years ago).

In fact, none of these calculations are complicated at all.

How This Book Helps

This book attempts to sort through the confusion and present you with a methodical, logical, and easy way to figure out the answers and interpret what you read and hear. Each chapter tackles a specific topic and provides examples of formulas in context. The topics covered include *returns* (return on investment and return on capital, which are not always the same); how leverage changes the equation; calculations over the long-term; adjusting for what corporations report versus what is accurate; fundamental and technical analysis of stocks; and tax-related calculations.

Remember this above all else: No investment calculation is so complex that you cannot figure it out. As long as you clarify what you are interested in calculating, you can crunch the numbers. At times, knowing the right questions to ask is the most difficult part of the calculation; this book shows you how to go through that initial phase and to articulate and compare risks. For those cases where the calculations can be complicated, which is most of them in the real world, the book provides you with the needed Excel solution, so that you can have your computer do the calculation. It is up to you to figure out what the solution means.

It helps to think of investment calculations in practical terms. Figuring out profitability is a method for keeping track of your investing success. Any series of calculations performed to figure out a percentage of profit has context and purpose. Unfortunately, it becomes complicated if and when you compare two different investments without making sure they are expressed on the same basis. It is all too easy to arrive at a distorted answer. For example, if you own two stocks and make a net profit of 10% on both, that is an identical outcome—if you owned those stocks for exactly the same time period. But if you owned one stock for exactly one year and another for two years, the outcome is not the same. If it takes two years to earn 10%, that is an average of only 5% per year—or half as high as earning the same percentage in half the time.

Many adjustments similar to this need to be made in order to arrive at an *accurate* outcome. This is one of the major problems you face in any type of financial study. Companies selling products make the issue more complex in the way they express numbers, often exaggerating outcomes so that what they offer seems more attractive than it is, or more profitable than it has been. Math is easily manipulated with the selective use of some, but not all, data.

When it comes to calculating outcomes, you are on your own. You need to take the information you are presented (or project into the future based on your assumptions) and take steps to make sure you are using like-kind comparisons. Many investors make mistakes in their assumptions and basis for comparison, leading to low quality information. If nothing else, improving the quality and consistency of calculations is going to help you to become a better informed and more confidant investor. In figuring out likely outcomes, one purpose is to evaluate risks—not only of specific products but also in comparing one to another—and this is an essential step in making any decision. So, the more reliable your calculations, the more likely you are to make *informed* decisions.

Using the Internet to Help Solve Problems

With the Internet, you can find a mind-numbing array of free information, much of it useful in performing investment calculations. Many websites will be included in this book to help you make calculations when necessary. But be aware that the Internet also offers a lot of misleading information and advice. One of the problems with free information is deciding which has value and which is useless. It makes sense to evaluate information as broadly as possible in your initial research and before making decisions; but once you have narrowed down your sources and determined which kinds of calculations are valid and useful, you may discover that the large volume of free online advice is mostly useless in the decision-making process. A lot of it is promotional, and the useful information can be divided into a limited number of categories, including four primary areas:

1. *Information and background.* One of the most amazing things about the Internet is the availability of free articles and tutorials on a vast number of topics. Many of these are provided on sites trying to attract subscribers, and that is not a problem. You can read the articles and follow links without being obligated to signing up, and the Internet is an excellent place to get a free financial education.

2. *Definitions.* Another good use of the Internet is for gaining an understanding of terms. The investment arena has thousands of specialized words and phrases that have specific meaning and importance and for the novice. This can be overwhelming, but the Internet makes it simple to look up words. For example, www.investopedia.com is a free site with many articles and tutorials and an excellent dictionary.

3. *Free quotes and research.* Numerous sites provide free market information. Most allow you to look up stock symbols by company name, and then find the current stock price and chart. You can also link directly to companies and view annual and quarterly reports online. This is very valuable. Before the Internet, investors depended on stockbrokers and mail to send away for annual reports, and often had to wait several weeks before receiving them.

4. *Calculators.* If you do an online search for some of the more complicated formulas, such as mortgage amortization for example, you will find dozens of free calculators to simplify the process. For these more complicated formulas, you don't need to know how to figure them out (although you will be better informed if you understand the basic reasoning for the calculation), you can simply go to one of the free sites and punch in the raw numbers. Where necessary, you can use the Excel solutions provided in this book to find your answers.

Chapter 1
Rates of Return on Investment:
What Goes In, What Comes Out

Even the most seemingly easy calculation can become quite involved.

For example, what is your "return?" If you invest money in a stock or mutual fund, you need to be able to figure out and compare the outcome; but as the following explanation demonstrates, there are many different versions of "return" and you need to be sure that when comparing two different outcomes, you are making a like-kind study. Otherwise, you can be deceived into drawing an inaccurate conclusion. And *accuracy* is one of your goals in going to the trouble of drawing conclusions in the first place.

The "return" you earn on your investments can be calculated and expressed in many different ways. This is why comparisons are difficult. If you read the promotional literature from mutual funds and other investments, the return provided in the brochure could be one of many different results.

This is why you need to be able to make distinctions between return on *investment* and return on *capital*. Your *investment return* is supposed to be calculated based on the amount of cash you put into a program, fund or stock. Most investors use "return on investment" in some form to calculate and compare. The *return on capital* is usually different and is used by corporations to judge operations. To further complicate matters, "capital" is not the same as "capitalization" so corporate return calculations can be difficult to compare. Return on capital normally means capital stock. Capitalization is the total funding of an organization, including stock and long-term debt.

A business model of return on capital may present problems, however. Accuracy is in question when the calculation is based on a fixed value, such as capital, versus current value of the same investment:

> The book value of capital might not be a good measure of the capital invested in existing investments, since it reflects the historical cost of these assets and accounting decisions on depreciation. [i]

The same question may be applied to capital invested in shares of stock. Since capital is a fixed value at a particular time (purchase of shares), but current valuation may be significantly different, the potential impact makes this calculation one that has to be considered with some qualification, perhaps even discounting its value in favor of return on cash invested.

DOI 10.1515/9781501507427-001

Judging the Outcome – What Did You Expect?

All investment calculations are done in order to monitor and judge standards. You enter an investment with a basic assumption, an expectation about the return you will be able to earn. In order to judge the quality of the investment and the reliability of your own decision-making capabilities, you will need to figure out how well the investment has performed. In so doing, you need to be aware of some popular mistakes investors make, including the following primary points:

1. *The purchase price is the assumed "starting point."* It is easy to fall into the trap of believing that the point of entry to any investment is the price-based starting point. Thus, the assumption is that price must move upward from that point. No consideration is given to the realistic point of view that price at any given moment is part of a continuum of ever-evolving upward and downward price point movements. As a starting point, price does not always move upward. In other words, profitability is not the only possible outcome; the rate of return may also be negative.

2. *A bail-out and/or profit goal is not specifically set.* Too often, an investment is made with little or no idea about the individual's expectations. Do you plan to double your money? Triple it? Or would you settle for a 15% return in one year? Equally important is the question of possible loss. How much of your investment capital will you lose before you cut your losses and close it out? If you don't set goals and identify the point at which you will close the investment, then you cannot know what to expect.

3. *The specific method of calculation is not understood.* It is difficult to determine whether an investment is a success of a failure unless you also know how the return calculation is made. This includes making clear distinctions between different types of returns, the effect of taxes, and how the formula works. All of these variables have to be considered with consistent comparisons between them or they will not be valid.

4. *The time factor is not considered.* You need to take into account the reality that not all investments produce a return in the same amount of time. The longer the time required (thus, the longer your capital is tied up), the less effective the return. So, the time element is crucial to the comparison of one investment to another.

5. *The varying degrees of risk are not taken into account.* Risk is not only as aspect of opportunity; it is really the reverse effect of it as well. Opportunity for profit and risk of loss are two sides of the same coin. This relationship between the two attributes is shown in Figure 1.1.

opportunity and risk

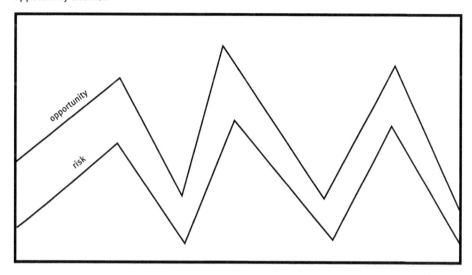

Figure 1.1: Relationship between opportunity for profit and risk of loss.

Even so, some investors focus only on the "heads" side and invest with the profitability potential in mind, but have made no plans for the contingency of loss. How much could you lose? How much can you afford? What criteria do you use to judge risk? For example, investors who base their decisions on fundamental analysis look for revenue and earnings trends and compute working capital and capitalization ratios. Investors who prefer to trust in technical signals check price volatility and look at charts. Whatever method you use, a decision should be assessed based on potential for both profit and loss.

6. *Comparisons fail to include compound rates of return versus simple return.* In calculating return, there are numerous methods in use and are explained later in this chapter. However, in estimating future returns, it is important to know whether you will earn a simple return or a compound rate of return. For example, if you are buying shares of a mutual fund, will you take your dividends and other distributions in cash? If so, your annual returns will be simple. But if you instruct the fund to reinvest your earnings, your investment account balance will increase each time you earn; the result is a compound rate of return and over many years it will be much higher. So without deciding in advance how your mutual fund or stock earnings are going to be treated, it is not possible to set profit goals for yourself.

The important determination of an investment's success has two components. First is the decision as to how much profit you expect (or how much loss you will accept). Second is deciding how to compute the outcome.

Setting goals involves identifying the profit you hope to earn and, if you do not plan to hold your investments indefinitely, the point at which you will sell. It also involves identifying when you will sell if the investment falls in value. At what point will you bail out and take a small loss to avoid a larger loss later on?

The second part— deciding how to compute profits and losses—is equally important because you need a consistent, reliable, and accurate method to assess your investing success and make valid comparisons between different investments.

The Basic Equation: Return on Cash Invested

Calculating return is perceived to be rather simple; and it is, as long as the amount of money placed into the investment is the entire amount invested. In some cases, though, you deposit only a portion of the investment's total value, deferring payment of the remainder. Anyone who has ever purchased a home knows that the down payment is only a small portion of the property's total value; the remainder is financed and paid over many years.

The same thing happens with investments. For example, if you use a margin account you are allowed to buy stock and pay for only one-half of the current market value. The balance is held in margin and interest is charged. The concept here is that when stock's price moves upward, margin investors make twice the profit (less interest) because they can afford to own twice as much stock. It's a great concept, unless your investments lose value or take too long to become profitable.

Another example involves the use of options, which is explained in greater detail later in this chapter. As one form of leverage, you can control shares of stock with the use of options for a fraction of their market value. So, calculating return will be more complicated when options are used.

The most basic calculation is *return on purchase price*, which is simply the return you earn or expect to earn when you put the entire amount of capital into the investment. For example, if you buy 100 shares of stock and pay $2,587 in cash, you have paid the entire purchase price in cash. If you later sell for a net of $2,934, your profit is $347.

Return on purchase price is calculated by dividing the profit by the original basis:

Formula: return on purchase price

$$(S - P) \div P = R$$

S = sales price
P = purchase price
R = return

Excel program

> A1 sales price
> B1 purchase price
> C1 =SUM(A1-B1)/B1

The result is expressed as a percentage. In the example, the return is calculated as:

($2,934 – $2,587) ÷ $2,587 = 13.4%

Return on purchase price is the calculation most investors are describing when discussing or thinking about their investments. It is the standard by which success is defined, and by which one investment is most likely to be compared to another. But what happens to the return calculation when you do not put the entire amount into the investment?

Return on purchase price may continue to be used as a common standard for the sake of ensuring consistency; but if you use a brokerage margin account to leverage your capital, you can expect two differences in the return. First, profitable returns are going to be much greater when you isolate the cash amount only; and second, risk is also considerably higher. So the higher return is accompanied by far greater risk. Thus, it is not realistic to prefer using margin for all investing just because returns are greater. You also must accept greater risk levels.

For example, if your cost for 100 shares of stock is $2,587 but you deposit only one-half using your margin account, you may continue to calculate return on purchase. But you will also want to figure out your *return on invested capital*. In this case, only the actual amount invested is involved in the final outcome. The "gross" return on invested capital (before deducting margin costs) will involve a 50% investment, or $1,294. The formula for this calculation is:

Formula: return on invested capital

[(S – I) ÷ I] * 100 = R

S = sales price
I = invested capital
R = return

Excel program

> A1 sales price
> B1 invested capital
> C1 =SUM((A1-B1)/B1)*100

Using the example and assuming a sales price of $2,934, your return would be:

*[($2,934 - $1,294) ÷ $1,294] * 100 = 126.7%*

This calculation is a theoretical outcome only. It is not realistic to count this triple-digit return as typical because not all investments are going to be profitable; it does not take into account the higher risk levels; and it ignores the fact that you continue to be obligated for the margin debt.

The advantage to using margin is that your capital can be leveraged; however, if a particular position loses money and you sell at a loss, you are still obligated for the amount borrowed. The return on invested capital formula is important in fixing the outcome, but only for a specific purpose: judging *overall* margin-based investing. So if you were to buy stocks only with cash, your outcome will be reviewed on the basis of the common formula: return on purchase price. If you use margin and invest only one-half, you double your opportunity *and* your exposure. A review of all outcomes on the basis of calculated return on invested capital will enable you to decide whether margin investing is more profitable or not. If your losses offset or surpass your gains, the added exposure to risk will not be worth the advantage (and greater risk) in leverage.

A third calculation that will help you to ensure like-kind comparisons in different markets and employing different strategies is *return on net investment*. This is the same calculation as both of the two previous formulas, but all outcomes are expressed on a net basis. So if you use margin, the actual profit is decreased (or loss is increased) by the interest cost of using margin. The formula is:

Formula: return on net investment

$$(S - I - C) \div I = R$$

S = sales price
I = invested capital
C = costs
R = return

Excel program

A1   sales price
B1   invested capital
C1   costs
D1   =SUM(A1-B1-C1)/B1

For example, if your sales price was $2,934, the basis (amount invested in a margin account) was $1,294, and margin interest was $78, the outcome would be:

($2,934 - $1,294 - $78) ÷ $1294 = 120.7%

An alternative method of computing this would assume that the margin cost should be added to the invested capital. The formula under this method is:

Formula: return on net investment with net cost basis

$(S - I) \div (I + C) = R$

S = sales price
I = invested capital
C = costs
R = return

Excel program

A1   sales price
B1   invested capital
C1   costs
D1   =SUM(A1-B1)/(B1+C1)

So rather than deducting interest costs from the sales price, they are simply added to the original basis. For example:

($2,934 - $1,294) ÷ ($1,294 + $78) = 119.5%

This outcome is not significantly different than the previous calculation. However, the longer the holding period, the higher the costs—and the more important this distinction becomes. It is also possible for this calculation to develop as a net loss. In that case, the return would be negative. For example, if the sales price had been $934 rather than $2,934, the outcome would be summarized as:

($934 - $1,294) ÷ ($1,294 + $78) = -26.2%

Two final versions of return involve calculations with the dividends earned. First is *total return* which includes a calculation net of costs, but adds in any dividends earned during the holding period. The formula:

Formula: total return with dividends

$$(S - I - C + D) \div I = R$$

S = sales price
I = invested capital
C = costs
D = dividends earned
R = return

Excel program

A1 sales price
B1 invested capital
C1 costs
D1 dividends earned
E1 =SUM(A1-B1-C1+D1)/B1

For example, if your sales price was $2,934, the basis (amount invested in a margin account) was $1,294, margin interest was $78, and dividends earned were $124, the outcome would be:

($2,934 - $1,294 - $78 + $124) ÷ $1,294 = 130.3%

The inclusion of dividends is complicated for two reasons. First, you are able to reinvest dividends for most listed companies and buy additional fractional shares rather than taking dividends in cash. So this creates a compound return and makes comparisons more elusive. Second, the holding period will also affect the total return. If you own stock up to a few days before ex-dividend date before selling, you will not earn the dividend for the last period, which also affects overall return. If you purchase shares immediately before ex-dividend date and sell on or after, you earn a full quarter's dividend even with a brief holding period.

Valuable resource: To find out more about reinvesting dividends in DRIP accounts (Dividend Reinvestment Plans), check the website http://www.dividend.com/dividend-investing-101/dividend-reinvestment-plans-drips/

The final calculation for return on cash invested is *dividend yield*, also called "current yield." This is the rate you earn on dividends, calculated as a percentage of the stock's market value. However, a distinction has to be made. This yield is reported every day in the financial press and is based on the stock's closing price. But if you buy stock, your actual yield will always be based on the price you pay and not on what is reported later. So for anyone who already owns shares, the daily changes in yield are meaningless. The formula for dividend yield is:

Formula: dividend yield

$D \div P = Y$

D = dividend per share
P = current price per share
Y = dividend yield

Excel program

A1   dividend per share
B1   current price per share
C1   =SUM(A1/B1)

For example, a particular stock closed yesterday at $48.86 per share. The dividend paid per share is $0.40 per quarter, or $1.60 per share, per year. Yield is:

$1.60 ÷ $48.86 = 3.3%

The higher the stock's price moves, the lower the yield (as long as dividend remains at the same amount per share) and the lower the price, the higher the yield. For example, if the market share price moved up to $55 per share, the $1.60 per share would represent a yield of 2.9% ($55 ÷ $1.60). And if share value fell to $40 per share, yield would increase to 4.0% ($40 ÷ $1.60). If you buy shares at the current price of $48.86 per share, your yield remains at 3.3% for as long as you own those shares.

This calculation becomes more complicated when you reinvest dividends, creating a compound rate of return. Although the actual yield values may be quite small, an exact calculation would assume a continuing 3.3% yield on the original shares, plus an adjusted yield calculated at the time dividends were posted in additional fractional shares. For example, if you own 100 shares and you receive the next quarterly dividend of 40 cents per share, or $40; and at that time the share price was $42 per share, you take the dividend in the form of shares, or an additional 0.95 share of stock ($40 ÷ $42) and the yield on that 0.95 share will be 3.8% per year. (The 40 cents per share is a quarterly dividend, so it is multiplied by 4 to arrive at the annual $1.60. Divide this by current share value of $42 per share to arrive at 3.8%.) The result:

100 shares earn 3.3% current yield
0.95 share earns 3.8% current yield

If this calculation is performed each quarter, you arrive at a very accurate overall yield. Even so, with only 100 shares the difference this makes is minimal. For portfolios with many more shares, the calculation is more significant because the dollar values are higher as well.

The importance of dividends as part of overall investment performance is not agreed upon by all. In fact, investors may tend to overlook or even ignore the role of dividends in their choice of equities and in portfolio performance:

> One school of thought called dividend irrelevance theory argues that what a firm pays in dividends is irrelevant and that stockholders are indifferent about receiving dividends ... Dividend policy is simply a way to package the return of the firm's cash flows. [ii]

The tendency to overlook the role of dividends is an error. Between 1926 and 2001, the total return in the market was approximately 11%, and 42.7% of that return was generated through dividend payments. [iii]

Calculating Option Trading Returns

The calculations of stock return and dividend yield involve subtle variations. The key thing to remember is that comparisons should be made consistently between different stocks, funds and other investments. The same level of calculation for options trading is far more complicated and involves many more variables.

An option is an intangible contract, a right. The owner of an option has the right to buy or to sell 100 shares of stock at a fixed price and for a very specific period of time. Once an option expires it becomes worthless.

There are two types of options. A *call* grants its owner the right but not the obligation to buy 100 shares of a stock at a fixed price. A *put* is the opposite, granting the right to sell 100 shares of stock. Every option is tied to one stock, called the *underlying security*, and it cannot be transferred to other stocks. The *strike price* is the fixed price the owner of an option can *exercise*. When a call owner exercises that call, it means 100 shares of the stock can be bought at the strike price, even when the stock price is substantially higher. If and when a put owner exercises a put, they sell 100 shares of stock at the fixed strike price even though the stock's current market price is far lower.

In a nutshell, that is how options work, but because option values change as stock prices change, not all options are exercised. In fact, about three out of every four options expires worthless. As the owner of an option, one of three things can happen: You can simply let it expire, in which case you lose the entire amount invested. Second, you can exercise the option and buy (with a call) or sell (with a put) 100 shares of stock. And third, you can sell the call or put and take a profit or loss on the transaction.

You can also act as seller rather than as buyer. In other words, instead of going through the sequence of buy-hold-sell, it is reversed to sell-hold-buy. Going short on options is far riskier than buying in most situations, because you may lose more money than you can afford. One exception to this is the *covered call*, a strategy in which you sell one call while also owning 100 shares of the underlying security. If the call is exercised by its buyer, you have 100 shares to deliver; so even if the stock price moves far higher, you do not lose on the option transaction (you do lose the increased market value of shares, however). You keep the money paid to you when you go short, called the option *premium*. The covered call is very conservative, and there are several possible outcomes. Analyzing these outcomes helps you to decide whether a particular position is worth the risks, or should be avoided.

The calculation of profit or loss for buyers is simple. You buy an option; and later you sell it. The difference is either profit or loss. (If you allow the option to expire worthless, your loss is 100%.) Even though three-fourths of options expire worthless, they remain popular as side-bets in the market. This is true partly because the options market holds a certain allure for the more speculative investor or trader. Options are also cheap. They can be bought for one-tenth or less of the price of stock. So rather than investing $4,000 in 100 shares of stock, you can spend $400 or less and own an option.

A comparative outcome is useful in identifying the attraction of options. For example, if you were to buy 100 shares of stock and the price rose four points, your profit upon sale (before calculating trading costs) would be $400, or 10%. However, if you bought a call option and spend $400 and the stock rose four points, you would double your money and sell for $800, or a 100% gain.

In the money and out of the money. The illustration of an option's value matching stock price point for point does not always occur. This is true only when the option is *in the money*. This means the stock price is higher than a call's strike price, or lower than a put's strike price. An in-the-money call will change in value point-for-point with the stock; as price of the stock rises, so does the call's value. An in-the-money put does the opposite; as the stock's price falls, an in-the-money put rises one point for each point the stock loses.

The comparison between a stock's profit and an option's demonstrates the power of leverage. For $400, the call buyer controls 100 shares of stock, but without carrying the risk of investing $4,000 in shares. The maximum loss, in fact, is limited to the price of the option. For example, if your $4,000 investment in stock falls to $3,800, your paper loss is $200 or 5%. However, you are not required to take that loss and you can hold onto shares indefinitely. The option buyer, however, has to be concerned with expiration. The two-point loss represents 50% of the premium value. So while profit and loss are far more substantial for options, their primary advantage is the lower dollar amount at risk, while the primary disadvantage is expiration.

The calculation of profit or loss for long positions is not complex. In comparison, when you go short with a covered call, your profit or loss is more complicated, for several reasons. First, there are three possible outcomes (expiration, exercise, or closing of the position). Second, because you also own shares of stock, exercise means that your stock will be sold; so you need to structure a covered call with the related capital gain on stock in mind.

The first calculation involving options involves selling covered calls and the sale of stock. Without options, the return on purchase price is easily calculated, because that price does not change. But when you sell covered calls, the outcome changes because the net basis in stock is reduced.

For example, if you own 100 shares of stock originally purchased at $40 per share, and you sell a covered call for 4 ($400), that may be viewed as a reduction in your basis. Most calculations of option return separate stock and options because it is complicated to try to figure out the overall return. But if you treat the covered call strictly as a form of reduced basis, then this calculation—*return if exercised*—can be very useful, especially in comparing one stock investment with another. The formula:

Formula: return if exercised

$$(S - I) \div (I - O) = R$$

S = sales price of stock
I = invested capital
O = option premium received
R = return

Excel program

A1 sales price of stock
B1 invested capital
C1 option premium received
D1 =SUM(A1-B1)/(B1-C1)

For example, if your covered call was sold with a strike price of 45 (or $45 per share) and ultimately exercised, the outcome in this case would be:

$$(\$4,500 - \$4,000) \div (\$4,000 - \$400) = 13.9\%$$

If the covered call had not been included, the two sides of the transactions would be calculated apart from one another. Thus, the capital gain on stock would be 10% ($400 ÷ $4,000). And the gain on the covered call would be 100% (because you received $100 upon sale, and it is all profit). But this is unrealistic; upon exercise, the premium you receive for selling a covered call reduces the basis.

The outcome may also involve keeping the call open until it expires. In this situation, the option premium is 100% profit; but it may also be used to reduce the basis in stock on an ongoing basis. You can write an unlimited number of calls against 100 shares of stock and allow each to expire in turn. Until one is actually exercised, you keep your stock. So, the true net basis in stock could be viewed as being discounted over a period of covered call writes.

Finally, a covered call may be closed and a profit taken. When you close a short position, it involves a closing purchase transaction. Your original order was a sell, so closing this requires a buy. For example, if you sell an option for $400 and later close it for $150, you have a $250 gain, or 62.5%. You may want to close the covered call for a number of reasons. For example, once it is closed you are free to write another one with a higher strike price and more time until expiration. That extended time means the option premium will be higher, so it is profitable for you to sell. Remember, upon sale, you receive the premium so the higher it is, the more profitable.

The discounting effect of covered call writing complicates the calculation of return on your investment. But it also discounts your basis in stock and provides a third way to gain (after capital gains and dividends) from investing in stock. Computing your investment return is also complicated by the effect of federal and state income taxes.

Taxes and Investment Return

There are two aspects to taxes that concern all investors: the *effective tax rate* and its impact on net returns, and the viability of tax-free investing (based on pre-tax and after-tax returns).

The effective tax rate is the rate that you pay on your taxable income, as an average tax rate. This is not the same as total income, gross income, or adjusted gross income. The formula for taxable income is:

Formula: taxable income

1) $I - A = G$
2) $G - E - D = T$

I = total income, all sources
A = adjustments
G = adjusted gross income
E = exemptions
D = deductions (itemized or standard)
T = taxable income

Excel program

> A1 total income, all sources
> B1 adjustments
> C1 exemptions
> D1 deductions
> E1 =SUM(A1-B1-C1-D1)

This formula describes federal taxable income. The formula used by various states will vary considerably. For the federal formula, assuming total income of $107,600, adjustments of $6,000, exemptions of $8,100, and deductions of $44,009:

> $107,600 – $6,000 – $8,100 – $44,009 = $49,491

The *effective tax rate* is the percentage that your total tax liability represents of your taxable income:

Formula: effective tax rate (federal)

> $L \div T = R$

> L = liability for taxes
> T = taxable income
> R = effective tax rate

Excel program

> A1 liability for taxes
> B1 taxable income
> C1 =SUM(A1/B1)

For example, with taxable income of $49,491, assume a tax liability of $12,373. The effective tax rate (federal) is:

> $12,373 \div $49,491 = 25\%$

This formula applies to the federal tax rate. To find your overall tax rate (combining both federal and state and, where applicable, local income taxes) add together the computed tax liability and federal liability; and divide the total by the federal taxable income:

Formula: effective tax rate (total)

$(FL + SL + LL) \div T = R$

FL = liability for taxes, federal
FT = liability for taxes, state
LL = liability for taxes, local
T = taxable income (on federal return)
R = effective tax rate, total

Excel program

A1 liability for taxes, federal
B1 liability for taxes, state
C1 liability for taxes, local
D1 taxable income
E1 =SUM(A1+B1+C1)/D1

For example, on income of $49,491, federal liability is $12,373, state tax liability is $990 and local tax is $49. The total effective tax rate is:

$(\$12{,}373 + \$990 + \$49) \div \$49{,}491 = 27.1\%$

The various state taxable income levels and income tax rates may not be identical to the federal rate; but based on the rationale that federal taxes are normally greater than those paid to the state or locality, using the federally-computed taxable income is the most logical.

Valuable resource: To check the rules for state taxes in your state, refer to the website http://www.statetaxcentral.com/

These calculations may be complicated by making a distinction between two separate definition of "effective tax rates" based on income or expected return:

Effective tax rates can be divided into two broad classifications: "average" effective tax rates and "marginal" effective tax rates. The first are generally defined as the amount of tax paid (or accrued) as a percentage of income. The marginal tax rate is the percentage of the expected return on an additional investment that is expected to be paid in tax. [iv]

This distinction is worth remembering, even though a majority of calculations are going to be based on the average effective tax rate known and readily discovered on financial statements or analysts' reports. Beyond the tax rate is another calculation for *after-tax income*. This requires a reduction of gross return by the percentage of your effective tax rate:

Formula: after-tax income

$$I * [(100 - R) \div 100] = A$$

I = income before taxes
R = effective tax rate
A = after-tax income

Excel program

A1   income before taxes
B1   effective tax rate
C1   =SUM(A1*(100-B1)/100)

For example, income before taxes is $49,491 and the effective tax rate is 27.1%. Applying this formula:

$$\$49,491 * [(100 - 27.1) \div 100] = \$36,079$$

By deducting your effective tax rate from 100, you arrive at the percentage of after-tax income you earn. Once you know your taxable income and tax bracket, you can simply subtract taxes from taxable income:

$$\$49,491 - \$13,412 = \$36,079$$

However, this second method is not practical prior to the conclusion of the year and calculation of exact taxable income and tax liability. The first method is preferable when attempting to calculate after-tax outcomes in advance of the tax calculation itself. This is useful as a planning tool or for means of comparisons of various investment outcomes based on tax bracket. However, the matter is not always so straightforward. As Chapter 5 reveals, reported earnings, tax earnings, and core earnings are not always the same. The after-tax income reported on an income statement could be inaccurate based on some reporting practices, including the fact that "... companies often record expenses for financial reporting purposes (for example, restructuring charges) that are not deductible for tax purposes. In this instance current tax payments are higher than reported on the income statement ..." [v]

This complexity should not change the calculation. However, any analysis of comparative after-tax returns should be made with this discrepancy in mind, and the potential distortions based on reporting methods and interpretations made by the reporting organization.

There are many forms of investing free of income tax altogether, or with taxes deferred until the future. For example, municipal bonds are issued without a liability for federal or state taxes. But the interest rate is lower than you would earn from buying other bonds, so a comparison is necessary. By computing your effective tax rate, you can determine whether you would be better off one way or the other. The comparison would be to reduce the income on a taxable bond by your effective tax rate, resulting in your after-tax income. Is this higher or lower than the yield from a tax-free bond?

Another type of tax deferral is that earned in qualified accounts such as individual retirement accounts. In these accounts, current income is not taxed until retirement or withdrawal and, in some types of IRA accounts, you can withdraw your principal and leave earnings to accumulate without paying tax until later. In calculating a true and comparative return on investment, you have to consider the true net basis, the time the investment was held, and the tax consequences of profits. In the case of capital gains, a lower rate applies if the gain is long-term; this affects your effective tax rate as well.

Conclusion

Return on investment is far from simple or consistent, which is why you need to ensure that the methods you use are applied in the same manner in each instance. A much different method of calculation is used by corporations. When you invest in a company and examine the balance sheet, you discover that returns on capital are key indicators in picking the stock of one company over another. This is the topic of the next chapter..

---

[i] Damodaran, A. (2002). *Investment Valuation: Tools and Techniques for Determining the Value of Any Asset*, 2nd Ed. Hoboken NJ: John Wiley & Sons, p. 289.

[ii] Baker, H. K. & Powell, G. E. (2005). *Understanding Financial Management: A Practical Guide*. Malden, MA: Blackwell Publishing, p. 407.

[iii] T. Rowe Price Investment Services, Inc. (Summer, 2003). Dividends and your total return. *Take Note*, 1-4.

[iv] Spooner, G. M. (September, 1986). Effective tax rates from financial statements. *National Tax Journal*, 39(3), 293-306.

[v] Stowe, J. D., Robinson, T. R., Pinto, J. E., & McLeavey, D. W. (2007). *Equity Asset Valuation*. Hoboken, NJ: John Wiley & Sons, p. 121.

Chapter 2
Returns on Capital: Putting Cash to Work

The investor is primarily concerned with calculating a rate of return on invested capital. "How much did I invest and how much did I take out? How long did it take? What is my return?" In comparison, the corporation looks at a range of "performance" returns in a much different manner. From a corporate perspective, use of capital and cash are more important than to the individual.

The two—individual investors and corporations—both want to maximize their available capital, and both are concerned with profitability. As an investor, you expect your capital to grow due to expanded market value. As a corporation, the expectation is based on profit and loss and how well that is accomplished. Corporate evaluation and judgment depends on many facets to this question: competition, keeping expenses under control, identifying and moving into many different product and geographic markets, and keeping a sensible balance between net worth (equity) and debt capitalization (borrowed money, or debt capital). The task faced by the corporation in setting up and monitoring these aspects to corporate returns on capital involve a few calculations that are much different than those executed by investors.

Calculating Returns from the Corporate View

The first question in the mind of a corporate analyst is, "How well did the company put its capital to work to produce profits?" This analysis is not performed only by the internal accounting or auditing departments. It is also performed by outside analysts advising clients to buy or not to buy the stock of a particular company. So, an analyst may make a recommendation to a client based on one company's superior return versus another.

This is not the same calculation as net return, which involves a study of revenues, costs, and expenses. In discussing fundamental analysis in Chapter 7, you will be provided with a complete list of calculations to evaluate profitability on the corporate level. For now, the concern is with return on capital, the profitability expressed as a percentage of corporate equity. Corporations are responsible to their shareholders, who expect to gain a better return on capital from their investments than other investors earn from the company's competitors.

If the calculation were to involve only net profits and capital stock, the return on capital or, more accurately, *return on equity* is not difficult to calculate. The basic formula assumes (a) that the dollar value of capital did not change during the year, and (b) the calculation is concerned only with equity (capital stock). To compute return on this basis, the formula is:

DOI 10.1515/9781501507427-002

Formula: return on equity

$$P \div E = R$$

P = profit for a one-year period
E = shareholders' equity
R = return on equity

Excel program

A1   profit for a one-year period
B1   shareholders' equity
C1   =SUM(A1/B1)

For example, last fiscal year's total profit was $845,057 and shareholder's equity was $8,832,401. The formula reveals a return on equity:

$$\$845{,}057 \div \$8{,}832{,}401 = 9.6\%$$

This formula is limited by what it excludes. It assumes that the value of net equity is the same at the beginning of the year as at the end of the year. In reality, capital stock may change due to new issues of stock, retirement of stock (companies may buy their own stock on the open market and permanently retire it as "Treasury Stock," for example), or the effects of mergers and acquisitions.

Furthermore, this formula can be affected in several ways, notably by financial leverage, which adjusts asset valuation; and by liability leverage obtained through the use of debt. This potential variability explains why return on equity varies as widely as it does among competing firms:

> To assess management's effectiveness in adding value, common equity investors evaluate the firm's profitability using various return measures. One of the most widely used measures for this purpose is the return on equity (ROE) calculated on the basis of the firm's financial statements. While the ratio is conceptually simple, several problems arise from its definition and use as well as the way it is often expressed in terms of other financial measures. [i]

The formula also is limited to its evaluation of equity. From a shareholder's point of view, this is valuable information; but return may further involve the use of debt. Total capitalization is the sum of capital stock and accumulated earnings, and bonds or long-term notes. So, in addition to return on equity, it is also important to calculate *return on total capitalization*. This includes both equity and long-term debt capitalization and presents a broader picture. Recognizing that corporations fund operations by selling stock and from borrowing money, this calculation can be revealing when tracked over many years. To calculate:

Formula: return on total capitalization

$$(P + I) \div (E + B) = R$$

P = profit for a one-year period
I = interest paid on long-term bonds
E = shareholders' equity
B = par value of long-term bonds
R = return on equity

Excel program

A1   profit for a one-year period
B1   interest paid on long-term bonds
C1   shareholders' equity
     D1 par value of long-term bonds
E1   =SUM(A1+B1)/(C1+D1)

For example, with a profit of $845,057 and shareholders' equity of $8,832,401, also assume par value of long-term bonds of $6,000,000 and interest paid of $194,055:

$$(\$845,057 + \$194,055) \div (\$8,832,401 + \$6,000,000) = 7.0\%$$

Total capitalization includes both shareholders' equity and long-term bond obligations. So "return" consists of profit on equity plus interest on bonds. Although that interest is an expense to the corporation, it is income to bondholders. This creates an equivalency between shareholders' profit and bondholders' interest. Some versions of this calculation include in "equity" both common and preferred shares, which makes the formula inclusive and more accurate than if preferred stock is excluded.

Par value of long-term bonds is the face amount of the debt, which is also the amount that will be repaid at the conclusion of the bond term. This distinction has to be made here because bond current value may be at a discount (lower than par value) or at a premium (above par value).

This calculation is more complex than a simple return on invested capital (shareholders' equity) because of the inclusion of interest expense as a form of "return." But this calculation includes both sides of the capitalization equation, so both forms of return have to be allowed for as well. The balance between equity and debt capitalization is an important and permanent concern for corporate management. For the long term, a balance between equity and debt—or, between production of profits versus payments of interest—may decide whether investors select one company over another. The higher the interest expense (due to heavy debt capitalization), the lower the net profit. For the shareholder, this also means there will be less cash available in future years to fund growth in operations and to pay dividends.

Calculating Average Net Worth

The calculation of return on capital is easily performed if capital value remains identical throughout the year. The "return" is an annual event; in other words, the profits (or, profits plus interest expense) occurring over a one-year period are simply divided by the capital stock (or capital stock plus par value of long-term bonds).

In practice, however, the capital stock dollar value does not always remain identical from beginning to end of the year. Because of this, the calculation is going to be inaccurate if it is restricted to either beginning balance or ending balance of capital. It is going to be necessary to calculate *average capital stock value* for the year. This cannot be done by merely adding beginning and ending balances together and dividing by two. You need to weight the average based on when the dollar value changes.

For example, if the beginning value is $4,500,000 and additional common stock is issued on March 1 for $1,200,000, the average net worth would be:

(2 months at $4,500,000 + 10 months at $5,700,000) ÷ 12
($9,000,000 + $57,000,000) ÷ 12
= $5,500,000

The formula for this *weighted average capital* is:

Formula: weighted average capital, months

$$[(P_1 * v) + (P_2 * v)] \div 12 = W$$

P_1 = period 1 (number of months)
P_2 = period 2 (number of months)
v = value
W = weighted average capital

Excel program

A1 period 1 (number of months)
B1 value (capital in period 1)
C1 period 2 (number of months)
D1 value (capital in period 2)
E1 =SUM((A1*B1) + (C1*D1))/12

For example, for the first two months of a year, capital was $6,000,000, and for the next 10 months, with a new stock issue, capital was raised to $7,500,000. The weighted average capital is:

$[(2 * \$6,000,000) + (10 * \$7,500,000)] \div 12 = \$7,250,000$

If more than two periods are involved, they would be added together and the total divided by the full year's periods, or 12 months.

The accurately calculated average net worth is used in the previous calculations of return on capital. However, the degree of accuracy you require depends on the amount of change during the year. For example, a significant level of change occurring in the middle of a month could make calculations of weighted average based on 12 months inaccurate. So in those instances, you can apply an assumption that all changes occurring in a particular month are assumed to occur at the mid-month level, and that the year consists of 24 equal periods. In this case, the previous calculation would involve adjusting the "period" calculation. For example, assume the organization's capital was $4,500,000 for four months, $5,700,000 for 15 months, and $5,340,000 for five months. The calculation based on 24 half-months would be:

$[(4 * \$4,500,000) + (15 * \$5,700,000) + (5 * \$5,340,000)] \div 24 = \$5,425,000$

The formula for the half-month method is:

Formula: weighted average capital, half-months

$[(P_1 * v) + (P_2 * v) + (P_3 * v)] \div 24 = W$

P_1 = period 1 (number of months)
P_2 = period 2 (number of months)
P_3 = period 3 (number of months)
v = value
P_t = 24 half-months per year
W = weighted average capital

Excel program

A1   period 1 (number of months)
B1   value (capital in period 1)
C1   period 2 (number of months)
D1   value (capital in period 2)
E1   period 3 (number of months)
F1   value (capital in period 3)

G1 =SUM((A1*B1) + (C1*D1) + (E1*F1))/24

As a weighted average, this lower result would be more accurate if changes actually occurred on days other than the end of the month. Each month's holding period is doubled with the assumption that changes take place halfway through the month, so this accomplishes an averaging effect and avoids the assumption that change must conform to the standard of a 12-month year. The need for this added complexity is dependent upon the dollar value of actual changes as well as the frequency of those changes.

The detail you employ in calculations of weighted average depends on the significance and timing of changes. The *average* of anything should be computed to be as fair and accurate as possible. In the case of capital stock, new issues of stock or retirement of outstanding shares can be significant, so steps should be taken to make the average as accurate as possible; this explains the mid-month application in which the year is divided into 24 half-month periods. However, in comparing formulas between two or more companies, you will also need to use the same weighted average formula in all instances. In cases of frequent changes during the year and large dollar amounts, a 365-day year can be employed rather than relying on 12 months or 24 half months.

Net Worth Versus Total Capitalization

Another range of calculations affecting judgments about corporate strength or weakness involves analysis of overall capitalization, the combination of shareholders' equity and long-term debt. How much of the total consists of debt?

If debt levels are allowed to rise over time, the corporation will be committed not only to repayments of the debt in the future, but also to ever-growing annual interest expense. For shareholders, this threatens the future dividends and also hampers a corporation's ability to continue funding growth and expansion. The more profits to be used to service ever-growing debt, the more restricted the corporation will be in the future.

The *debt capitalization ratio* is the calculation of long-term debt as a percentage of total capitalization. This is one of the key tests of a company and, although often overlooked, may be used to compare one company to another. Three separate debt-related ratios should be distinguished. The most important of the three is the debt capitalization ratio.

Formula: debt capitalization ratio

$$D \div C = R$$

D = long-term debt
C = total capital
R = debt capitalization ratio

Excel program

A1 long-term debt
B1 total capital
C1 =SUM(A1/B1) * 100

For example, if total capitalization is $23.6 billion and long-term debt listed on the company's balance sheet is shown as $4.7 billion, the debt ratio is:

$4.7 ÷ $23.6 = 19.9$

The outcome is expressed as a numerical value to one decimal point, without percentage signs. Confusion arises when the debt capitalization is referred to as either the debt equity ratio or simply as the debt ratio. These are two entirely different formulas:

Formula: debt equity ratio

$$L \div E = R$$

L = total liabilities
E = total equity
R = debt equity ratio

Excel program

A1 total liabilities
B1 total equity
C1 =SUM(A1/B1)

For example, assume total liabilities (long-term and current) of $7.0 billion and total equity of $23.6 billion. The debt/equity ratio is expressed as a reduced percentage relationship. To find the percentage, multiply the result by 100. The result for this calculation is:

$7.0 ÷ $23.6 = 0.297 (29.7\%)$

This ratio often is confused with the previously explained debt capitalization ratio. Thus, when using either of these, the correct and descriptive terminology makes a difference. The final ratio, called the *debt ratio* (also called the debt-to-assets ratio), is an unfortunate name because of its similarity to the previous two calculations. However, it is quite different as it compares total liabilities to total assets.

Formula: debt ratio

$$L \div A = R$$

L = total liabilities
A = total assets
D = debt ratio

Excel program

A1 total liabilities
B1 total assets
C1 =SUM(A1/B1)*100

For example, total liabilities are $7.0 billion and total assets are $13.3 billion. The debt ratio is expressed as a percentage. In this example, the ratio is:

$$\$7.0 \div \$13.3 = 52.6\%$$

An example of how the ratios are applied is instructive. If you are considering investing in a retail corporation, you may check a series of ratios for a particular date. As of 2006, latest reported annual year-end results for all three ratios for four retail corporations showed the results summarized in Table 2.1.

Table 2.1: Debt-based ratio comparisons.

Company	Debt Capitalization Ratio (Long-Term Debt ÷ Total Capital	Debt Equity Ratio (Total liabilities ÷ Total Equity	Debt Ratio (Total Liabilities ÷ Total Assets
Wal-Mart (WMT)	38,214 ÷ 124,570 = 30.7	102,833 ÷ 124,570 = 0.826	102,833 ÷ 199,581 = 51.5%
Macy's (M)	6,966 ÷ 11,855 = 58.8	12,694 ÷ 11,855 = 1.071	12,694 ÷ 20,576 = 61.7%
Target (TGT)	11,945 ÷ 25,717 = 46.4	24,567 ÷ 25,717 = 0.956	24,567 ÷ 40,262 = 61.0%
J.C. Penney (JCP)	4,696 ÷ 6,106 = 76.9	7,108 ÷ 6,106 = 1.164	7,108 ÷ 9,442 = 75.3%

Source: *CFRA Stock Reports*

The results demonstrate the often-significant differences in outcomes between the three similarly-named ratios. The debt-based ratios may be overlooked in the overall analysis of companies, and more information about this problem is provided in coming chapters involving fundamental analysis (Chapters 6 and 7). For example, some investors will focus only on the current ratio (a comparison between current assets and liabilities) as a test of cash flow. However, when corporations report net losses, it is possible to bolster the current ratio by accumulating a growing level of long-term debt. The borrowed funds are kept in the form cash, for example, to offset annual net losses. By doing so, the current ratio is not affected and investors whose analysis is limited to that test may be misled.

The solution is to check both current ratio *and* debt ratio. As long as both remain consistent from one year to the next, the conclusion that money is being managed well is confirmed. The purpose of performing any tests on reported corporate assets or liabilities (as well as profits) is to identify trends. But a single trend is not always reliable. When a corporation keeps its current ratio level by allowing its long-term debt to rise each year, it is creating future problems to satisfy short-term requirements. So, confirming the apparent trend is essential. You confirm cash flow trends by checking both current ratio and debt ratio. By the same argument, the effectiveness of internal controls is checked by comparing increased revenues with expense levels, hoping to find improved margins. However, it is a danger signal if you discover that the growth in expenses is keeping pace with higher revenues or outpacing that trend.

All financial tests can be confirmed by checking beyond a single ratio, and your ability to draw well-informed conclusions is vastly improved when you get a broader view of the corporation's financial status.

Like all financial tests, however, there are complications once core earnings adjustments are made. One type of stock—preferred stock—may behave as a hybrid form of capitalization, and this raises questions about capitalization ratios in general.

Preferred Stock as Hybrid Capitalization

The complexity of identifying the accurate capitalization value demonstrates the problem faced in accurately reporting returns: Identifying a means for consistent and accurate judgment of a company's basic value is no easy matter.

Capitalization itself is an elusive concept for most non-accountants. Even if you know the meaning of capital, distinctions between equity (stock) and debt (bonds and notes) capital are not always clear. But if you think of equity as a means of ownership with long-term risk/reward features (that is, dividend income and increased market value), it makes the distinction clear. Bondholders do not stand to earn capital gains, and rely on interest as well as repayment of principal.

Another risk factor is based on priority of repayment. In the worst-case scenario, a company goes broke, who gets paid first? Because bonds are contracted and have priority over common stock, bondholders get repaid before stockholders; but one class of stock gets paid before even bondholders. Preferred stock is so-called because in the event of complete liquidation of the company, they are paid first. So, the sequence in priority is usually: (1) preferred stockholders, (2) bondholders, and (3) common stockholders.

Some types of preferred stock are described as "mandatorily redeemable," meaning the stockholder will be repaid at an identified future date, and there is no choice involved. Preferred stock is often referred to as a hybrid investment because it has features of both equity and debt. Mandatory redemption makes this type of stock debt. However, preferred stockholders are paid a dividend which is generally fixed. Just as bondholders get a fixed rate of interest, preferred stockholders' dividends are customarily identified in advance.

Preferred stock can represent a substantial portion of total capitalization, although it is normally only a small percentage of total capital. Tracking this factor in total capitalization helps identify ways that companies use hybrid investments. If the *preferred stock ratio* climbs over time, that could be a sign the company is trying to keep the debt ratio low while accumulating a form of stock (preferred) that is really more like debt than equity. The formula:

Formula: preferred stock ratio

$$P \div C = R$$

P = preferred stock
C = total capitalization
R = preferred stock ratio

Excel program

A1 Preferred stock
B1 total capitalization
C1 =SUM(A1/B1)

For example, preferred stock is $30,000, equity capital is $56,405, and long-term debt is $51,000. The preferred stock ratio is:

$30,000 ÷ ($56,405 + $51,000) = 27.9%

Total capitalization consists of long-term debt plus preferred and common stock; all three are included.

The actual configuration of "stock" can be very complex, with multiple classes of stock involved, both preferred and common. In addition, "total capital" consists not only of stock, but of retained earnings, the accumulated profits and losses from prior years. This is also reduced by dividends declared and paid. So "total capital" for the purpose of the various return calculations should exclude current-year earnings but should include retained earnings less dividends.

A related calculation is *preferred dividend coverage*. This is a calculation of the company's available resources to make dividend payments when applicable on preferred stock. The higher the ratio, the stronger the company's position. This ratio also informs common stockholders about the company's dividend policies toward them. If the preferred dividend coverage is marginal, future common stock dividends might be in jeopardy.

The ratio is calculated by dividing net income by the amount of preferred dividend.

Formula: preferred dividend coverage ratio

$$N \div P = R$$

N = net income
P = preferred dividend
R = ratio

Excel program

A1   net income
B1   preferred dividend
C1   =SUM(A1/B1)

For example, net income for the period is $2,774 and preferred dividend is $500. The preferred dividend coverage ratio is:

$$\$2,774 \div \$500 = 5.55$$

A high ratio such as this indicates the company can easily afford preferred dividends as well as dividends in common stock. As long as dividends are paid quarterly, the need to find a fair weighted average can become quite important. For the sake of simplicity, an argument can be made that annual return should be made based strictly on the balance of the net worth section of the balance sheet as of the beginning of the year. This argument reduces the complexity of computations and gets around the question of ever-changing equity due to payment of quarterly dividends and issue of new classes of stock.

When a company issues a new class of preferred stock, it makes sense to evaluate its characteristics. For example, if the class is mandatorily redeemable, it is a form of debt. To accurately calculate a debt ratio in the case where mandatorily redeemable preferred stock has been issued during the year, it is reasonable to change the calculation of the debt ratio to the *adjusted debt ratio* calculation:

Formula: adjusted debt ratio

$$(D + S) \div C = R$$

D = long-term debt
S = mandatorily redeemable preferred stock
C = total capitalization
R = adjusted debt ratio

Excel program

A1 long-term debt
B1 mandatorily redeemable preferred stock
C1 total capitalization
D1 =SUM(A1+B1)/C1

For example, long-term debt is $56,405 and redeemable preferred stock is $30,000. Total capitalization is $161,996. The adjusted debt ratio is:

$$(\$56,405 + \$30,000) \div \$161,996 = 53.3\%$$

Some rationale may be argued to include all preferred stock in this calculation. As long as the same rules are applied consistently from one year to the next and between organizations, the adjusted ratio can be performed on either basis. If you do decide to move any or all preferred stock over to be counted as part of debt, this also alters your computation of return on equity. The formula for *net return on equity* is:

Formula: net return on equity

$$P \div (E - S) = R$$

P = profit for a one-year period
E = shareholders' equity
S = mandatorily redeemable preferred stock
R = net return on equity

Excel program

    A1 net profit
    B1 shareholders' equity
    C1 mandatorily redeemable preferred stock
    D1 =SUM(A1)/(B1-C1)

For example, when net profit is $2,774, shareholders' equity is $75,591 and preferred stock is $30,000, net return on equity is:

    $2,774 ÷ ($75,591 - $30,000) = 6.1%

Reducing "equity" to reflect non-hybrid forms makes both the debt ratio and return on equity consistent and reasonable. When preferred stock represents a significant share of overall shareholders' equity, the return calculation is not reliable without this reduction. If the organization wants to use preferred stock in place of bonds (application of a *de facto* form of debt) it will distort the traditional calculations, and these adjustments become essential for tracking long-term trends.

The Importance of "Use of Capital"

The return on capital calculations and tests of capitalization are best used as part of a trend. A single entry in that trend is not as meaningful as the long-term direction it is moving. For example, consider the ramifications for stockholders of GM's ever-rising debt ratio between 1996 and 2005. As shown in Figure 2.1, in 10 years debt rose from 58% of total capitalization to 91% by the end of 2005.

The obvious problem here is growing dependence on debt, meaning a requirement to repay borrowed money *and* to pay ever-higher interest each year. This erodes profits and ruins future dividend payments for stockholders. GM finally filed for Chapter 11 bankruptcy protection in 2009, when its debt capitalization ratio had risen to 209.6.

This leads to another important financial issue: the use of capital. Whether that capital is derived from equity or debt, the corporation must be concerned with its annual cash flow. With 209.6% of capitalization represented by debt, it is clear that a great burden on the use of capital will be in the form of annual interest payments. If the organization is not profitable, where will it find additional money to retool plants, expand operations, or develop new products?

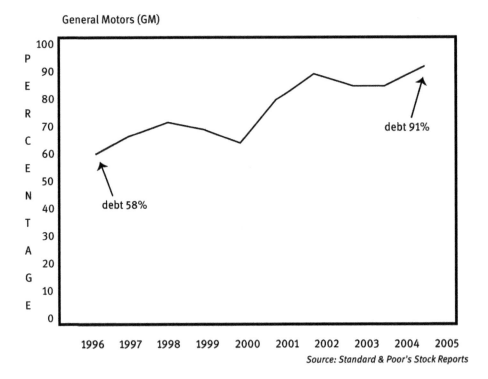

Figure 2.1: General Motors' debt ratios 1996–2005.

The best-known way to judge corporate management's effectiveness is through its use of capital. If management allows the debt ratio to rise over time, it is most difficult to imagine how management will be able to create strong and sustained growth in the future. Just as homeowners cannot expect to be able to afford ever-higher mortgage payments, management in a corporate environment cannot depend on endless profits to fund growing long-term debt.

The long-term trend in maintaining a cap on debt capitalization is one of the best signs that management is using capital wisely. Growth of current operations (and excluding acquisitions or expansion into new markets) should be affordable from current profits. In the most ideal situation, a company is able to pay competitive dividends, fund growth and current operations, and keep long-term debt under control. For example, one of the best-managed companies on the New York Stock Exchange is Altria (MO), which sells the Philip Morris line of tobacco. As of 2016, the company was paying dividends of over 3.44%. A look at its numbers shows that net income rose each year while long-term debt changed very little. The results for five years are shown in Table 2.2.

Table 2.2: Altria five-year results, net income to long-term debt.

Year	Net Income ($ millions)	Long-Term Debt ($ millions)	Debt to Cap. Ratio
2016	$14,239	$13,881	52.0
2015	5,241	12,915	81.6
2014	5,070	13,693	77.2
2013	4,535	13,992	74.9
2012	4,180	12,419	72.7

Source: *CFRA Stock Reports*

These trends were positive. It is clear that Altria has adequate current income to manage long-term debt and pay an exceptionally high dividend while its revenues and profits continue to rise. From the investor's point of view, the individual yield (from dividends) and the strong financial results make Altria attractive.

Conclusion

This is not to say that borrowing money is a negative attribute. Most corporations borrow. But if the debt is allowed to run out of control, it foreshadows bigger problems ahead. Investors can learn valuable lessons from the corporate world in this regard, and can use leverage wisely to augment their investment returns. The next chapters explain this is more detail.

---

[i] Tezel, A. & McManus, G. M. (Spring/Summer, 2003). Disaggregating the Return on Equity: An Expanded Leverage Approach. *Journal of Applied Finance*, 13.1, 66–71.

Chapter 3
Leverage and Risk Analysis:
Maximizing Other People's Money

The concept of "using other people's money" is an appealing one. Many investors like to use margin accounts or even borrow money to build a portfolio. But an inescapable reality about leverage is that it comes with risk.

The correlation between potential profit and risk is a reality every investor needs to resolve. In determining your personal risk tolerance, a key issue is identification of the amount of risk you consider appropriate. That is determined by your income, assets, investing experience, family situation, and long-term goals. For example, if you are single and earning a high salary, own your home free and clear, and have a large cash reserve, you can afford to take relatively high risks in exchange for potential profits. But if you are married with children, buying a home and paying on a large mortgage, and your income and investing experience are limited, you need to move more slowly. Everyone has to equate their personal situation, knowledge and goals with the appropriate risk level.

If you decide that leverage will work for you, then you will also be interested in some of the popular methods of leveraging your portfolio. These include simply borrowing money (for example, refinancing your home to get cash or applying for a home equity loan); using your brokerage margin account; or using options to control blocks of stock for relatively small cost. While there are many other potential ways to leverage your capital, these are the most obvious and among the most popular.

Calculating the Cost of Money

Are you willing to place your home at risk to increase your investing power? For many, the answer is no. When you refinance and increase your mortgage balance, you are increasing the debt on your home. When you apply for a home equity line of credit, it is like using a credit card. As you accumulate balances on that equity line, you add to your debt burden and to the amount owed for your home. The risk is that your use of funds may not be profitable. So if you lose money in the market, you have the worst of both worlds: You still have to repay the amount borrowed, but you have a depreciated asset in your portfolio. There is little doubt that anyone who increases the debt on their home intends to repay that debt with their profits; but there are no guarantees that the plan will work out that way.

This is not to say that leverage should not be used, only that you should be aware of the risks. It is important to determine whether you can afford those risks before going into debt. The best way to quantify risk is through comparison of the cost of

DOI 10.1515/9781501507427-003

leverage, both between two or more alternative investments, and between leverage and non-leverage as separate strategies.

Calculating *interest expense* is crucial as it represents the cost for leverage. The time element comes into this as well. The cost of a one-month move into and out of a position is clearly less than a full year's exposure. The time factor makes a significant difference; the longer you have to keep borrowed money outstanding, the higher the cost and the lower your profit. To calculate interest, the basic formula is:

Formula: simple interest

$P * R = I$

P = principal amount
R = annual rate
I = interest (per year)

Excel program

A1   principal amount
B1   annual rate
C1   =SUM(A1*B1)

The interest rate is always expressed as a one-year expense. Thus, a 5% interest charge would express the amount of interest you have to pay over one full year. In Chapter 4, you will see how different calculations of interest change the annual percentage rate (APR) you actually pay. If interest is computed annually, you pay the nominal or expressed amount; but if interest is calculated quarterly, monthly, or daily, the APR will be higher due to compounding.

In this chapter, the simple interest example is used. Simple interest is an annual charge only, so 5% means just that. Using simple interest, a 5% charge on $1,000 borrowed is going to be $50:

$1,000 * .05 = $50

Note that to multiple by a percentage, the interest rate is converted to decimal form. This involves moving the decimal point two places to the left. So, 5% becomes .05 and 35% would become .35. This makes multiplication easier to perform accurately, as long as the decimal places are included in the operation.

To calculate net profit on an investment, deduct interest expense from proceeds. For example, if you invest on margin, you need to account for the cost of borrowed money in order to compare the outcome realistically. It would make outcomes highly unreliable to base profits on the full value of an investment when only a portion of the value had been placed; however, the interest expense must also be part of the equation. The formula for *return on investment net of margin* is:

Formula: return on investment net of margin

$$(V - B - I) \div C = R$$

V = current market value
B = basis (including leveraged portion)
I = interest cost
C = cash invested net of margin
R = return on investment net of margin

Excel program

A1 current market value
B1 basis
C1 interest cost
D1 cash invested
E1 =SUM(A1-B1-C1)/D1

For example, assume that you purchased 100 shares of stock at $50 per share; invested $2,500 in cash with the balance carried on margin; sold after a four-point rise; and with interest expense of $85.00. The net return is:

$$(\$5,400 - \$5,000 - \$85) \div \$2,500 = 12.6\%$$

This rate of return points out the great advantages of using leverage. If you had invested the full $5,000, your $400 profit would represent only an 8% return ($400 ÷ $5,000). However, it is equally important to recognize the high risks associated with leverage. For example, if you sold after the investment had fallen four points, losing a net of $485 due to interest, the outcome would show a substantial loss:

$$(\$4,600 - \$5,000 - \$85) \div \$2,500 = -19.4\%$$

This loss is far different than a 12.6% return: a 32% swing.

An alternative calculation considers *capital* as the denominator for calculation, specifically *invested capital*. This value may also be called original investment in capital, versus current market value of equity. So, *return on book value of capital* adjusts net operating income by marginal taxes (adjusted taxes paid or incurred), and then divides by the value of invested capital. This means that the calculator is based on book value rather than on market value.[i]

Formula: return on book value of capital

$$(P - T) \div C = R$$

P = net operating profit
T = taxes
C = invested capital
R = return on invested capital

Excel program

A1 net operating profit
B1 taxes
C1 invested capital
D1 =SUM(A1-B1)/C1

For example, net operating profit was $68,450 and taxes were $17,100. Invested capital was $235,500:

$$(\$68,450 - \$17,100) \div \$235,500 = 21.8\%$$

Annualized Return

The associated potential for profit and risk is a feature of leverage, but another element has to be taken into account as well. How long do you keep a position open? The longer you have to wait before closing the position, the higher your interest cost. To make any comparisons truly valid, you need to consider the time element. A 5% cost over 12 months is just that, 5%. But if it takes only three months (one-fourth of the full year) to complete and close a position, your actual cost will be only 1.25%. It is still an *annual* rate of 5%, but only one-fourth of a full year. On the other hand, if it takes 15 months to finalize a leveraged transaction, your cost will cover 1¼ years. So that 5% per year comes out of 6.25% overall (again, still 5% *per year* but a higher overall cost).

To make any investments comparable to one another, the net return has to be expressed on an annualized basis. How much would your net profit be if held for exactly one year? How much would the interest expense be? Annualizing can be applied both to cost and to net profit (or loss). To annualize, use either a number of months or actual days. Using the months method to compute *annualized rate*, divide the rate by the number of months the position was open, and then multiply by 12 (months):

Formula: annualized rate (months)

$(R \div M) * 12 = A$

R = net return
M = months the position was open
A = annualized yield

Excel program

A1 net return
B1 = months the position was open
C1 =SUM(A1/B1) * 12

For example, if you opened two different positions and sold both once you had made a 10% profit, are these identical outcomes? If you owned one stock for 8 months and the other for 14 months, the annualized returns are quite different.

To annualize 10% over seven months:

$(10\% \div 7) * 12 = 17.1\%$

Over 14 months:

$(10\% \div 14) * 12 = 8.6\%$

This example demonstrates that the longer the holding period, the lower the annualized interest. Using months as a base for calculation is the easiest method. You can estimate partial months by assuming a four-week period per month. So if you own a stock for three months and a week, that would be 3.25 months; if 6 months and 3 weeks, it would be 6.75 months. As long as you are consistent in these calculations, stock-to-stock comparisons will be accurate. You can also perform annualization using the number of weeks and multiplying by 52; or even the exact number of days a position is owned, with a multiplier of 365. The actual days method is the most accurate.

Formula: annualized rate (days)

$(R \div D) * 365 = A$

R = net return
M = days the position was open
A = annualized yield

Excel program

> A1   net return
> B1 = days the position was open
> C1   =SUM(A1/B1) * 365

For example, for a 10% yield for a position held open 212 days:

> *(10% ÷ 212) * 365 = 17.2%*

For the same yield but with the investment kept open for 427 days:

> *(10% ÷ 427) * 365 = 8.5%*

The comparisons should be kept realistic. Extremely short-term holding periods are not reliably profitable, so it is not accurate to use a strict form of annualization to draw conclusions. For example, an investment of $5,000 in a stock sold one week later for $5,400, annualizes on either monthly or weekly basis, to an impressive result. However, the outcome cannot be expected to recur on an annual basis. So annualizing is valuable only for comparative purposes, and not as a means to estimate likely annual yields.

Using 365 days to annualize method is called the Stated Rate Method and is the most accurate. An alternative, called the Bank Method, is based on 360 days. This is used commonly in the mortgage lending business, based on 12 months of 30 days each; and in some accounting applications.

Leverage-Based Risk—the P/E Ratio as a Way to Quantify

The difficulty in contending with higher than average returns is factoring in the risk. Stocks that move rapidly either upward or downward—the more volatile issues—are by definition accompanied by higher risks. Profits may be short-term and higher than average, but so might losses.

Valuation risk—the risk that a particular stock could be overvalued at the time you buy—is probably the most common of all risks. The advice to "buy low and sell high" is profound because so many people do exactly the opposite. When stock prices rise, more and more people want to get in on the action, so the tendency to buy at the very height of the price curve can be strong. Likewise, when prices fall, investors might panic and sell at the depth of the same price curve. So, a common pattern is to "buy high and sell low" instead.

Even this observation concerning the timing of trades is only part of the challenge in understanding broader risk. Because P/E (price/earnings ratio) is one of the most popular indicators of value in stock prices, the question of its accuracy fails to take into account any factors other than the most recent year's earnings:

> The price-earnings (P/E) ratio is a widely used measure of the expected performance of companies, and it has almost invariably been calculated as the ratio of the current share price to the previous year's earnings. The P/E of a particular stock, however, is partly determined by outside influences such as the year in which it is measured, the size of the company, and the sector in which the company operates.[ii]

Various adjustments, such as using the average of recent years' earnings rather than only the latest year, may significantly change the P/E outcome. This is one of many forms of adjustment possible, adding to the potential for valuation risk. Distortions in P/E may occur during times of profound changes in the market, such as a collapse in earnings or acceleration in bullish sentiment. The typical limitation to the latest year's P/E is useful only when studied as part of a longer-term trend, and employing annual high and low P/E to judge the range of variability and spot trends in valuation over a period of several years.

To judge valuation risk, the *price/earnings ratio* is presented in its traditional form, limited to the current year. However, a more expansive analysis of the range of P/E provides the most useful and reliable conclusions about pricing of a stock. As a general rule, P/E is a means to determine whether a stock is fairly priced or overpriced. This ratio compares price (a technical indicator that is very current) and earnings per share (a fundamental indicator that may be dated). To compute:

Formula: price/earnings ratio

$$P \div E = R$$

P = price per share
E = earnings per share
R = P/E ratio

Excel program

A1 price per share
B1 earnings per share
C1 =SUM(A1/B1)

This ratio is significant because it can be used to judge whether a stock's price is "too high" if we assume some standards. The P/E is also called a *multiple* of earnings. The result of this formula tells you how many multiples of earnings are represented in the current price. For example, if today's price is $32 per share and the most recently reported earnings per share (EPS) was $2.90, the P/E is:

32 ÷ 2.90 = 11

Today's price is equal to 11 times earnings. This tells you a lot, given the following qualifications of the P/E ratio:

1. *EPS (earnings per share) is historical and may be out of date.* If you are reviewing P/E three months after the end of a company's fiscal year, you are using outdated earnings information, especially in cyclical industries. For example, in the retail sector the fourth quarter is usually the most profitable. So if your latest published EPS is for December 31, but the current price is as of March 15, the two sides of the equation are not as closely related as you might prefer.

2. *EPS counts only one form of capitalization.* The EPS includes only earnings per common share of stock. So in situations where debt capitalization is quite high, the earnings are reduced by higher than average interest expense. When a company has issued a large volume of preferred stock, it also distorts the true EPS value.

3. *Current market value could be untypical.* If today's stock price is a spike above or below the more typical trading range, it is not reliable for calculating P/E. It makes more sense to base P/E calculations on an established mid-range price of the stock. For example, if the stock has been trading between $25 and $35 per share but today's price spiked at $39, using the $39 value for P/E is unrealistic (especially since earnings are historical). It would be more accurate to use a mid-range price of $30 per share.

4. *Tracking indicators by a moment in time is unreliable.* No single indicator can be used reliably without also tracking how it has evolved over time. For cyclical stocks, a review of quarter-end P/E is more revealing than today's single P/E outcome. In this way, you can see how P/E has changed over time and you can also recognize cyclical changes. By using historical data, you are also able to match quarter-ending price with quarter-ending earnings, which overcomes the big problem with moment-in-time analysis, where the two time factors are mismatched.

Given the problems of dissimilar time factors in the two sides of the P/E ratio, to make valid comparisons, study the annual high and low P/E over a number of years. The higher the P/E range each year, the greater the chance of an inflated stock price. The previous example yielded the following formula:

32 ÷ 2.90 = 11

If the stock price were to rise over time, the P/E would rise as well, but the established latest EPS remains the same:

42 ÷ 2.90 = 14.5
52 ÷ 2.90 = 17.9
62 ÷ 2.90 = 21.4

In the third case, the price of $62 per share is over 21 times current earnings. Over long periods of time, lower-P/E stocks have tended to out-perform higher-P/E stocks. The market tends to over-value stocks when those stocks are in favor, thus prices may be driven too high. From the individual investor's point of view, this valuation risk can be quantified by comparing P/E levels among several stocks, as one of several means for selection. For example, you can make a rule for yourself that you will not buy any stock whose P/E is greater than 15. This level is provided as an example only. However, you will discover that a comparative analysis of P/E shows that stocks with exceptionally low P/E may be conservative choices but the chances for profit will be limited as well; and that exceptionally high P/E stocks tend to be more volatile than average.

A reasonable conclusion is that picking mid-range P/E stocks is a sensible way to reduce valuation risk. It is not fool-proof, but it is the closest thing to a formula that allows you to quantify the relationship between risk and reward.

One way to make good use of the P/E ratio is to limit your range of comparisons between stocks. If you were to study all stocks in a single sector, you would be likely to find variation among the P/E levels. If you ignore these variations, you gain no insight into how or why to pick one stock over another. However, if you further limit your comparison to those stocks with P/E between 11 and 16, the list narrows considerably. This "rule" eliminates stocks of little immediate interest in the market as well as those with greater price volatility. By limiting the range of P/E, you also are better able to analyze valuation risk between stocks in different sectors. For example, you have the means with P/E to compare valuation risk between retail, energy, and pharmaceutical issues. While the attributes of these sectors are vastly dissimilar, valuation risk through P/E is far more uniform. Given the need to ensure accuracy and reliability of both the EPS and current price levels employed, this comparative study is useful.

When the study is used in conjunction with an analysis of debt ratio, revenue and earnings, and other fundamental tests, valid comparisons between stocks is more reliable and realistic. The P/E, like all ratios, is useful when viewed over a length of time and when the factors employed are matched in time factors.

When comparing stocks using P/E as one of the analytical tools for the task, be aware of other types of risk worth considering. These include business risk (critical analysis of a company's solvency, gained from bond ratings, profitability, and capitalization trends); and basic market risk (the timing of your investment decision). Many tools, both fundamental and technical, can help in reducing these risks. For example, technical investors use specific chart patterns to time their decisions. While this is extremely short-term in a strategic sense, timing a buy or sell decision can help you to avoid poor timing. *Swing traders*, for example, use a limited number of charting patterns to recognize and anticipate when prices are about to turn.

Swing trading is only one of many technical methods traders employ. A sub-set of day trading, swing traders generally prefer to identify trends evolving over a two- to five-day period. Fundamental investors rely more on financial information and view short-term price as chaotic and unpredictable. Both technical and fundamental sides can offer valuable and useful information to improve trading profits, which is why an indicator like the P/E (which uses both fundamental and technical information) is so popular.

Using Options as a Form of Leverage

One purpose in evaluating the mathematical returns on specific strategies is to help identify the risk involved. The P/E ratio is useful in some respects because it can be used to compare stocks to one another, and to modify perceptions of profit potential. The greater the profit potential appears to be, the greater the risk. When you compare P/E's between stocks, you can also observe a correlation between interest in the market (higher than average volume and more volatile trading range, for example) and higher than average P/E. This is a good example of matching between profit and risk of a decision.

The options market allows you to manage risks while continuing to seek profits, *and* to use leverage while managing the amount of capital placed at risk. This often-overlooked feature makes options one of the best vehicles for a leveraged strategy.

Since an option is a wasting asset (meaning it will expire in the future) it cannot be compared to the purchase of stock in every respect. As a stockholder, you can afford to keep a long position open as long as you wish, and wait for the price to rise. You also earn dividends as long as you own the stock. With options, there are no dividends and expiration is an ever-present problem.

On the other side of the analysis, you can control 100 shares of stock for a small fraction of the cost in buying stock in the traditional manner. The price of the option varies based on proximity between strike price and current price; time to go until expiration; and the volatility in trading on the stock. These three elements are *intrinsic value*, *time value*, and *extrinsic value*:

1. *Intrinsic value* is any portion of the option premium "in the money." Call options are in the money whenever the current value of stock is higher than the strike price of the call. For example, if the strike price is 55 and the current market value is $57 per share, there are two points of intrinsic value in that call. For puts, it is opposite. For example, if the strike price of a put is 55 and the stock is currently at $52, the put has three points of in-the-money value.

2. *Time value* is the actual value of time itself. The longer the time to go until the expiration date arrives, the higher the time value. As expiration approaches, time value evaporates so that on expiration day, it falls to zero.

3. *Extrinsic value* is most often simply lumped in with time value and explained as a variable based on stock volatility. However, there is an element related to interest in the stock, and just as stocks are more volatile with broader trading ranges, options are going to follow that same tendency. So, when you look at identical options on two different stocks—expiring at the same time, with the same strike

price, and with similar or identical proximity to current value—why is the option value different? The answer is found in extrinsic value, that portion of premium reflecting the risk factor.

With option valuation as elusive as it is, one way to approach the leverage potential of options is to consider profit potential to various strategies, but in a comparative manner. This is the only reliable way to develop sound judgment about the potential and risk of one option over another or between options in general versus stock purchase.

The calculation of a simple purchase and sale of an option is not complicated. It works the same as return on investment for a stock purchase. There are two elements: first is the percentage of return, and second is the annualization of that return. In the typical transaction, a trader buys a call or a put and closes the position before expiration. The net difference between purchase and sale price is profit or loss. Calculation for *return on long options* is:

Formula: return on long options

$$(S - P) \div P = R$$

S = closing net sales price
P = opening net purchase price
R = net return

Excel program

A1   closing net sales price
B1   opening net purchase price
C1   =SUM(A1-B1)/B1

For example, if you buy a call at 6 ($600) and three months later close the position at a net of 8 ($800), the net return is $200, or:

$$(\$800 - \$600) \div \$600 = 33.3\%$$

To annualize this return, divide by the number of months held, and multiply by 12:

$$(33.3\% \div 3) * 12 = 133.2\%$$

Annualized return in this example creates a triple-digit outcome. However, the calculation is of limited value. It is useful for comparisons, but is not indicative of an outcome that should be expected to recur consistently.

Annualized return demonstrates the optimal positive outcome of a long position. Historically, 75% of all options held until expiration are worthless, so this exceptionally high return has a trade-off. This disturbing statistic relates only to options held to expiration. It does not take into consideration those options exercised or closed prior to expiration; so the actual percentage of worthless expirations is far lower.

The great advantage to buying options is that for the period those options are held, the buyer has the right to buy or sell 100 shares of the underlying stock at the fixed strike price, no matter what the market price of the stock. Plus, risk is strictly limited. You can only lose the amount of the option premium and no more. In this example, the maximum risk was $600. Were you to buy stock instead, the entire amount invested is at risk. There is no expiration involved in stock ownership, but capital has to be committed and, even employing leverage through a margin account, there is an on-going interest expense to consider in the overall comparison.

Calculations for short positions in options are far more complex. In this variety, the well-known sequence of buy-hold-sell is reversed to sell-hold-buy. The potential profits are higher for short options than for long options, but the risks are also radically altered and often much greater. Based on the specific strategy employed, short options can be high-risk or extremely conservative. A summary of this range of risks:

1. *Uncovered calls* are the highest-risk strategy possible using options. In theory, a stock's price could rise indefinitely, so when you have sold a call you could face an undefined risk. If the call is exercised, you are on the hook for the difference between the strike price and the current market value (minus the premium you were paid).

Formula: return on uncovered calls

$$P - C - S = R$$

P = premium received
C = current market value of stock
S = strike price of call
R = return (profit or loss)

Excel program

A1 premium received
B1 strike price of call
C1 current market value of stock
D1 =SUM(A1-B1-C1)

For example, you sell an uncovered call and receive a premium of 6 ($600). The strike price is 40. However, the stock soars to $62 per share and the call is exercised. Your loss is:

$600 – (6,200 – $4,000) = –$1,600$

If the net difference between strike and price is lower than the premium received, the outcome will be profitable. The loss level depends on the movement in the stock, of course, and because 75% of all options held to expiration expire worthless, there may be only a small chance of exercise—all depending on how the underlying stock price behaves. Even so, because in theory the upside price movement is unlimited, the uncovered short call is a high-risk strategy.

2. *Covered calls.* When you own 100 shares of stock and sell a call, it is "covered" because you can sell the stock to satisfy exercise. Because of this, the covered call is a very conservative strategy. Your only potential loss is increased value in the stock if and when the stock rises. Upon exercise, the stock must be given up at the strike price. The formula for covered call returns is shown below.

Formula: return on covered calls

$(S – B) + P = R$
S = strike of the option (* 100)
B = basis in underlying stock
P = premium received for option
R = return

Excel program

A1 strike of the option
B1 basis in the stock
C1 premium received
D1 =SUM(A1-B1) + C1

For example, you bought 100 shares of stock at $48 per share and sold a covered call with a strike price of 50. The stock rises to 62 and upon exercise, you receive only $50 per share. One way to look at this is as a missed opportunity of $1,200 (difference between price per share of $62 and strike of $50). However, the actual outcome is profitable as long as the basis in stock is lower than the strike of the call. If you were paid $400 in call premium, your net profit on the overall trade is computed by taking into account the net profit on both stock and option:

$($5,000 – $4,800) + $400 = 600

Selling a covered call produces immediate income, but the transaction is not taxed until one of three events occurs: (1) you close the position with a closing purchase transaction, (2) exercise of the call, or (3) expiration. So, it is possible to receive proceeds in one year and not be taxed until the following year.

The covered call can also be looked at as a discount in your basis, thus a reduction of market risk. If you purchase 100 shares at $48 per share and sell a call for 4 ($400), your basis in the stock is reduced to $4,400. So, describing covered calls as conservative is intended as a comparative analysis. On the one hand, owning shares exposes you to market risk as well as offering the potential for gain. But owning shares and selling a covered call reduces your basis in stock, and provides an income stream; the major risk is lost opportunity if and when the stock's price rises.

3. *Uncovered put.* A put cannot be covered in the same manner as a call. In theory, an investor who has gone short on 100 shares of stock could "cover" the position with a short put, but the outcome would not be favorable. Costs would offset any mitigating features. The market risk of the uncovered put is the same as market risk for the covered call.

There are dozens of other options strategies that may be employed to exert leverage or to hedge equity positions in a portfolio. Although most listed options have a relatively short life span, some options extend beyond one year, in which case annualizing is important to judge net returns on a comparative basis with shorter-term options. These long-term options, called *LEAPS* (Long-Term Equity Anticipation Securities) are written out as far as 30 months.

Because stock and option outcomes are two separate transactions, combining them may be viewed as a distortion of option return and risk. Accordingly, the accurate system for risk comparison is to calculate option returns and stock-based capital gains separately.

Conclusion

The first three chapters focused on calculations of returns using various methods. These essential calculations are a base for determining profit or loss; but as the examples of annualized return calculations have shown, time affects your profits as well as changes in the dollar value of investments. The following chapter delves into long-term trends, and shows how time works for you or against you.

---

[i] Damodaran, A. (July 2007). Return on Capital (ROC), Return on Invested Capital (ROIC), and Return on Equity (ROE): Measurement and Implications. *New York University Stern School of Business.*

[ii] Anderson, K. & Brooks, C. (March 2006). Decomposing the price/earnings ratio. *Journal of Asset Management.* Vol. 6, No. 6, pp. 456–469.

Chapter 4
Long-Term Trends:
Patience Rewarded

The methods by which returns are calculated can be deceiving. When you look at the long-term outcome of an investment, how can you decide whether a particular investment has been better than average, or worse? To get the answer, you need to look at compound return on investment over many years.

For example, everyone has heard promotions by mutual funds claiming incredible returns if you had invested $10,000 on a specific date 20 years earlier. You may read that "if you had invested $10,000 exactly 20 years ago, it would be worth more than $26,500 today." As good as this may sound, there are several problems with the claim:

1. *The fund picked a specific date.* If your timing is poor and you invest your $10,000 at a moment when the market is high, it could take many years to recover from a subsequent correction. For example, following the 1929 market crash, it took the market 25 years to recover its losses from a single month. When a mutual fund or other company makes claims about what would have happened to your money, they are able to select a specific date when the market was at a low level.

2. *The outcome is only equal to 5% per year.* The change from $10,000 to more than $26,500 only represents income of slightly over 5% per year. This is not an exceptional return at all over a 20-year period. When you consider inflation and taxes in the mix, a 5% return is a net loss after reduced purchasing power is considered. To calculate this, multiply 1.05 x $10,000, resulting in $10,500 after one year. Multiply 1.05 by that total, and so forth, 20 times, and the final value is $26,533. The 5% per year more than doubles the fund due to compounding.

3. *No consideration is provided for the effect of taxes.* The claims invariably leave out the likely effect of federal and state income taxes. For higher-earning investors, the tax bite is considerable and is likely to affect a decision about where and how to invest.

4. *The fund does not explain its level of fees or charges in the claim.* The claimed outcome might have been a lot higher before the fund deducted its fees. In picking any investment, one of the many comparisons worth making is how much you will be charged per year out of your earnings.

In this chapter, methods for calculating a realistic return on your money over many years are offered, whether the investment is in stocks, bonds, or mutual funds. The annual return might or might not be representative in any given year, so evaluation of any investment strategy has to consider the potential for consistent returns year after year. One poor year can wipe out gains for many previous profitable years; so reviewing risk levels continually is necessary to prevent losses that would be unaffordable.

DOI 10.1515/781501507427-004

A Realistic View: Long-Term Returns and Annual Rates

There are no definitive or universally agreed upon methods for describing the success of an investment. A friend tells you, "I made a 35% profit on that stock," and this can have several different meanings, including:
- The stock was owned for exactly one year and produced a 35% return.
- The stock was held for 10 years and produced an average annual return of 3.5%.
- The stock was bought on margin, meaning the actual return was greater if based on actual amount invested; but lower because interest expenses were paid as well.
- The transaction was the result of buying a call option, so it was highly leveraged but also probably difficult to repeat.
- Most important of all: This was the one success story in a friend's portfolio versus a series of disastrous outcomes.

No one can know the whole story from a single statement. It is, in fact, far more important to know how the entire portfolio performs per year versus the history of investing in a single stock. You should be dubious about such isolated claims because they are part of a larger outcome; you don't know how long the stock was held or how it was purchased; and even if it was a spectacular success, it would not make sense for you to buy shares today . . . the stock apparently has already produced a 35% return, so the opportunity—if it is accurately portrayed—has passed.

Putting aside the possibility that there is more to the story, you also need to appreciate the difference between a one-time outcome and annual performance. The tendency to focus on the exceptional successes is very human, but it distorts the more important picture of how portfolio performance ends up. The real question should be: How does your portfolio perform from year to year?

If you profit by 35% in a single stock but otherwise lose money, it is not a positive outcome. If your average portfolio return is only 3% (or a loss of 5%), it is more revealing than what a single stock's price did. The average annual return is the real bottom line of the portfolio. Because annual average returns are going to vary, it is important to calculate outcomes using an average. To calculate an average, add together the number of entries (in this case, rates of return) and then divide the total by the number of periods involved. The formula for *average* is:

Formula: average

$$(O_1 + O_2 + \ldots O_n) \div E = A$$

O = outcomes
E = number of entries ($_n$)
A = average

Excel program

A1 entry 1
B1 entry 2
C1 entry 3
D1 entry 4
D2 =AVERAGE(A1:D1)

In this example, the average involved four values, listed in cells A1 through D1. The Excel function "Average" adds these together and divides by the number of entries. Assuming the following values, the outcome of averaging is:

(56 + 334 + 32 + 696) ÷ 4 = 279.5

The use of averaging in technical analysis involves numerous price, volume, and momentum indicators. Among the best-known are the 50- and 200-day moving averages (MA). Calculating the average of such a large number of closing prices would be labor intensive. Fortunately, online free charting services perform these and other complex calculations instantly, saving time and effort for the investor intent on tracking average in many different ways.

Reporting a rate of return leads to chronic inaccuracy, which is why averaging is worth the effort. It would not be accurate to tell someone, "I make between 8 and 10 percent return on my portfolio." While that describes two years out of the six, it is far from typical and does not reflect the true average. Another approach, one that reflects the most recent information more than older information, is to use a moving average. For example, you can track your portfolio using the three latest years as summarized in Table 4.1:

Table 4.1: Moving Averages

Year	Number of values	Average
3	4.5 + 7.0 - 1.6 (1, 2 and 3)	3.3%
4	7.0 – 1.6 + 8.4 (2, 3 and 4)	4.6
5	-1.6 + 8.4 + 9.3 (3, 4 and 5)	5.4
6	8.4 + 9.3 -0.7 (4, 5 and 6)	5.7

A comparison between simple average and moving average based on this example is summarized in Figure 4.1.

Average and Moving Average

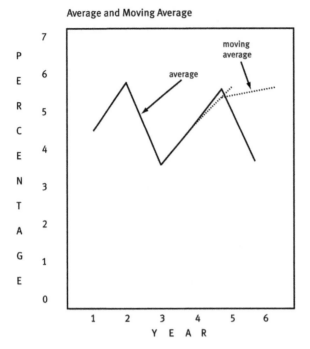

Figure 4.1: Average and Moving Average

The moving average may be a more accurate indicator of the portfolio performance in this case. The gradually rising line reflects the most recent three years rather than an ever-larger field of years, and because the information is perpetually more recent, the smoothing effect translates to greater reliability.

Using averages to track your portfolio will provide you with an evolving trend over time. It would be inaccurate to focus only on the successful outcomes and to ignore the losses. For example, in any of the six years in the example, you might have had one investment that earned you 12% in only three months. That is a 48% return when annualized. But the obvious fact that you did not make 48% overall that year or in any other year demonstrates that it was not *typical*. Investors—chronically optimistic about the future, but also about parts of the past—do tend to focus on their successes and that is a positive trait. At the same time, you want to develop and employ a practical and reliable method for judging your portfolio performance.

In the example provided, the moving average rose each year. This trend line should not be expected to move upward relentlessly; but it may indicate that over time, your ability to choose and time investments is improving. That is the kind of conclusion that is valuable in your self-assessment and in any study of your portfolio. You may apply this logic to your own portfolio management or to that provided by a mutual fund, to determine whether your portfolio is succeeding, and to what degree.

Total Net Annualized Return

In previous chapters, some versions of annualized returns were explained in context. A simple annualized return involves only the basic return on a single transaction; a more complex one involved option premiums and dividend payments received. In practice, the most accurate study of return on investment should not only be annualized; it should also be expressed net of your tax liability, which affects outcomes differently based on overall income and tax bracket.

This is important for a number of reasons, including:

1. *Tax rates at the state level vary considerably.* It is not realistic to assume a universal return on investment. Every state's tax rules are unique and there is no uniformity. A few states apply zero income taxes; others tax only investment returns but not ordinary income. So your net annualized return will depend on your state tax rules.

Valuable website: Check http://www.statetaxcentral.com to find the tax rules and rates in your state.

---

2. *Some investment accounts are not taxable, so results in an IRA account cannot be accurately compared on a pre-tax level to those in your taxable portfolio.* The calculation of net return will also vary based on the environment where you invest. Thus, if you compare your individual (fully taxable) account to investment return in your IRA (where taxes are deferred until withdrawal or retirement) you will find a completely different result. An assumed "equal" tax rate won't apply to the IRA either, based on the theory that after retirement your effective tax rate probably will be lower than today's rate.

3. *Some investments, such as municipal bonds, are either partially or wholly exempt from income taxes.* To compare taxable to non-taxable investments, the tax rate has to be taken into account. The nature of the investment itself also has to be considered. Certain investments are completely tax-free, others only partially taxable. In fact, the comparison between municipal bonds and fully taxable investments has to be made on a net after-tax basis. Many investors discover that they come out slightly ahead with fully taxable investments because (a) the interest rates are higher, and (b) the costs are lower. This is especially true if you purchase tax-free bonds through a mutual fund, where costs can be extremely high.

4. *Your individual tax rate changes as income grows, and is not identical to after-tax returns earned by other investors.* Even within a single state, your after-tax net return will not be identical with your neighbor's return. As your income increases, so does your tax rate. Deductions and exemptions also affect everyone's tax liability. A family with a mortgage deduction and several children will get

more tax breaks than a higher-income working couple with no children and no home mortgage deduction, for example.

The calculation of *net after-tax annualized return* should include both federal and state tax liabilities. For example, if your state's tax rate is 9% and your effective federal rate is 25%, then you will need to use a rate of 34% to figure out your tax. Even though you may be allowed deductions and exemptions that reduce your taxable income, any returns you gain from investment activity will apply at the effective tax rate involving both federal and state taxes together. The "effective" tax rate is the rate applicable to net taxable income after deductions, exemptions, and adjustments are taken into account. The formula:

Formula: net after-tax annualized return

$$I\,((100 - R) \div 100)\,(\div M * 12) = A$$

I = income from investments
R = effective tax rate (federal and state)
M = months held
A = net after-tax annualized return

Excel program

A1 income from investments
B1 effective tax rate
C1 months held
D1 =SUM(A1*(100-B1)/100)
E1 =SUM(D1/C1*12)

For example, investment income for one full year was $18,623. The combined federal and state tax rate was 28%, and the position was held for 8 months. The outcome:

$$\$18{,}623\left((100 - 28) \div 100\right)(\div 8 * 12) = \$20{,}112.84$$

After-tax annualized income is greater than the stated annual income due to annualizing. The position was held only 8 months, so the initial return is reduced by taxes to $13,408.56. Because it was not held for the full year, the annualized result is adjusted to $20,112.84.

This calculation is complicated further by the lower federal rate for long-term capital gains; for exclusion from tax of some types of investments, such as losses on real estate or income on municipal bonds; and great variation in individual state rules. For example, some states tax *only* interest and dividends but not on other forms of income.

Assuming that all investment income is subject to the same rules, this formula can be applied as stated. If other forms of income are taxed at lower rates (such as long-term capital gains) those should be excluded from this calculation and calculated separately; and the two separate calculations added together to find the overall return.

When investments are held for different numbers of months, the calculations have to be performed separately. This calculation has to be applied to each investment; and the purpose to the calculation is to be able to make valid comparisons of outcomes between two or more investments in your portfolio.

You have a lot of control over the net outcome. The tax liability is not going to apply until you close a position, so if your overall income and tax rate were high this year, you can defer selling a stock until the following year as one example of tax avoidance. You can also time sales of profitable portfolio positions to offset losses in other investments. This helps avoid carrying over losses greater than $3,000 (the annual limitation in capital gains). You can also time the sale of stock or mutual funds to report current-year capital gains when you already have a large carry-over loss to absorb.

Annualized return, especially when adjusted for tax considerations, makes side-by-side comparisons accurate. A related calculation is *cumulative return*, which is a calculation of aggregate profit or loss based on overall performance between the purchase date and the current date. This gain or loss may be expressed on either a pretax or after-tax basis. The method should be applied consistently among all positions, to ensure that comparisons are accurate.

Formula: cumulative return

$$(C - I) \div I = R$$

C = current value
I = initial value
R = cumulative return

Excel program

A1   current value
B1   initial value
C1   =SUM(A1-B1)/B1

For example, 37 months ago, you purchased stock with a net cost of $5,716.29. Today, the value has grown to $6,601.77. Cumulative return is:

($6,601.77 – $5,716.29) ÷ $5,716.29 = 15.5%

This is an impressive return; however, it took more than three years to reach that level. Thus, cumulative return should always be annualized to reflect a like-kind comparison between several different investments:

*15.5% ÷ 37 * 12 = 5.0%*

The overall success of this investment was equal to 5% per year. This may be further adjusted for dividends as well as tax liabilities.

Carryover Losses and Net Return

When you do apply current-year gains against carry-over losses, it affects your after-tax calculation as well. Because the carry-over loss may in fact reduce your tax liability to zero, the comparison is complex. You will report a zero tax liability on a particular transaction due to the carry-over loss; but next year an identical sale (when no carry-over loss will be available) may well be taxed at a substantial rate.

These variations should always be remembered so that your comparisons will remain valid. Even when you do use a carry-over loss to reduce or eliminate a tax liability, it makes sense to calculate an after-tax return. The carry-over loss does not change the effective tax rate, it simply eliminates the tax for the current year. So in order to ensure that your comparisons are valid, your calculation will remain consistent when you apply your effective combined (federal and state) tax rate whether you have to pay it or not.

The implications of loss carryover go beyond the initial and obvious point that the tax liability in future periods is reduced. The question of leverage and risk also comes into consideration when calculating the effect of a loss carryover:

> The allowance of offsetting losses has several economic implications . . . it might have an impact on the willingness to employ financial leverage. To be more specific, taxation reduces the average expected yield to investors but it also reduces their risk. However, the higher the financial leverage (i.e., the higher the stockholders' risk) the smaller the probability that loss offsetting would take place. Hence, the structure of the tax offsetting allowance has a direct impact on the desired financial leverage.[i]

The complexity of this calculation also requires consideration of state-level income taxes. Because state taxes are computed using different methods and allow dissimilar deductions than federal, the net outcome often ends up with a different carry-over number. The federal carry-over may be more or less than the state carry-over. The annual allowance for deduction may be different as well. The carry-over application will distort the actual tax liability, perhaps significantly; but because it applies overall, it is going to be extremely difficult to apply it to any one investment. For example, if your current-year carry-over loss is $4,000 but current-year investment income is $9,000, which specific investments should be assumed to benefit from zero tax? Or should the benefit of the carry-over loss be applied equally to all of your investment profits?

Because this carry-over provision applies to your entire investment portfolio and to all of your profits in the current year, there is no equitable way to apply the loss. So there is only one possible method to use: Estimate your after-tax profit assuming that there is no carry-over loss. Compare all of your profits on the same basis—as they would be taxed without a carry-over—and separate the calculation from the actual outcome.

Some carry-over losses may be significant. Those investors who lost a lot of money in the market crash of 2008 and 2009 may never fully absorb their carry-over losses. It is possible that these investors will not have an actual tax liability for many years to come, and perhaps never. But it remains important to compare outcomes between two or more investments on a taxable basis as though no carry-over losses were available, even when none of your investment gains will be taxed this year. Only by using this assumption can you realistically compare investment outcome in your taxable portfolio, your tax-deferred portfolio (an IRA or pension plan, for example), and tax-exempt investments like municipal bonds. If you were to use a zero tax in your computations, it distorts the outcome even when you owe no tax.

This argument also applies when your overall income is lower than your investment profits. For example, if you operate your own business and report a profit each year, your effective tax rate reflects the dollar level of those annual profits. But what happens if your business income is exceptionally low one year? For example, assume your annual return on investments is $15,000 in capital gains, interest and dividends; and your taxable business income averages $85,000. Your gross income before deductions and exemptions is $100,000. But if your business income next year is only $10,000, your overall gross would be only $25,000. It does not take much in the way of itemized deductions and exemptions to bring your taxable income down to zero.

In this situation, should you use a zero tax rate to compare investments? A valid and realistic comparison of portfolio performance in this situation would be invalid if you expect the overall gross income level to return to more typical levels the following year. So when you calculate your after-tax returns, it makes the most sense to use a *typical* tax rate rather than the actual rate you will pay this year. The specific circumstances distorting the actual tax liability (carry-over loss or business loss) distort these outcomes and should not be compared to net return in other, more typical years.

The same rationale should be applied in years when your tax rate is exceptionally high. A large profit in your business or in the market can take your federal and state effective tax rates up to the highest brackets; but if those rates are unusual and not typical, it doesn't make sense to compare after-tax returns in those years to after-tax returns in more typical years.

Because of the complexity of tax calculations, attempt to identify a realistic and typical tax rate and apply that to all investment returns, whether you will pay much less or much more in any one year. The comparison should not be distorted by one-time changes in your taxable income. The tax affect cannot be ignored, especially when the overall rate is high; but in years when that rate spikes up or down and away from the average, that typical rate should still be used.

Realistic Expectations: Inflation and Taxes

Taxes alone are not the only factor reducing your net return from investments. Inflation also has to be considered in the mix. One consequence of inflation is reduced purchasing power of your money. In other words, a dollar today will buy only 97 cents worth of goods after a 3% inflation year.

The ramifications of inflation and the extent to which it impacts not only net returns, but also taxation itself, are severe. The inflation factor makes year-to-year comparisons of unchanging effective tax rates less and less applicable. The higher the inflation rate, the less reliable the comparisons of annual tax liabilities:

> Inflation affects tax liabilities in three ways. First, it may alter real factor incomes. Second, it affects the measurement of taxable income. Third, it changes the real value of deductions, exemptions, credits, ceilings and floors, bracket widths, and all other tax provisions legally fixed in nominal terms.[ii]

These considerations affect analysis of tax policy and liabilities from year to year. On an annual basis and from the investor's point of view, the combination of inflation and taxes is equally profound. One of the most important calculations every investor needs to perform is the *breakeven return* they need to earn net of inflation and taxes. In the interest of avoiding risk, if you select investments with returns lower than your breakeven point, you end up losing money on a post-tax, post-inflation basis.

The calculation of breakeven return is:

Formula: breakeven return

$$I \div (100 - R) = B$$

I = rate of inflation
R = effective tax rate (federal and state)
B = breakeven return

Excel program

A1 rate of inflation
B1 effective tax rate
C1 =-SUM(A1/(100-B1))

For example, if the current rate of inflation is 3% per year and your effective tax rate (federal and state combined) is 34%, your breakeven return is:

3% ÷ (100 – 34) = 4.5%

Valuable website: Current inflation rates are provided free of charge at https://inflationdata.com/Inflation/Inflation_Rate/CurrentInflation.asp and also from the Bureau of Labor Statistics at https://www.bls.gov/cpi/.

This formula demonstrates that you need to earn 4.5% on your money just to break even, considering both taxes and inflation:

Basis invested	$100.00
Assumed gross return, 4.5%$	4.50
Less: 34% tax	− 1.53
Less: Inflation, 3%	− 3.00
Total reductions	$ 4.53
Net return	$ − 0.03

This example shows that on a "net, net" basis—reducing the 4.5% return for both taxes and inflation—the investment yielded nothing (except three cents due to rounding). To calculate the breakeven point, use the chart in Table 4.2.

A stark reality is that when both taxes and inflation are taken into account, simply keeping pace with the purchasing power of your capital is a challenge. It makes no sense to select investments that are extremely safe but yield a return below your breakeven; to do so means to lose. At the same time, as the breakeven rises due to the double effect of taxes and inflation, it becomes ever more difficult to consistently achieve a breakeven. To do so requires greater market risks.

These realities about taxes and inflation demonstrate the importance of tax deferral and reinvesting earnings. When you reinvest capital gains, interest and dividends, you achieve a compound return on your money.

The effect of inflation and taxes on a single year's return may be a serious reduction in actual profitability. But because compound returns accelerate over time, reinvestment makes sense. Mutual funds allow reinvestment of all forms of income, as an automatic occurrence; other than electing to receive dividends in additional partial shares, you need to take steps on your own to create compound returns. When you create a capital gain by selling stock, for example, you need to figure out how to reinvest those funds as quickly as possible to continue keeping your capital at work. If you time your decisions based on market movements and trends, this may be quite difficult. For example, if you believe you should be out of the market right now, where do you invest your funds?

Table 4.2: Calculating the Breakeven Point

Effective Tax Rate	Inflation Rate					
	1%	2%	3%	4%	5%	6%
14%	1.2%	2.3%	3.5%	4.7%	5.8%	7.0%
16%	1.2	2.4	3.6	4.8	6.0	7.1
18%	1.2	2.4	3.7	4.9	6.1	7.3
20%	1.3	2.5	3.8	5.0	6.3	7.5
22%	1.3	2.6	3.8	5.1	6.4	7/7
24%	1.3%	2.6%	3/9%	5.3%	6.6%	7.9%
26%	1.4	2.7	4.1	5.4	6.8	8.1
28%	1.4	2.8	4.2	5.6	6.9	8.3
30%	1.4	2.9	4.3	5.7	7.1	8.6
32%	1.5	2.9	4.4	5.9	7.4	8.8
34%	1.5%	3.0%	4.5%	6.1%	7.6%	9.1%
36%	1.6	3.1	4.7	6.3	7.8	9.4
38%	1.6	3.2	4.8	6.5	8.1	9.7
40%	1.6	3.2	5.0	6.7	8.3	10.0
42%	1.7	3.4	5.2	6.9	8.6	10.3

At the very least, available funds should be kept in a money market account and allowed to earn interest until you select another investment. The importance of compound returns is best understood when you see how the time value of money works. In fact, *time* is the essential element in creating powerful long-term returns by keeping money at work.

Compound Return Calculations

Investors need to track their investments in terms of how their capital is put to work. As a stockholder, you can afford to wait out a slow period in the market. However, if it takes five years for you to realize a 20% return, that is only 5% per year. The time element is an essential ingredient in comparative judgment about the success of an investment program and the effectiveness of your decisions. This argument applies not only to capital gains and dividends, but also to interest on money market accounts or bond funds. If your bond fund invests in long-term but low-yielding high-grade bonds, it is possible that these "safe" decisions will lag behind your required breakeven return.

Whether applied to interest, dividends, or capital gains, figuring out your annual returns is the most reliable method for comparison. The annualization formula is easily applied to any simple return; but in fact, the stated interest rate can also vary depending on compounding methods. When interest is compounded, it means the calculation is performed more than once per year; or that year-to-year interest is added to the principal balance and carried forward. With a compounding effect, you gain an accelerating return over many years. This is why the claims that $10,000 turns into $26,500 over 20 years sounds good, but is dismal. It is only a 5% return per year, but this is compounded year after year, so an investment earns interest not only on the amount invested, but on accumulated interest as well. This interest on interest (compounding) is what makes the time element so critical. Thus, the first year's return is $500 (1.05 * $10,000 = $10,500). The second year is 1.05 * $10,500, or $11,025. Carried out for 20 years, this shows how compounding works. The principal value rises each year as interest is added; and then the account earns interest on interest.

Compounding methods describe the number of times per year that interest is calculated. For example, when you are told that an investment earns 6%, is this an annual rate without adjustment? Or is the calculation of interest performed semi-annually, quarterly, monthly, or daily? These distinctions make a difference in the *Annual Percentage Rate* (APR) of the investment.

The basic interest computation involves three elements: principal, interest, and time. The formula for *interest* is:

Formula: interest

$$P * R * T = I$$

P = principal
R = interest rate
T = time
I = interest

Excel program

A1 principal
B1 interest rate
C1 time

D1 =SUM(A1*B1*C1)

For example, assuming that interest is calculated only once per year, a 6% rate applied to $100 would be:

$100 * 6% * 1 = $6.00

In calculating interest, the stated rate is actually expressed in decimal form; so 6% becomes .06. The annual interest is $100 * .06, or $6.00 per year.

This process becomes more involved when interest is calculated on a compounded method. For example, if 6% is to apply on a semi-annual basis (twice per year), the annual rate is divided by the number of periods and then multiplied twice. The formula for *semiannual compounding* is:

Formula: semiannual compounding

$$(1 + (R \div 2))^2 = I$$

R = stated interest rate
I = annual percentage rate (APR)

For example, if the $100 deposit is to be compounded semiannually, it should be multiplied by the APR as calculated above:

$(1 + (.06 \div 2))^2 = I$
$(1 + .03)^2 = I$
$1.03 * 1.03 = 1.0609$

The $100 deposit will grow annually at a rate of 6.09% using semiannual compounding:

$100.00 * 1.0609 = $106.09

The calculation, performed twice per year, provides a simplified version of how compounding works. Semiannual compounding involves two periods per year. Quarterly compounding requires the use of four periods, each equal to one-fourth of the annual rate. Monthly compounding divides the annual interest into 12. And daily compounding is the most involved, dividing the stated annual rate into either 360 or 365 portions.

Most stock investors use compound interest only for calculation of interest on savings, or to calculate the effect of reinvesting dividends. The formulas are available online with useful compound interest calculators.

The Securities and Exchange Commission (SEC) provides a free online compound interest calculator, at https://www.investor.gov/additional-resources/free-financial-planning-tools/compound-interest-calculator

---

Compound interest works to make your money grow faster. For example, if money is invested in a mutual fund with instructions to reinvest dividends and capital gains, a compounding effect is possible. Compounding can also work against you. When you owe money, compounding more frequently translates into greater interest. For example, home mortgage debt is usually subject to monthly compounding. Your monthly interest consists of 1/12th of the annual rate, multiplied by the loan's balance forward. This explains why interest is quite high during the early years of the loan and much smaller in the later years. If your mortgage rate is 6% and you are paying over 30 years, the loan is only one-half paid off during the twenty-first year.

Other Cash Flow Trends

Every investor tracking money-related trends understands that money placed at risk should come back at some point. Otherwise, the investment does not make sense. The analysis of cash flow in an investment refers to periodic dividends and capital gains. The question is, how long will it take to retrieve the initial investment from cash flow? This question is complex because investing on margin allows you to finance 50% of a stock purchase, so the true "investment" consists of net cash paid, minus the interest cost of borrowing on margin. The *payback ratio* is calculated by dividing the investment by calculated cash flow.

Formula: payback ratio

$$I \div C = R$$

I = cash invested
C = net cash flow
R = ratio

Excel program

A1   cash invested
B1   net cash flow
C1   =SUM(A1/B1)

For example, $60,000 is invested initially, and annual cash flow is estimated to net $3,275. The payback ratio is

$$\$60,000 \div \$3,275 = 18.3 \text{ years}$$

The payback ratio is an excellent comparative tool. If a particular investment produces a faster payback ratio than another, this is a positive indicator.

A second cash flow–related calculation is *cash-on-cash return*. This ratio is also called the *equity dividend yield*. This is a return calculation used in pooled programs such as limited partnerships. Usually limited to evaluation of programs based on projections of the first-year cash flow, the ratio provides a comparative analysis. Limited partnerships are concerned with annual cash flow, just as all investors have to be, and they try to raise investment capital by presenting cash flow projections; one method of analyzing and comparing the cash flow risk of different programs is to study the relative health of cash flow. This can be done in two ways: historically and as projected. Historical cash-on-cash return is the actual results reported by a program, and projections are estimates of the future.

Formula: cash-on-cash return

$$C \div I = R$$

C = annual cash flow
   I = cash investment
   R = cash-on-cash return

Excel program

A1 annual cash flow
B1 cash investment
C1 =SUM(A1/B1)

In addition to providing a comparison of cash-on-cash return between different investments, the ratio can also be used to get a sense of how programs compare to other investments. For example, if you can earn an estimated 7 percent in the stock market compared to 13.7 percent in a limited partnership, it adds to your insight. Comparisons between dissimilar investments are not easily made; all of the factors have to be considered in the mix, including degrees of risk, levels of capital required, personal risk tolerance, liquidity, and investing goals.

Return Formulas

Calculating *return on investment* can mean many things. Some may prefer calculating the increase in a property's market value as the benchmark of success. This is also the most common method of comparison among properties, regions, and other markets. In considering realistically how "return" really applies, however, the real return to an individual also depends on the cash investment. Consider the differences between the *rate of return* and *current yield*.

Rate of return is a calculation that is used in different markets to describe and compare how investments have performed. It is universally accepted as the ultimate measurement of an investment's success. For example, if you purchase stock at $20 per share and later sell it for $30, your rate of return is 50 percent (profit of $10 ÷ $20 original cost). Even for investments not yet sold, current market value is often used as a way of explaining how investments have performed.

Formula: rate of return

$$(C - B) \div B = R$$

C = current value (or sales price)
B = original cost or basis
R = rate of return

Excel program

A1   current value
B1   original cost or basis
C1   =SUM(A1-B1)/B1

For example, today's estimated market value of 100 shares of stock is $300,000 and original cost was $23,500. The rate of return in this example is computed by dividing the difference between cost and value by original cost:

$$(\$30,000 - \$23,500) \div \$23,500 = 0.2766 \ (27.66\%)$$

To make the calculation reliable (and comparable between different properties), it is also important to annualize the return. Adjust the percentage outcome as it would have been reflected on a one-year holding period. For example, if a property had been purchased for $23,500 and is worth $30,000 today, the annualized rate of return over five years would be:

$$((\$30,000 - \$23,500) \div \$23,500)) \div 5 = 5.53\%$$

Annualizing makes a profound difference in how one investment compares to another. For example, the outcome is much different if the same investment had been held for only four months:

$(($30,000 - $23,500) \div $23,500)) \div 4 * 12 = 83.0\%$

The use of the rate of return formula to calculate paper profit is valid also. Without disposing of holdings, this calculation enables you to determine the current return if sold. However, in this situation, the details of cash flow and tax benefits over the holding period would not be considered. Thus, rate of return may be viewed as an estimate of how investment values have grown in gross market value; as long as the same exclusions are applied to all holdings, the comparison remains valid. As in all cases, comparisons are reliable only if performed on the same basis.

To judge returns realistically, especially upon the sale of investments, you need to use an annualized basis that accounts for *all* types of income or loss. This *total return* calculation is the dollar amount of net gains from the investment; it includes the net income earned during the period that the property was held on an after-tax basis and capital gains net of income tax liabilities.

This raises an interesting question. In calculating total return, should you base it on the outcome as completed or on an *as if* basis? That would include a calculation of the federal and state tax liabilities that would be incurred upon sale, or may be deferred by taking no action. It is appropriate to compute the tax liability for two reasons. First, you continue to owe the tax, although it won't be paid until later. Second, to make the calculation comparable to other properties, you will need to make the two calculations comparable.

Formula: total return per year

$(C + I - B) \div B \div Y = R$

C = capital gains
I = total net income
B = basis
Y = years held
R = total return

Excel program

A1   capital gains
B1   total net income
C1   basis
D1   years held

E1 =SUM((A1+B1-C1)/C1/D1)

The calculation of total return involves several steps. For example, a stock purchase was made at a net cost of $10,500. The adjusted sale price consists of the net sales price after trading fees. If the stock were sold for $13,950 net, it represents a capital gain. Federal and state taxes due on the capital gains depends on holding period and state tax rules.

Total return also includes the sum of net income received during the holding period. This includes dividends received. For the purposes of showing the calculation, assume a five-year net dividend income was $1,500. The annualized five-year total return on this example is:

(($13,950 +$1,500 − $10,500) ÷ $10,500)) ÷ 5 = 9.4%

Total return often is named *return on investment* or *return on equity*. Total return considers the change in overall value including dividend income and net cost of trading, so under that calculation, "investment" is the same as market value, even though various levels of cost and benefit can be involved. The return on equity will vary considerably based on the eventual federal and state tax liability upon completion of a sale.

Total return is a reliable method for calculating the "net net" outcome of an investment, even when the full trade may take just a matter of days or several years. By annualizing the return, outcomes among different investments are expressed on a consistent basis. An investor relying on cash flow to judge investments may easily overlook this nuance unless all returns are annualized between original date of entry and final date of exit. Many consider annualizing an unnecessary extra step. However, a 9.4% return over five years is not as attractive as the same return over five weeks . . . or five days.

The range of calculation is further complicated when considering *current yield*, the income per year from dividend income paid to those holding dividend-paying stock. As an initial consideration, two different companies with similar fundamental attributes should be further quantified by their current yield. One stock paying a low dividend (or no dividend) will not be as attractive as another paying an exceptional dividend. The same comparison applies to investors who choose to buy bonds and similar debt instruments. In that case, current yield (the percentage yield based on whether the bond trades at a premium or a discount) is not the same as the stated yield, or *nominal yield* on the bond. So current yield is the percentage on the current price of the bond, which is not always the same as the face value.

Formula: nominal yield (bond)

$$A \div F = N$$

A = annual interest
F = face value of the bond
N = nominal yield

Excel program

A1   annual interest
B1   face value of the bond
C1   =SUM(A1/B1)

A bond of $1,000 paying $20 per year has nominal yield of:

$$\$20 \div \$1,000 = 2\%$$

Current yield is calculated based on adjustments to face value for discount or premium of the bond.

Formula: current yield (bond)

$$A \div P = Y$$

A = annual interest
P = price of the bond
Y = current yield

Excel program

A1   annual yield
B1   price of the bond
C1   =SUM(A1/B1)

For example, a bond with face value of $1,000 pays nominal yield of 2%, or $20 per year. However, that bond currently is priced at a discount of 97, or $970. Current yield is:

$$\$20 \div \$970 = 2.06\%$$

If the same bond were priced at a premium of 103, the current yield would be:

$20 ÷ $1,003 = 1.99%

Current yield of stock is calculated to reflect dividend yield as a percentage of current price per share. This is more popularly known as *dividend yield*. If the stock price rises, current yield declines and if the stock price declines, current yield rises.

Formula: dividend yield

$$D ÷ P = Y$$

D = dividend per share
P = current price per share
Y = dividend yield

Excel program

A1   dividend per share
B1   current price per share
C1   =SUM(A1/B1)

For example, one company has declared a dividend of $1.50 per share and the current price at time of purchase is $51.00. Current yield is 2.94%. If the stock price rises to $58, yield changes to 2.59%. If the price declines to $46 per share, current yield changes to 3.26%.

Another calculation is based on a comparison between original discount and cash flow. The *equity dividend yield* should also be made consistently to ensure like-kind comparisons. One investment, for example, might yield dividend of 2% average per year, while another yields 5%. Equity dividend yield can be used as a means for determining whether to keep or dispose of one investment or another. The formula is based on cash dividends received per year.

Formula: equity dividend yield

$$C ÷ N = Y$$

C = net cash flow
N = net cash paid
Y = equity dividend yield

Excel program

> A1 net cash flow
> B1 down payment
> C1 =SUM(A1/B1)

For example, you are holding two investments, both based on net cost of $8,000. Of this, $4,000 was paid and the balance of $4,000 is financed by your brokerage company. One of the two yields average annual dividend of $360, and the other produces $105. The first property's equity dividend yield is:

> $360 ÷ $4,000 = 9.0%

In the second case:

> $105 ÷ $4,000 = 2.6%

Even though the difference in dividend yield is based on the full purchase price, the net cash paid is only half of that amount, so a higher dividend translates to a substantially higher comparative equity dividend yield. The difference could affect a selection of one company's stock over the other when stock is purchased on margin.

Useful Return Shortcuts

The comparison between return calculations can be considerably reduced to a series of useful shortcuts, designed to help investors develop a comparative tool to judge one stock against another, especially with dividend yield in mind. Among these, the best-known is the *rule of 72*. This tells you approximately how long it will take for an investment to double in value, based on the combination of current dividend yield plus estimated annual price appreciation. The number 72 is divided by the estimated yield.

Formula: rule of 72

> $72 \div i = Y$

> i = interest rate
> Y = years required to double

Excel program

A1 =SUM(72/interest rate)

For example, assume the current dividend yield of 4% will be accompanied by annual average increase in stock price of 5%. The total will average 9%. How long will it take for your original investment to double:

$$72 \div 9 = 8$$

It will take eight years for your investment to double in value, based on your assumption of price increase and a second assumption that dividend yield will remain as a constant.

This outcome can be proven based on annual compounding. For example, investing $8,000 and expecting to yield $320 per year in dividends plus $400 per year in price appreciation provides a basic, pre-tax net return:

$$\$8,000 * (1.09)^8 = \$15,941$$

The outcome is within $50 of the estimated 8-year time required to double the investment's value. A slightly more accurate calculation is called the *rule of 69*. In this variation, 69 is divided by the assumed annual yield and 0.35 is added to the result.

Formula: rule of 69

$$(69 \div i) + 0.35 = Y$$

i = interest rate
Y = years required to double

Excel program

A1 =SUM (69/interest rate)+0.35

Applying this adjusted formula to the previous example:

$$(69 \div 9\%) + 0.35 = 8.02 \ years$$

A third formula helps estimate the length of time required for an investment to triple in value. As with all estimates based on assumptions, the longer the time involved, the less reliable the outcome. With this in mind, when using the *rule of 113*, greater time converts to less certainty but the application is very similar to the rule of 72. Divide 113 by the annual interest rate to determine the years until the investment will triple in value.

Formula: rule of 113

$$113 \div i = Y$$

i = interest rate
Y = years required to triple

Excel program

A1 =SUM(113/interest rate)

For example, with assumed annual yield of 9%, an investment will triple in:

113 ÷ 9% = 12.56 years

The many ways of calculating "return" on investment point out why confusion reigns among investors and why so many sources of advice (in person and online) publish conflicting or inconsistent reports on the potential for a particular plan of investing. The only solution is to ensure that in any comparative analysis, the same methods and assumptions are applied to each case.

Estimating the Value of Deposits over Time

Beyond calculating returns, investors are also interested in estimating outcomes when a series of deposits are made every month. What will that fund be worth after several years? To know the answer, an assumed average rate of return has to be applied. For example, an investment program may involve depositing $100 per month over several years. Assuming a given rate of return, what will the total of those deposits be worth years later?

The *accumulated value of 1 per period* is calculated by applying the assumptions about the period (a month, for example), amount of deposit each period ($100), the assumed rate of return (4% per year, for example), and the number of periods overall. The system of depositing a fixed amount over time is used commonly for investment in mutual funds. As long as all income is reinvested to purchase additional shares, the result is a compounding effect.

Formula: accumulated value of 1 per period

$$[D [(1 + R)^n - 1] \div R] * P = A$$

D = periodic deposit amount
R = periodic interest rate
n = number of periods
P = principal
A = accumulated value of 1 per period

Excel program

A1 $=FV(r/n,y*n,d)$

r = interest rate
n = number of periods per year
y = number of years
d = amount of periodic deposits

On an Excel spreadsheet, the 'FV' function ("future value) reduces this calculation to a simple set of inputs. All of the information required in entered in a single line of code: interest rate, periods per year (such as 12 months), and amount of the deposit per month. Assuming 4% interest and $100 per month over 36 months (three years):

$=FV(4\%/12,3*12,100)$

This yields a result of $3,818.16 on the Excel spreadsheet. The outcome is proven with the formula:

$$\$100 [(1 + 0.00333)^{36} - 1] \div 0.00333 = \$3,818.16$$

If the assumption about the number of deposits is other than monthly, change the number of periods to reflect the difference. For example, for quarterly deposits of $100 (total of $1,200):

$=FV(4\%/4,3*4,100)$

This yields $1,268.25. Proof:

$$\$100 [(1 + 0.01)^{12} - 1] \div 0.01 = \$1,268.25$$

With these simplified Excel formulas, calculating the effect of making periodic deposits for any number of years is vastly simplified.

The opposite of accumulated value is *present value*. Also based on periodic rates and dollar amounts, present value is the calculation of how today's starting value grows over time. For example, a fixed amount of money placed into an investment today will grow based on compound interest and the amount of time the funds are left on deposit. The *present value of 1 per period* shows how much you need to deposit periodically to reach a target value, based on assumed annual yield and the time allowed.

Formula: present value of 1 per period

$$1 \div (1 + R)^n = P$$

R = periodic interest rate
n = periods
P = present value factor

Excel program

A1 = PV(r,p,0,FV)

r = interest rate
P = number of periods
0 = starting point (beginning of period)
FV = future value

On Excel, the PV function (present value) allows you to reduce an otherwise complex formula down to a single line of code. The elements are the interest rate, number of periods, starting point (zero), and the amount to be achieved in the future. Assuming 4% compounded monthly over three years, how much has to be deposited today in a single deposit to achieve a balance of $1,000 in three years?

=PV(0.333%,36,0,1000)

This produces an answer of $887.20. Placing this amount into an account, if the yield is consistently at 4%, it will grow to $1,000 in three years.

A final aspect of interest rates applies when the rate is not identical for two separate investments. For example, you average 4% from a stock portfolio, and only 2.5% in a series of mutual fund investments. To discover the *weighted average interest rate*, a specific calculation has to be applied, because the investment value of each segment within your portfolio is not likely to be identical.

Formula: weighted average interest rate

$$[(L_1 * R_1) + (L_2 * R_2)] \div L_t = A$$

L_1 = balance, investment 1
L_2 = balance, investment 2
L_t = total balances of investments
R_1 = rate on investment 1
R_2 = rate on investment 2
A = average rate

Excel program

A1 investment balance #1
A2 investment balance #2
A3 =SUM(A1 + A2)
B1 rate, investment #1 (decimal form)
B2 rate, investment #2 (decimal form)
C1 =SUM(A1 * B1)
C2 =SUM(A2 * B2)
C3 =SUM(C1 + C2)
D1 =SUM(C3/A3) * 100

For example, two segments of a portfolio involve directly owned stocks and mutual funds. The stock portfolio has a balance of $80,000 and has yielded a combined dividend and capital gain profit of 7% over the past year. The mutual fund portfolio has a balance of $20,000 and has yielded 11% for one year. Applying the formula:

$$[(\$80,000 * 7\%) + (\$20,000 * 11\%)] \div \$100,000 = 7.8\%$$

This disproportionate average reflects the greater weighting in the stock portfolio with a lower overall interest rate. The weighting is taken into account, making the calculation easier.

An alternative method would be simpler but less accurate. Simply averaging the two rates of return of 11% and 7% yields an average of 9%. However, because of the disproportionate investment value on each side, this average yield would not reflect the accurate results uncovered through using a weighting formula.

The same formulas can be expanded for three or more portfolio segments, or even to discover average returns for individual components within a single portfolio, such as several different stocks, ETFs, or mutual funds. For example, assume you want to analyze three portfolio components. One has a balance of $85,000 and a 7% return;

another of $25,000 has an 11% return; and the third with a balance of $10,000 has a 14% return:

$$[(\$85,000 * 7\%) + (\$25,000 * 11\%) + (\$10,000 * 14\%)] \div \$120,000 = 8.4\%$$

Conclusion

The calculation of trends over time relies on several variables. These include annualizing and applying a variety of methods for determining accurate outcomes. Relying on moving averages helps smooth out an otherwise erratic year-to-year result. As this chapter reveals, there are many similar but distinctly different calculations involved in tracking results over time. Making this even more complex is yet another adjustment, from reported net earnings to core net earnings. The "core" calculation, developed by *Standard & Poor's Corporation,* often changes results substantially. This reflects removal of non-recurring elements within GAAP-based earnings reports, but the adjustment is overlooked in most trend analysis and return calculations. The next chapter examines the core earnings adjustment and how it impacts net returns.

---

[i] Barlev, B. and Levy, H. (June 1975). Loss Carryback and Carryover Provision: Effectiveness and Economic Implications. *National Tax Journal.* Vol. 28, No. 2, pp. 173–184.
[ii] Aaron, H. (May 1976). Inflation and the Income Tax. *The American Economic Review.* Vol. 6, No. 2, pp. 193–199.

Chapter 5
Core Earnings and Net Worth Adjustments: Making the Numbers Real

Before embarking on a discussion of fundamental analysis (Chapters 6 and 7) a distinction must be made—between what is reported on financial statements and what is real. In fact, if fundamental analysis is to be reliable and accurate, making core earnings adjustments is a necessary first step.

When Standard & Poor's Corporation (S&P) developed its concept of "*core earnings*," the estimate was that the S&P 500 corporations saw earnings overstated by about 30% during the first year the adjustment was calculated.[i] The core earnings (or "true economic profit") of a company may be significantly different than the earnings a company reports under the GAAP (Generally Accepted Accounting Principles) system. What is allowed and what is accurate are not the same, and this is where the problem arises. A 30% downward adjustment affects not only the profitability and equity of a company; it also makes most forms of financially-based analysis useless. For this reason, using the core net profit and core net worth values are a reliable means for applying financial formulas and ratios. Essentially, core earnings adjustments are an attempt to remove non-recurring and non-operational sources for reported profits and reflect the remainder, the *core* generated from business activity (and not from exchange rate adjustments, capital gains, and accounting elections, for example).

Where do you find these data? Fortunately, S&P calculates the often complex adjustments between reported and core earnings on its *CFRA Stock Reports* service. The reports for each company, including a 10-year financial summary, are provided by the major online brokerage services free of charge. Charles Schwab, for example, contains a link for each listed company to the Stock Reports and other analytical services. As of 2016, the *CFRA Stock Reports* format remained unchanged, but the service was acquired from S&P by CFRA Research. This is the title employed by online brokerage services for reporting the S&P data.

S&P devised core earnings as adjustments due to the inaccuracies in how financial information is reported. They made a distinction between three separate versions of "earnings" used in the accounting and corporate worlds. Reported, operating, and *pro forma* earnings are all used in various ways. The S&P comment regarding *pro forma* earnings made an important point regarding the rationale for core earnings adjustments:

> Originally, the use of the term pro forma meant a special analysis of a major change, such as a merger, where adjustments were made for an "as if" review. In such cases, pro forma measures are very useful. However, the specific items being considered in an "as if" review must be clear. In some recent cases, "as if" has come to mean "as if the company didn't have to cover proper

DOI 10.1515/9781501507427-005

expenses." In the most extreme cases, pro forma is nicknamed EBBS, or "earnings before bad stuff."[ii]

The observation of flaws in how earnings are reported led S&P to devise the concept of core earnings adjustments, which is defined by S&P specifically:

> Core Earnings refer to the after-tax earnings generated from a corporation's principal business or businesses. Since there is a general understanding of what is included in as reported earnings, the definition of Core Earnings begins with as reported earnings and then makes a series of adjustments. As Reported is earnings as defined by GAAP, with three exclusions—extraordinary items, cumulative effect of accounting changes, and discontinued operations, all as defined by GAAP.[iii]

The Problem with Today's Accounting Rules

The accounting industry is assumed to be the watchdog of publicly listed companies. Every company trading stock is required to undergo periodic independent audits and produce certified financial statements. For decades, the investing public has viewed this process as its line of defense against fraud and inaccuracy.

The confidence placed in the independent audit is misplaced.

The audit process is not proactive. Many investors assume that the audit is designed to discover and fix problems, but in fact it is a very passive activity. The audit is designed to ensure that the accounting decisions conform to GAAP (Generally Accepted Accounting Principles). These standards are complex and at times contradictory, so in practice the audit team will only insist on changes when accounting decisions are glaringly wrong. Even then, there have been numerous instances in which incorrect or even dishonest accounting decisions have not been reversed during an audit. The extreme case of Enron is only one of many instances where corporations have deceived investors and the independent audit has not fixed the problem.

The reasons are many, including:

1. *Basic conflict of interest.* The audit firm doesn't restrict its activities to an annual audit. Most firms also perform numerous consulting tasks for their audit clients, including design of internal systems, legal and personnel work, and accounting functions themselves. This involvement creates two problems. First, the auditing firm often ends up auditing its own work. Second, revenues from consultation are approximately equal to revenues from auditing, and at times far greater. So consulting has become a major source of revenue for the auditing firms. The conflict of interest is glaring. And the legislation passed in 2002 (Sarbanes-Oxley Act) was designed to fix this problem, but it has had little effect.

2. *Close relationships between executives and auditors.* Historically, the audit team worked closely with the CEO and CFO, often negotiating and compromising on

proposed changes in accounting policies. If an audit team was too inflexible in its insistence that certain decisions had to be changed, the company might decide to change to another auditing firm. Because auditors are judged within their firm by revenue production, losing a big client could be disastrous for a person's career. The case of Arthur Andersen and its close ties to Enron was the most glaring example of this problem.

In addition, many auditors have always been recruited from client ranks, so an accounting executive may easily end up working for the auditing firm. The Sarbanes-Oxley Act (SOX) places restrictions on audit work by anyone working for a client in the recent past; but this situation only augments the degree of the problem. The failure of the accounting industry to maintain distance between itself and its clients is disturbing.

3. *Failure to take the auditing role as a public responsibility.* In theory, the audit is independent and it is performed on behalf of the company's shareholders. In practice, executives and the board's audit committee decide which firm to hire (or fire) and the auditing industry has not taken its role seriously. The idea that the independent audit is designed to protect shareholders from unethical executives has simply not worked. And SOX has not fixed that problem. Several years after the Enron scandal, the financial news consistently reveals corporate financial problems.

4. *A cultural desire to keep stock prices high.* Auditors understand that corporations want their stock price to remain high. A CEO and CFO depend on ever-higher prices to earn their incentive compensation. These bonus and option packages often exceed their base pay significantly and represent millions of dollars per year. This creates an obvious secondary conflict for the executive. If earnings fall below expectations this year, the stock price is likely to fall as well. If a drop of several points in the stock's value represents several million dollars in compensation, it is important. The auditor may not directly conspire with an executive to artificially inflate earnings, but this cultural aspect to accounting is widely understood. When earnings meet expectations, everyone is happy.

The problems of how the numbers get reported are significant. For anyone depending on audited financial statements to perform an analysis of a corporation, this is a disturbing reality. But the numbers do reveal the truth in many ways. The following guidelines help to get around the deception and inaccuracy of audited financial statements:

1. *Long-term trends reveal the truth.* Studying one year's financial statements does not tell you much at all. You need to (a) identify the ratios you find most useful, and (b) look for long-term trends in those ratios. Chapters 6 and 7 help to reduce the number of possible ratios to a few of the most valuable financial tests to perform over many years.

2. *Using specific formulas in combination reveals hidden facts.* The use of any one ratio reveals part of the picture. But to truly understand what is going on, you need to have all of the pieces. For example, testing working capital by tracking current assets and liabilities (through the current ratio) is instructive; but to see the entire picture, you also need to track long-term debt trends. Watching revenues over time is also useful and most investors like to see revenues rise each year. But if profits are flat or falling, the rise in revenues is not useful; so you also need to track expense levels and profits each year.

3. *Inconsistent results are a danger signal.* Investors naturally like predictability in the financial results of companies. When revenues and earnings gyrate wildly from one year to the next, it is impossible to estimate a direction. You often see a corresponding level of volatility in stock prices, so big changes from year to year may indicate that the company is not in control of its markets and sales; or even worse, it may indicate that some accounting shenanigans are in practice.

4. *Big changes between reported earnings and core earnings may serve as the most important red flag of all.* When Standard & Poor's developed its core earnings concept, it provided a valuable service to investors. Core earnings—earnings from a primary product or service and excluding non-recurring items—is the true picture of corporate performance. This number is easily found in the *CFRA Stock Reports*, which include a 10-year history of key financial results. You will discover that well-managed companies tend to have relatively low core earnings adjustments in most years. (When a company sells off an operating segment or acquires a competing company, for example, a large core earnings adjustment will result; otherwise, core earnings adjustments should be minor.) Companies with low core earnings adjustments tend to report lower than average stock price volatility; and companies with exceptionally high core earnings adjustments tend to reveal higher than average price volatility, as a general observation.

Flaws in the GAAP System – a Passive Approach to Reporting

There is no single, central control of the GAAP system. In fact, it is a loosely organized set of rules, guidelines, and opinions. The two major organizations involved in development of these rules are the Financial Accounting Standards Board (FASB), an independent organization; and the American Institute of Certified Public Accountants (AICPA), the organization overseeing the accounting industry.

Valuable Resource: To find out how the major GAAP organizations function, check their websites: www.fasb.org and www.aicpa.org

---

The entire GAAP structure is managed by these two organizations, but "GAAP" includes much more. Publications include high-level interpretations, opinions, and research bulletins; guidelines and statements of position; task force publications and practice bulletins; implementation guides; and issue papers, technical practice aids, pronouncements, and accounting textbooks, trade books, and articles.

It is fair to say that GAAP consists of all current opinions, observations and interpretations of how the industry is supposed to work. Change within this complex structure takes time, because any proposed new approach is subject to a lengthy review process on several levels. Within such a highly technical but loosely organized structure, many different opinions exist and justification for a particular interpretation may easily be found. So in spite of its public image, the accounting and auditing industry is far from specific in its determinations. When a senior auditor confronts a decision that seems to not conform to GAAP, discussions with the company's financial employees may result in (a) a change in the financial outcome, (b) modification of the transaction, or (c) no change whatsoever. It depends on how aggressively the auditor takes a stand and whether or not some justification can be found in the vast publication universe of GAAP.

Because auditors have a well-known conflict of interest in working on both audits and consultation projects for the same companies, the Sarbanes-Oxley Act attempted to inhibit some of the more egregious problems in five ways:

1. The Act set up a Public Company Accounting Oversight Board (PCAOB) to supervise firm practices and, if necessary, to impose sanctions. The Board is a private sector, non-profit organization, but it reports to the Securities and Exchange Commission (SEC). However, the effectiveness of this oversight board is difficult to judge; between 2005 and 2017, 209 sanctions were imposed against accounting firms, a relatively small number considering the tens of thousands of audit activities performed each year.[iv]

Valuable Resource: Check the work of the SEC and PCAOB by visiting their websites: www.sec.gov and www.pcaobus.org

---

2. Non-audit services were restricted. SOX named many services that auditing firms were no longer allowed to provide for those companies for whom auditing work is also performed. However, this provision has not affected accounting firms' ability to generate non-audit revenues. In fact, there is no apparent reduction in revenues among any of the large accounting firms since SOX was enacted. Within the first year following SOX, the Big Four firms continued reporting between $3 and $5 billion per year in non-audit revenues.[v]

3. Auditors have to rotate off accounts. In the past, senior auditors were fixtures in the offices of larger clients. Maintaining objectivity is impossible when people

become so familiar with those being audited. SOX requires partners to rotate off accounts within a five-year period.

4. Auditors report to the audit committee, not to financial executives. Before SOX, auditors met regularly with the CEO or CFO and negotiated changes to accounting decisions. This led to many problems, not the least of which was loss of objectivity for auditors themselves. Executives made decisions to hire or fire firms, giving them tremendous control. Now, however, the board's audit committee makes those decisions and meets with auditors directly.

5. Auditors cannot move into positions with a client's company. In the past, companies hired financial executives from the audit team directly, so that the current year's audit was conducted with a recent employee of the accounting firm itself. Under SOX, the auditing firm cannot conduct an audit for any company that has hired a member of senior management from that firm within the past year.

Have these provisions fixed the problems? There remains a widespread cultural attitude in the accounting industry that views past compliance problems as matters of public relations rather than as potential internal flaws. This means that in order to be able to rely on financial statements, you cannot simply accept a certification from an "independent" auditing firm as the last word. Real independence remains elusive. So in calculating valuation and profitability of a company, you need to be able to isolate non-core earnings and make adjustments on your own. *CFRA Stock Reports* summarize the core earnings numbers, which helps considerably by providing reliable numbers; but going beyond the one-line identification of *core earnings*, it is also necessary to look critically at (a) the level of adjustments a company needs each year and the trend in those adjustments; (b) the degree of disclosure and explanation the company provides; and (c) efforts to achieve genuine transparency.

It is clear that the accounting industry has no interest in true reform of its practices. It is up to corporations to make meaningful change. For example, it would be simple for corporations to decide to not use their auditing firm for any non-audit work. This may result in short-term problems, but it would send the message to the investing public that corporate management is serious about fixing its own problems.

Examples of Material Expenses

A core earnings adjustment is necessary when any *material* expense is improperly excluded from the list of expenses; or when any *material* revenue is included, but is a one-time event. "Material" simply means that the dollar value of the transaction makes a difference in the outcome of the financial report (the valuation of the company as reported on its balance sheet or the earnings as reported on its operating statement).

Typically, material expenses that may be left off the GAAP-approved operating statement include:

Stock options granted to executive or employees. The stock option is a form of compensation, but under traditional accounting rules, the value of these options was never reported as an expense—even though their value could be huge. So the expense simply vanished and investors had no idea how much compensation executives earned if and when they cashed in their options. Because stockholders have to pay for those options out of the company's assets, the effect is very real even though it did not show up anywhere. The large dollar value of stock options has led some companies to voluntarily report the expense, and others to do away with options altogether. Gradually, the system is reforming and stock option expense is showing up in some instances.

Contingent liabilities. Many companies *might* owe a great deal of money to others, while the contingent expense is not shown on the operating statement. For example, Merck (MRK) faced thousands of lawsuits due to the company's Vioxx-related problems. The court granted awards to Merck shareholders from 1999 to 2004 in a total of $830 million (plus an additional $232 million for attorney fees and other expenses). The final judgment was entered in 2016.[vi]

This is a huge sum of money. However, until a settlement is final, the potential liability is *contingent* and under GAAP it is not part of a liability section of the financial report. It shows up only in the footnotes. Under GAAP rules, expenses are to be shown in the year *incurred*, so realistically the expense of losing a lawsuit cannot be recorded until the loss is determined, in the case of a lawsuit, by the court. Nevertheless, it would make sense for companies to set up loss reserves as liabilities and record an annual expense in anticipation of future litigation losses – especially when those potential losses will be large. A formula similar to that used to set up bad debt reserves would mitigate this problem.

Core earnings can also go the other way. Companies may include revenue that will not recur; as a result, these items should be removed from the operating statement:

Capital gains from the sale of assets. When companies sell off assets they book the revenue; however, this is a non-recurring form of revenue and will not recur in the future in the same way that core revenue would be expected to recur. Capital gains are usually listed below the operating net earnings as a form of "other income," but the question should be raised as to whether the earnings per share (EPS) includes capital gains. If it does, then the EPS is inaccurate.

Revenue from selling operating segments. Companies also may sell off operating segments. For example, in 2002 Philip Morris sold its Miller Brewing segment and booked $2.6 billion in revenue from the sale, as well as gaining a net 27% stake in the purchasing company, South African Breweries. But this was non-core revenue because it was not profit derived from recurring sales of product. In any study of revenue and earnings for Philip Morris (now renamed Altria), earnings have to be restated to (a) remove the non-recurring earnings from Miller Brewing operations; and (b) also remove Miller

Brewing revenues from previous years to accurately track remaining revenues into the future. These are large and very significant core earnings adjustments.

Revenue from non-recurring accounting changes. Companies make technical changes in the way they value some of their assets. For example, calculating bad debt reserves or setting valuation of inventory may be changed, affecting earnings during the year the change goes into effect. These are non-core adjustments and should be removed from the recalculated core earnings.

Altering the reported outcome on the operating statement does not negate the transactions. For example, when a company is paid for selling an operating unit, the money received is real. But under core earnings adjustments, these items have to be excluded in order to estimate fundamental trends and to judge how growth is likely to occur in the future. Non-core items distort this analysis; so before embarking on development of any fundamental trends, these core earnings adjustments should be made to ensure consistency in trends and accuracy over time.

Balance Sheet Problems – Inaccurate Valuation

Adjusting core earnings is only half of the picture of the problems with GAAP reporting. When revenues and earnings are distorted by non-core transactions, the balance sheet—where assets, liabilities and net worth are reported—is also altered as a consequence.

It may be shocking for investors to learn that some very large liabilities are routinely excluded from the balance sheet. In fact, the balance sheet does not provide an accurate summary of assets, liabilities, or net worth. The accounting standards applied to how these items are valued fall short of what investors should expect. Some examples:

Pension liabilities. The ever-growing pension liabilities of many large corporations are not reported anywhere. General Motors owed billions in its pension liability by the time the company went bankrupt.

Long-term lease obligations. Many corporations enter into long-term leases for their plant or equipment, often going out 30 years or more. These obligations show up from year to year as current expenses, but the contractual obligation—tangible liabilities—are not shown in the list of corporate liabilities, and this reporting is not required under GAAP rules.

Contingent liabilities. Just as expenses may be understated due to contingent liabilities, the liability itself is not reported anywhere except in a footnote of the annual report. In those cases where the contingent liability could be significant, companies should set up a reserve in its liability section and add to it each year; but under GAAP this is not required.

Stock option liability. Stock options granted to executives and employees in past years remain as obligations of the corporation. If those options are exercised, the employee is able to purchase stock below current market value. This dilutes the value of stock for the remaining stockholders, especially since many such transactions involve purchases of stock at the option price and an immediate sale at market price. That difference is an expense to the company, but the liability does not show up anywhere on the balance sheet.

Asset valuation. Just as liabilities are understated, assets may be as well. Under GAAP rules, depreciable assets are always booked at purchase price and depreciated over a number of years. So while real estate net values on the balance sheet decline each year due to depreciation (until their book value is zero), market value may be rising substantially. This does not show up anywhere. It is commonplace for corporations to own vast holdings of real estate with little or no book value. As a result, GAAP requires these assets to be treated like equipment and vehicles which do truly lose value. Real estate often appreciates, so under GAAP rules, the asset section of the balance sheet is often far below true market value, and the real estimated value reported only in a footnote.

An effort has been underway for many years to resolve differences between GAAP and International Financial Reporting Standards (IFRS), which is used in most of the world outside of the U.S. Many of the IFRS rules, such as valuation of real estate and principles-based recognition rules (as opposed to GAAP's rules-based approach), are more accurate and less complicated than GAAP; the process of reconciliation has been pursued over many years, but a genuine consolidation is not likely.

The solution to the many material problems in GAAP is to reform the system, but that is not realistic. In order for investors to gain a true picture of the companies whose stock they own, transparency requires a recalculation of asset, liability, and net worth values; and operating statement revenue and earnings. Companies could easily summarize their results in two columns. The first column would be the GAAP-based outcome you see currently, and the second would be the core valuation (balance sheet) and core earnings (operating statement). However, the assignment of accurate valuation is more complex than just making a side-by-side comparison, and opens up the possibility of manipulation.

Recalculating the Key Ratios

The importance of core earnings and core valuation adjustments cannot be overemphasized. In many instances, these adjustments radically change the outlook for corporations. Until reform occurs, investors need to continue performing their own fundamental analysis, but with accurately adjusted valuation. When you determine a number of important ratios, both core earnings and core valuation questions have to be addressed, especially when those adjustments are large. For example, *earnings per share (EPS)* is considered a key ratio and is widely used as a means for judging the value of a stock. The formula:

Formula: earnings per share

$$N \div S = E$$

N = net earnings
S = shares outstanding
E = earnings per share

Excel program

A1 net earnings
B1 shares outstanding
C1 =SUM(A1/B1)

The shares outstanding is computed at an annual level throughout the year (compared to earnings for the entire year). For example, if a company reports 5.218 million shares and its latest year's earnings were $1.185 million, then EPS would be:

$$\$1.185 \div 5.218 = \$0.23$$

If the number of shares changes during the year, one of two methods are employed for the EPS calculation. First, the average number of shares can be calculated and applied. Second, the entire year's earnings can be expressed on a per-share basis according to the number of shares outstanding at the end of the fiscal year. The first method is preferred. Since earnings are reported and analyzed on a quarterly basis, any change in the number of shares also changes EPS. Even though this adds more work, the accurate method is to calculate actual average shares for each quarter and throughout the entire year.

A second issue is raised in comparing *reported* earnings per share to core earnings. If the core earnings are considerably lower, then the EPS is distorted. For example, consider the effect on the above calculation if core earnings were $0.202 million:

$$\$0.202 \div 5.218 = \$0.04$$

The difference between 23 cents per share EPS and four cents is considerable. This is not an exaggerated example. It is based on the 2005 results for Lucent Technologies (LU). The calculation of *core earnings per share (CEPS)* is:

Formula: core earnings per share

$$(N \pm A) \div S = C$$

N = net earnings
A = core earnings adjustments
S = shares outstanding
C = core earnings per share

Excel program

A1 net earnings
B1 core earnings adjustments
C1 shares outstanding
D1 =SUM(A1-B1)/C1

For example, net earnings and core net earnings might appear as:

$$(\$1.185 - \$0.983) \div 5.218 = \$0.04$$

The adjustments may either increase or decrease the reported net earnings. In this example, a reduction occurred, so the adjustments were subtracted from earnings.

The difference between EPS and core EPS can be substantial. For example, someone considering a purchase of shares might review EPS and conclude that the company has consistently produced profitable results. But when the core numbers are studied, the picture is far more dismal.

Two additional ratios should also be adjusted to ensure the accuracy of fundamental analysis. The debt capitalization ratio is among the most important tests of a company's ability to maintain a balance between equity and debt. But what about unreported liabilities? For example, General Motors' reported common equity at the end of 2005 was $14.597 billion; but its *unrecorded* pension liabilities were about $37 billion. The effect of this was that GM's negative net worth was over $22 billion.[vii] This profoundly affected the debt capitalization ratio, in fact throwing the calculation into complete disarray. GM's reported debt capitalization ratio at the end of 2005 was 91% (2001 through 2005 showed the ratio growing from 79% up to 91%, increasing every year). The "core net worth" of GM was obviously negative if pension liabilities were counted. In recalculating the debt capitalization ratio, net worth is a key element to the adjustments. In the case of GM, the ratio could not be calculated because net worth was negative. To recalculate the debt ratio to the *core debt to capitalization ratio*, make adjustments to total capitalization (which consists of net worth and long-term debt):

Formula: core debt to capitalization ratio

$L \div (T \pm A) = C$

L = long-term debt
T = total capitalization
A = core valuation adjustments
C = core debt to capitalization ratio

Excel program

A1 long-term debt
B1 total capitalization
C1 core valuation adjustments
D1 =SUM(A1/((B1-C1))

For example, assume long-term debt of $3.007 million, total capitalization of $7.382 million, and core valuation adjustments of $1.653 million:

$\$3.007 \div (\$7.382 - 1.653) = .52$

In this example, adjustments were subtracted. In other cases, the adjustment may involve adding to capitalization for core items.

The same type of adjustment can be required for the P/E ratio as well. P/E is calculated by dividing the current price per share of stock by the EPS. But recalling the dramatic difference between EPS and core EPS in many instances, adjustments can alter the outcome. An organization not showing substantial pension liabilities, contingent liabilities, and similar items on its balance sheet is reporting inaccurately to shareholders and regulators.

These off-balance-sheet liabilities affect virtually all ratios you would perform in trying to place any kind of value in the stock of a company with large adjustments. It brings into question the calculation of earnings as well. Since pension liabilities can represent rather large annual expenses—which also remain unreported on the company's operating statement—the P/E ratio is inaccurate as well. Numerous adjustments to earnings further affect the earnings used in the P/E. To calculate the *core P/E ratio:*

Formula: core P/E ratio

$P \div (E \pm A) = C$

P = price per share

E = earnings per share as reported
A = core earnings adjustments
C = core P/E ratio

Excel program

A1   price per share
B1   earnings per share
C1   core earnings adjustments per share
D1   =SUM(A1/(B1-C1))

The adjustment is shown in the formula as a reduction. Core earnings per share may also be increased for core earnings adjustments. Changes in P/E due to recalculated earnings can be significant. For example, if earnings were reported at $4.55 per share and core earnings adjustments were $3.15, an adjustment takes core EPS down to $1.40. If the current stock price was $92 per share, P/E is first calculated as:

$$\$92 \div \$4.55 = 20$$

However, with the core adjustments, core P/E is changed to:

$$\$92 \div (\$4.55 - \$3.15) = 66$$

Rather than the GAAP-based P/E ratio reflecting that current price represents 20 years of earnings (well within what is considered an acceptable range), the actual core P/E is more than three times higher with price equal to 66 years of earnings, indicating that the stock is extremely overpriced.

Any ratio—including the P/E—is only as valuable as the information used. If P/E is to be used to estimate future trends in stock and corporate value, the core P/E should be the ratio of choice.

Recalculating Net Worth

Adjusting any ratio involving values reported on the balance sheet or income statement will also affect net worth. An accurate net worth value should be reported accurately with core earnings adjustments. To arrive at the *core net worth* of a corporation, it is necessary to adjust the reported value of both assets and liabilities. Because this may involve a great amount of detail, identifying the major adjustments may be enough. The formula for core net worth is:

Formula: core net worth

$$N \pm A \pm L = C$$

N = net worth as reported
A = adjustments to reported value of assets
L = adjustments to reported value of liabilities
C = core net worth

Excel program

A1 net worth
B1 adjustments to assets
C1 adjustments to liabilities
D1 =SUM(A1+B1-C1)

The formula sets up assumed increased in assets and decreases in liabilities. These adjustments can go in either direction. For example, net worth was reported for the most recent fiscal year in the amount of $13,667 (in millions). Adjustments to assets require adding $10.68 and to liabilities requires adding $2,005.05 (both in millions of dollars). Core net worth is:

$$\$13,667 + \$10.68 - \$2,005.05 = \$11,672.63$$

In this example, net core is adjusted significantly due to the core adjustments to assets and, even more so, the core adjustments to liabilities. Inconsistencies and exclusions of GAAP apply to all corporations and to all years. With this in mind, trends need to be evaluated not only in the current year but as part of an ongoing trend over many years. An evaluation of a 10-year record of a company's reported *statutory* (pre-core adjustment) stock price, debt ratio, revenues, and earnings might reveal potentially significant adjustments.

A symptom of problems involving adjustments to core net worth is also found in the core earnings adjustments. It is a fair assumption that companies with large core earnings adjustments (from reported earnings to core business-based earnings) are also likely to have large core net worth adjustments. As a general rule, companies with relatively small core adjustments also tend to report less volatility in stock price trading ranges. The fundamental (financial) volatility reflected in core adjustments translates to a corresponding high or low volatility level in the stock price; and this itself is a key indicator. An evaluation of volatility in financial reports is discussed in greater detail in Chapters 6 and 7; calculating return on capital can be elusive with core adjustments in mind.

This raises another question: Even if you accept the reported value of net worth as accurate, what number should you use for net profits? Most analysts accept the reported net earnings on the company's income statement as the accurate number; but a company-to-company comparison will be far more accurate and reliable if, instead, you use the reported core earnings for the year.

The importance of using core earnings in place of reported earnings will also affect how return is calculated. The non-core earnings may be very real in terms of profit and loss, but cannot be relied upon over the long-term as a summary of non-recurring results based on a company's core business and excluding all else. So restricting your analysis to core earnings, an analysis of return on equity also becomes inaccurate unless adjustments are a part of the calculation. The following revised formulas accurately adjusts "core" return on equity:

Formula: core return on equity

$$C \div E = R$$

C = core earnings (profit) for a one-year period
E = shareholders' equity
R = core return on equity

Excel program

A1 core earnings
B1 shareholders' equity
C1 =SUM(A1/B1)

For example, the net profit adjusted to reflect core earnings for the most recent fiscal year equaled $2,774. Shareholders' equity is $56,405. Core return on equity is:

$$\$2,774 \div \$56,405 = 4.9\%$$

A closely related and popularly used formula is return on total capitalization. To adjust this to reflect the core return, a new formula is needed:

Formula: core return on total capitalization

$$(C + I) \div (E + B) = R$$

C = core earnings (profit) for a one-year period
I = interest paid on long-term bonds
E = shareholders' equity

B = par value of long-term bonds

R = core return on total capitalization

Excel program

A1   core earnings, one year

B1   interest paid

C1   shareholders' equity

D1   par value, long-term bonds

E1   =SUM((A1+B1)/(C1+D1))

For example, core earnings for the past year was $2,774 and interest on long-term debt was $1,652. Shareholders' equity was $56,405 and par value of bonds was $51,000. Core return on total capitalization was:

($2,774 + $1,652) ÷ ($56,405 + $51,000) = 4.1%

Finding Core Earnings – Comparative Analysis

The detailed calculation of core earnings becomes complex when all of its aspects are explored. In fact, an online search on the subject of core earnings is not especially helpful, and there are no services or shortcuts available for making the calculations.

Standard & Poor's originally developed this system of adjustments as part of its effort to accurately rate bonds issued by listed companies. It continues to emphasize credit ratings on its own website. However, the *CFRA Stock Reports* provide a one-line annual summary of net earnings and core net earnings.

As the mood for accounting reform moves forward, investors may hope that corporations will take the lead in disclosure with transparency, voluntarily showing core-adjusted earnings as part of its report to investors. S&P would provide a valuable service to investors by expanding its core reporting to include estimates of core valuation. That would include adjustments for off-balance sheet liabilities like pension obligations; employee stock option debt; the current and long-term liability of lease commitments; and a reserve-calculated expense based on an approximation of the value of contingent liabilities. On its Stock Reports, further breakdowns of key ratios (like the debt ratio, current ratio, EPS and P/E) could also be provided on two levels: GAAP and core.

All of these changes would be valuable to any investor who wants to track the fundamentals accurately. Without core earnings adjustments, it is virtually impossible to make reliable comparisons between companies, even when they are in the same industry.

Conclusion

You will not always find such glaring discrepancies within a single industry. But the chance that the numbers you rely upon—the *same* numbers certified by an independent audit—may, in fact, be highly inaccurate. With this information as a premise for beginning a program of fundamental analysis, the next two chapters provide explanations for the major tests worth using on the balance sheet and on the operating statement of a company.

---

[i] "2002 S&P Core Earnings," *Business Week online,* October 2002 through June 2002 reported profits for the 500 corporations totaled $26.74 per share, versus a core net profit of only $18.48, a reduction of 30%.

[ii] Blitzer, D. M, Ph.D., Friedman, R. E., CPA, and Silverblatt, H. J. (May 14, 2002). Measures of Corporate Earnings. *Standard & Poor's.* p. 4.

[iii] *Ibid.*

[iv] Enforcement link on PCAOB (Public Company Accounting Oversight Board) website, https://pcaobus.org/Enforcement/Decisions/Pages/default.aspx, accessed May 17, 2017.

[v] Bryan-Low, C. "Accounting Firms Are Still Consulting," *Wall Street Journal*, September 23, 2002, pp. C1 and C7.

[vi] https://www.merckvioxxsecuritieslitigation.com/, accessed May 18, 2017.

[vii] GM reported in 2005 a total of $9 billion in pension liabilities plus an additional $28 billion for "other postretirement pensions."? Source: General Motors 10-K filings.

Chapter 6
Fundamentals:
Balance Sheet Tests You Need to Know

The "fundamentals" refers to financial information a company reports. In the last chapter, the discussion of core earnings demonstrated that the official GAAP version of accounting is unreliable and often distorts the picture completely. This often overlooked problem indicates a general lack of reliability in fundamental reporting, especially when core earnings adjustments are significant.

The widespread distrust of technical indicators leads many conservative investors to reliance on the fundamental signals. There are solid justifications for this, and as a result:

> ... the typical analyst adheres to a technique known as fundamental analysis or the intrinsic value method. The assumption of the fundamental analysis approach is that at any point in time an individual security has an intrinsic value (or in the terms of the economist, an equilibrium price) which depends on the earning potential of the security. The earning potential of the security depends in turn on such fundamental factors as quality of management, outlook for the industry and the economy, etc. Through a careful study of these fundamental factors the analyst should, in principle, be able to determine whether the actual price of a security is above or below its intrinsic value. If actual prices tend to move toward intrinsic values, then attempting to determine the intrinsic value of a security is equivalent to making a prediction of its future price; and this is the essence of the predictive procedure implicit in fundamental analysis. [i]

The belief among fundamental analysts is, in fact, that financial trends can be used to determine whether current pricing of stocks is reasonable. An overpriced or underpriced stock indicates specific judgment regarding whether or not to buy or sell shares; and for this reason, the many formulas related to fundamental analysis are worthy of review.

In this chapter, the balance sheet ratios and formulas are examined and, in the next chapter, fundamentals on the company's operating statement are explained. A case could be made for restricting core earnings adjustments to earnings-related indicators. For trend analysis, earnings trends studied on a core basis makes sense. For working capital analysis, however, non-core items contribute to a longer-term trend and could be overlooked. Thus, return on capital, debt capitalization, and similar ratios could be allowed to include non-core items such as capital gains, changes in accounting methods, and foreign exchange profit or loss. However, in the interest of core-based analysis across a spectrum of indicators-including non-earnings items-is also justified. It enables investors to better understand all attributes of "core outcomes" for their holdings.

DOI 10.1515/9781501507427-006

The Nature of Fundamental Analysis

The fundamentals are nothing more than a financial history of a company. It is not necessarily a presentation of the whole truth, or even a complete picture; financial statements at their very best only conform to GAAP standards. This means that they may be quite unreliable as a means for judging a company's value, notably as matters evolve in fundamental trends over time. A few essential points concerning fundamental analysis:

1. *All analysis is meant only to improve your estimation; nothing ensures success.* The purpose in studying the numbers is that they reveal trends. They show clearly what has occurred in the past, which gives you some fairly reliable ideas about how the future might shape up. But there are no guarantees. A "best estimate" is worthwhile, however. Consider a comparison of ten years' revenue among Wal-Mart, Sears and J.C. Penney, shown on Table 6.1. [ii]

Table 6.1: Revenue Comparisons

	In Millions of dollars		
Year	WMT	SHLD	JCP
2016	$482,130	$ 25,146	$ 12,625
2015	485,651	31,198	12,257
2014	476,294	36,188	11,854
2013	469,162	39,854	12,985
2012	446,950	41,567	17,260

Source: *CFRA Stock Reports*

This historical summary of revenues demonstrates that while Wal-Mart's growth is consistent and predictable, Sears was just as consistently on the decline during the same period. J.C. Penney's revenues were flat. These are three distinct and different types of revenue trends, and they are revealing. As a fundamental indicator, the revenue trend exhibits growth, decline, or a flat movement over several years.

2. The fundamentals are always historical, so be aware of the potential for change between the latest report and today's situation. Whenever you study a financial statement, you have a time problem. It takes quite a while to audit a company's books and to produce a final version of the statements. So from the cut-off date of the statements, it is quite likely that a final report will not be available for at least two months. A lot can happen in that time. For example, if the company closes its books at the end of its highest-volume quarter and you are reviewing results two

to three months later, the quarterly results you are looking at are (a) out of date and (b) not accurate for judging the current level of revenue and earnings.

3. *No single indicator should be used alone; the best analysis gathers data from many sources.* Virtually every fundamental indicator has to be reviewed in conjunction with other indicators. For example, tracking revenues alone is not enough; you also need to track earnings. A five-year comparison among Wal-Mart, Sears and J. C. Penney is as revealing as the previous revenue trend, as shown in Table 6.2. [iii]

Table 6.2: Earnings Comparison

Year	In Millions of dollars		
	WMT	**SHLD**	**JCP**
2016	$14,694	$-1,129	$- 513
2015	16,078	-1,682	- 771
2014	15,878	-1,385	-1,388
2013	16,999	- 930	- 985
2012	15,766	-3,113	- 152

Source: *CFRA Stock Reports*

The earnings trend revealed that, as with revenue, earnings followed a specific pattern. Walmart reported steady results year after year; Sears and Penney's both reported losses for the entire period.

Applying a similar form of analysis from year to year, tracking working capital reveals trends. For example, organizations reporting net losses are likely to acquire ever higher levels of long-term debt, aggravating a negative situation. Reviewed collectively, a range of trend analyses reveals what is occurring in the fundamental strength or weakness of an organization. Well-informed investors never depend on any single ratios or formulas; they review a series of valuable tests together. This does not mean that dozens of tests have to be performed; but a few important indicators can reveal a lot.

4. Before drawing conclusions from a published financial statement, check the difference between reported earnings and core earnings. There may be important differences between reported earnings and core earnings. These differences will affect all ratios. In the retail sector, these adjustments have not been historically significant. But in many other sectors, they have been enormous. For example, when S&P first began publishing its core earnings adjustments, many corporations had adjustments in the billions of dollars. Several of the most significant of the initial adjustments are summarized in Table 6.3. [iv]

Table 6.3: Core Earnings Adjustments

Company	2002 Earnings (In $ Millions)		
	Reported	Core	Difference
Boeing	$ 2,107.0	$- 315.5	$ - 2,422.5
Citicorp	15,930.0	13,708.8	- 2,221.2
Du Pont de Nemours	5,069.0	- 346.6	- 5,415.6
Ford Motor Co.	- 5,297.0	- 8,412.7	- 3,115.7
General Electric	15,158.0	11,225.4	- 3,932.6
General Motors	1,829.0	- 2,363.5	- 4,192.5
IBM	5,657.0	287.3	- 5,369.7
SBC Communications	6,872.0	4,107.6	- 2,764.4
Total	**$47,325.0**	**$17,890.8**	**$−29,434.2**

Source: *Business Week Online*

These adjustments, all more than two billion dollars, show that virtually no fundamental analysis can be accurate based on the GAAP-approved methods of reporting. Both Du Pont Nemours and IBM were over $5 billion in that first year that core earnings calculations were performed. Overall, core earnings adjustments to all of the companies on this list came up to over $29 billion. Without those adjustments, investors were expected to accept the numbers as reported (and still are expected to do so today). Any earnings values used in calculating ratios based on financial reports should be based on core earnings and not on reported earnings.

Basics of the Balance Sheet

The balance sheet is the proper starting point in fundamental analysis. This financial report is so-called because it reports the balances of all asset, liability and net worth accounts on a specific date. (This date is the same date as the end of the quarter or year reported on the operating statement.) In addition, the sum of all assets must equal the sum of liabilities plus net worth. This is accomplished by the fact that in the double-entry system, every transaction contains a debit and a credit, so that the sum of all entries is always zero. At the end of a reporting period, the profit or loss is "closed" and the value transferred to net worth. This account, retained earnings, becomes a part of the shareholders' equity. Figure 6.1 summarizes the features of the balance sheet.

Balance Sheet

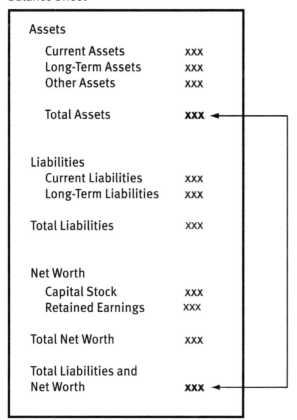

Figure 6.1: Balance Sheet

The figure demonstrates how the balance sheet appears in summarized form. Each account's balance is listed as a single value as of the date of the financial report.

Current assets are those assets in the form of cash or readily convertible to cash within 12 months. (cash, accounts receivable, notes receivable, marketable securities, inventory.)

Long-term assets are the capital assets of the company, net of accumulated depreciation. (real estate, vehicles, machinery and equipment.)

Other assets include any tangible or intangible assets not included in the other categories. (prepaid or deferred assets and intangibles such as goodwill.)

Current liabilities are all debts payable within 12 months, including 12 months' payments on notes and contracts.

Long-term liabilities are all liabilities payable beyond the next 12 months. (notes and bonds.)

Capital stock is the issued value of all outstanding shares of stock. (common and preferred stock.)

Retained earnings is the accumulated net earnings or losses during each year.

Valuation on the balance sheet includes many subjective accounting decisions, notably in two areas: long-term assets and intangible assets. Long-term assets are valued under GAAP rules at original cost, minus accumulated depreciation. Consequently, an asset such as a building may be worth considerably more 20 years after acquisition than its original purchase price. However, the net balance sheet value moves lower every year due to depreciation. Under IFRS rules, standards have been set to adjust asset values to current market value. For U.S.-based companies, balance sheets prepared under GAAP standards may undervalue assets significantly.

Placing a dollar value on intangible assets is the second area where balance sheets do not reflect accurate valuation. Because "value" is elusive and, often, is exaggerated on balance sheets for items such as goodwill, brand, and intellectual property, this is not easily reconciled. However, although these intangible assets have value, the exact value is not easily defined:

> Intangibles include all economic values of investment that does not dress up the physical form of the material goods, used in your own organisation or entrusted to third parties to be used by them. Even if they don't dress up a concrete material form, intangible assets are valuable to a company and can be critical to the success or failure in the long run. For example, an international renowned company like Coca Cola, would not be as profitable if the brand name would not have been recognized all over the world. Another example just as valuable intangible property *(sic)*, the row is "Barbie Doll" that along with the entire system material built around the property, valued at $ 2 billion. [v]

The balance sheet is the source for many important ratios. Working capital is tested from balance sheet accounts. The trend in working capital is among the most important fundamental tests; a company that cannot maintain healthy working capital cannot pay its bills or finance its own growth.

Another important area to test on the balance sheet is trends in capitalization. A corporation funds its operations through equity (capital stock) and debt (notes and long-term bonds). The higher the debt, the greater the future burden on operations. Not only do these debts have to be repaid, but interest has to be paid to debtors as well. The greater the percentage of debt as part of total capitalization, the more profits have to be paid out in interest. This means that as debt rises, less profit remains for future growth or to pay dividends. An exceptionally high debt capitalization ratio is a sign of trouble. And if the debt capitalization ratio is rising each year, that means the problems are getting worse.

There is often a direct correlation between ever-growing debt levels and core earnings adjustments. A study of the *CFRA Stock Reports* for three retail corporations-Wal-Mart, Sears and J.C. Penney makes this point, as summarized in Table 6.4. [vi]

Table 6.4: Debt Capitalization Ratio Comparisons

Year	WMT	SHLD	JCP
2016	31	246	77
2015	31	149	73
2014	33	60	61
2013	31	41	48
2012	35	33	40

Source: *CFRA Stock Reports*

The clear differences in the trends for these three makes the point that capitalization trends matter in any program of fundamental analysis. Whereas Wal-Mart's ratio has been steady over five years, Shear has experienced a dramatic rise in its long-term debt. To the extent that equity is valued below zero (any time the debt capitalization is greater than 100, net equity becomes negative). J.C. Penney's debt capitalization was not as severe, but the trend clearly was negative, with debt nearly doubling as a percentage of capitalization over five years.

Working Capital Tests

Several working capital tests help identify growth potential (or emerging problems) on the balance sheet. As with all ratio analysis, it is the trend that matters and not only the latest ratio itself. Companies that consistently maintain working capital at an acceptable level compare favorably with those who working capital tests are trending negatively.

The first of these is the *current ratio*, a comparison between the balances of current assets and current liabilities. By definition, current assets are all assets in the form of cash or are convertible to cash within 12 months (accounts receivable, inventory, marketable securities, and similar holdings). Current liabilities are debts payable within 12 months, including accounts and taxes payable, accrued liabilities, and the next 12 months' payments due on long-term debt. The current ratio is intended as a test of liquidity, based on comparison between these current accounts. To calculate current ratio, divide current assets by current liabilities:

Formula: current ratio

$$A \div L = R$$

A = current assets
L = current liabilities
R = current ratio

Excel program

A1 current assets
B1 current liabilities
C1 =SUM(A1/B1)

The ratio is expressed as a single digit. For example, if assets are $546,097 million and liabilities are $483,955 million, the current ratio is 1.1:

$546,097 \div $483,955 = 1.1$

A popular standard for current ratio is "2 or better." You would expect to see a consistent ratio at or above 2 based on this standard. But the current ratio is a limited indicator. In many very well capitalized and well managed companies, a current ratio of 1 is acceptable as long as the dollar values of current assets are strong and earnings are consistent. However, the current ratio, even though a popular indicator, is not an accurate test of working capital. For example, a five-year summary of the current ratio for Wal-Mart, Sears and J.C. Penney demonstrates that the current ratio can be artificially maintained even as the company loses money each year. This is shown in Table 6.5. [vii]

Table 6.5: Current Ratio Comparisons

Year	WMT	SHLD	JCP
2016	0.9	1.1	1.7
2015	1.0	1.0	1.9
2014	0.9	1.1	1.7
2013	0.8	1.1	1.4
2012	0.9	1.1	1.8

Source: *CFRA Stock Reports*

All five companies maintained consistent current ratios throughout the period. However, Wal-Mart reported strong profitability and level debt capitalization ratio; in comparison, Sers and J.C. Penney reported net losses and worsening levels of debt capitalization. These trends are not revealed in the current ratio.

A closely related ratio is the *quick assets ratio* (also called the acid test). This is a variation on the current assets which excludes inventory values. To compute the quick assets ratio:

Formula: quick assets ratio

$(A-I) \div L = R$

A = current assets
I = inventory
L = current liabilities
R = quick assets ratio

Excel program

A1 current assets
B1 inventory
C1 current liabilities
D1 =SUM(A1-B1)/C1

For example, current assets are $546,097; inventory is valued at $209,000; and current liabilities are $483,955. The quick assets ratio is:

$(\$546,097\text{-}\$209,000) \div \$483,955 = 0.7$

The distinction between current ratio and quick assets ratio becomes significant in industries with large or widely fluctuating inventory levels, especially those where inventory levels change frequently through the year due to seasonal cycles. This makes quarterly review of current ratio difficult and year-end review unreliable in some instances. When this is the case, the quick assets ratio may provide a better tracking history.

The most conservative test of working capital is the *cash ratio*. This tests the highly liquid asset relationship to current obligations. The formula:

Formula: cash ratio

$(C + M) \div L = R$

C = cash
M = marketable securities
L = current liabilities
R = cash ratio

Excel program

> A1 current assets
> B1 marketable securities
> C1 current liabilities
> D1 =SUM(A1 + B1)/C1

For example, the balance of cash is $107,044; marketable securities total is $105,800; and current liabilities balance is $483,955:

> *($107,044 + $105,800) ÷ $483,955 = 0.4*

This ratio demonstrates the most stringent test of liquidity. Cash and marketable securities are immediately available to pay off debts, and other current assets (such as inventory and accounts receivable) are intentionally excluded.

The last in this group of ratios is *working capital turnover*. This is an average of the number of times per year working capital is replaced. In accounting, this concept is often used. However, it does not mean that the actual assets and liabilities are eliminated and replaced; it is an estimate based on comparisons between balances. The formula is:

Formula: working capital turnover

> $R \div (A\text{-}L) = T$

> R = one year's revenue
> A = current assets
> L = current liabilities
> T = working capital turnover

Excel program

> A1 one year's revenue
> B1 current assets
> C1 current liabilities
> D1 =SUM(A1/(B1-C1))

For example, one year's revenue was $434,897. Current assets were valued at $546,097 and current liabilities at $483,955. The result is expressed as a number representing the number of "turns."

> *$434,897 ÷ ($546,097-$483,955) = 7 turns*

This reveals that working capital generated 7 times its net value in annual revenues. By itself, this is not especially revealing. But as part of a longer-term trend, as the turnover declines or grows, the effectiveness of management's control of working capital is revealed.

Accounts Receivable Tests

The current asset named "accounts receivable" represents the balance of money owed to the company by its customers. Since some portion of receivables will eventually be written off as bad debts, the asset is reduced by a *reserve* for bad debts. Periodic entries are made into this reserve, offset by an annual bad debt expense. When accounts receivable are identified as bad debts, they are removed from the asset and placed into the reserve. The net asset consists of the asset account, minus the bad debt reserve. For example, accounts receivable are currently $423,660 and the bad debt reserve is $7,215:

Accounts receivable	423,660
Reserve for bad debts	(7,215)
Net accounts receivable	416,445

The entry to increase bad debt reserve involves a credit to the reserve, offset by a debt to the expense account. For example, this year a company determines that its bad debt reserve should be increased by $900:

	debit	credit
Bad debt expense	900.00	
Reserve for bad debts		900.00

The determination about how much to place into the reserve is an accounting issue. Generally, a company will base its reserve decisions on recent history of bad debts and current and anticipated changes in activity. The reserve is only an estimate, so actual levels are constantly adjusted.

The corporate policy regarding its reserve requirements can be tested with the *bad debts to accounts receivable ratio*. This formula, expressed as a percentage, should remain fairly level even when receivable levels grow. So if a company's revenues expand rapidly (meaning accounts receivable balances are likely to grow as well) you would not expect to see an increased level of bad debt reserves. No matter what dollar value of accounts receivable is on the books, the bad debt reserve should remain approximately the same on a percentage basis. The formula:

Formula: bad debts to accounts receivable ratio

$$B \div A = R$$

B = bad debts reserve
A = accounts receivable
R = bad debts to accounts receivable ratio

Excel program

A1   bad debt reserve
B1   accounts receivable
C1   =SUM(A1/B1)

In the example of accounts receivable of $423,660 and a reserve of $7,215, the outcome is:

$$\$7,215 \div \$423,660 = 1.7\%$$

Another way to track this asset is by comparing receivable levels to credit-based sales. A consistent relationship between the two accounts should appear. In other words, if accounts receivable is increasing at a greater rate than credit sales, that can spell trouble for working capital. The *accounts receivable turnover* is a calculation of this relationship. The formula:

Formula: accounts receivable turnover

$$S \div A = T$$

S = credit sales
A = average accounts receivable
T = accounts receivable turnover

Excel program

A1   credit sales
B1   average accounts receivable
C1   =SUM(A1/B1)

Inclusion of average accounts receivable requires an additional adjustment. Using month=-end receivables for three months, and devising their simple average is one method. However, if the largest accounts receivable balance spikes much higher than previous averages, the average itself may deceptively understate the turnover rate. In that case, the latest entry may be weighted; or the highest recent balance may be used in place of an average. The purpose is to uncover a trend moving higher than recent turnover rates.

For example, latest month's accounts receivable balance was $423,660. The two previous months were $398,007 and $402,114. The average was:

$$(\$423,660 + \$398,007 + \$402,114) \div 3 = \$407,927$$

The turnover rate, based on credit sales of $4,799,502, is:

$$\$4,799,502 \div \$407,927 = 11.8 \text{ turns}$$

This formula may change drastically when the mix of business changes. So a company that either acquires a new subsidiary or spins off an operating unit might experience a change in this ratio (as well as many others). As with all ratio analysis, you only develop reliable trends when the values you use are consistent and accurate.

Another important test of how well a company is managing its accounts receivable is the *average collection period*, which tests the time required to collect debts. During times when revenues are expanding rapidly, there is a tendency to relax collection efforts and internal controls. As a consequence, you often see rapid growth accompanied by lower net profits. The collection period ratio is:

Formula: average collection period

$$365 \div T = A$$

T = accounts receivable turnover
A = average collection period

Excel program

A1 accounts receivable turnover
B1 =SUM(365/A1)

Based on the previous example of 11.8 turns, average collection period is:

$$365 \div 11.8 = 30.9$$

The average collection period is approximately one month, of 30.9 days.

Inventory Tests

In addition to cash, marketable securities and accounts receivable, current assets include inventory. This is the value of goods the company holds for sale. Inventory is most often valued at actual cost, but numerous inventory valuation methods are in use and may affect profits. This becomes an issue in those organizations depending on significant inventory levels, notably manufacturing concerns. In manufacturing, inventory may be subdivided into several subcategories, including raw material, work in progress, and finished goods. In retail organizations, inventory tends to be turned over rapidly as it is stored in warehouses for fast turnaround (just in time delivery) into retail outlets.

While inventory levels have to be expected to vary by industry, they may also vary by season. For example, higher inventory levels are expected in the retail sector in the high-volume holiday season, and relatively low inventory levels in the first quarter. The complexity and variation of inventory levels makes it important that an accurate *average* inventory level be used in tracking inventory trends. The average inventory is determined in one of several ways. If inventory levels remain fairly consistent throughout the year, the beginning and ending balances may be added together and divided by 2. If quarterly levels change significantly, add quarter-end values together and divide by four. In cases where inventory levels are more volatile, monthly totals may be used and averaged. However, whereas quarterly and annual inventory values are readily found on corporate websites and on SEC filings, monthly totals are not as accessible. In the majority of instances, quarterly or annual averages will be sufficient. To compute *average inventory*, apply this formula:

Formula: average inventory

$$(I_a + I_b + ... I_n) \div n = A$$

I = inventory value
a, b = period used in calculation
n = total number of periods
A = average inventory

Excel program

A1 inventory value a
B1 inventory value b
C1 ... inventory value n
C2 =SUM(A1 + B1 + C1)/n

In this Excel formula, 'n' represents the total number of values in use (12 monthly, four quarterly, or two values for beginning and ending inventory levels.

In a case where four values are in use, assume inventory levels of $446,412, $592,004, $455,700, and $481,532:

$$(\$446{,}412 + \$592{,}004 + \$455{,}700 + \$481{,}532) \div 4 = \$493{,}912$$

This average is used in calculation of *inventory turnover,* which is an estimate of the number of times inventory is sold and replaced. In actual practice, the goods in inventory are not completely disposed of and replaced; this is only an average. The turnover reflects management's efficiency at keeping inventory at the best possible level. If inventory levels go too high, it ties up cash and adds to storage costs and insurance. If levels go too low, it becomes increasingly difficult to fulfill orders and revenue is lost. To calculate inventory turnover:

Formula: inventory turnover

$$C \div A = T$$

C = cost of goods sold (annual)
A = average inventory
T = turnover

Excel program

A1   cost of goods sold (annual)
B1   average inventory
C1   =SUM(A1/B1)

Some formulas involve the use of sales in calculating inventory turnover. This is an unreliable alternative. Sales (or, revenues) are recorded on a marked-up basis, whereas inventory is reported at actual cost. Using the cost of goods sold is much more accurate. So if a company reports annual cost of goods sold of $4.72 billion and average inventory $1.09 billion, turnover is:

$$\$4.72 \div \$1.09 = 4.3 \ turns$$

This reveals that turnover occurred 4.3 times during the year. If the historical average has been in the range of 4.0 to 4.5, this is a typical year. However, if the turnover begins to decline in future years, that may be a sign that the company is investing too much in its inventory and that improved inventory controls are required.

Long-Term Asset Tests

While current assets define working capital trends, long-term assets (capital assets) may define the company's long-term commitment to growth and to creation and maintenance of its infrastructure and investment over many years.

By definition, a capital asset is any asset with a "useful life" greater than one to two years. When an asset is capitalized, it is set up as an asset (rather than as an expense) and written off over several years. The write-off is made in the form of annual depreciation.

Valuable resource: To get information on depreciation rules and calculations, go to the website of the Internal Revenue Service and download a free instruction manual, at https://www.irs.gov/pub/irs-pdf/i4562.pdf

---

The IRS publishes charts with pre-calculated depreciation in recovery classes. This includes depreciation for vehicles, machinery and equipment, and real estate. The basic formulas for calculating the best-known and most often used forms of depreciation are summarized below:

The easiest calculation is for *straight-line depreciation*, in which the same amount is deducted each year. The asset is divided by the number of years in the recovery period, and the result is the dollar amount of straight-line depreciation deducted each year. The formula:

Formula: straight-line depreciation

$A \div R = D$

A = basis of asset
R = recovery period
D = annual depreciation

Excel program

A1 basis of asset
B1 recovery period
C1 =SUM(A1/B1)

For example, a company purchases an asset worth $189,000. Its recovery period is 7 years. Straight-line depreciation is:

$189,000 ÷ 7 = $27,000

The first year's depreciation is allowed for only a portion of the year, based on when the asset was placed in service. This is calculated in a variety of ways, and the IRS publication explains the first-year rules.

A variation on straight-line is declining-balance depreciation, which is calculated using either 150% or 200% of the straight-line method. For example, under the 200% method (200DB), the first year's depreciation is doubled; the basis for depreciation in the following year is the original basis minus depreciation previous written off. The formula for *declining-balance depreciation* is:

Formula: declining balance depreciation

$$((B\text{-}P) \div R) * A = D$$

B = basis of asset
P = prior depreciation deducted
R = recovery period
A = acceleration percentage
D = annual depreciation

Excel program

A1 basis of asset
B1 prior depreciation deducted
C1 recovery period
D1 acceleration percentage
E1 =SUM((A1-B1)/C1)*D1

For example, a company purchases an asset for $189,000 and its recovery period is 7 years. The annual depreciation for the first year using 200DB is:

$$(($189,000\text{-}$0) \div 7) * 200\% = $54,000$$

For the second year:

$$(($189,000\text{-}$54,000) \div 7) * 200\% = $38,571$$

The rules for deducting depreciation in the first year reduce the claimed amount, based on when the asset was purchased during the year. The same calculations using 150DB would be:

year 1: $(($189,000\text{-}$0) \div 7) *150\% = $40,500$
year 2: $(($189,000\text{-}$40,500) \div 7) * 150\% = $31,821$

Capitalization

A lot of confusion arises about the concept of "capitalization," which often is confused with the vastly different "capital." A company's capital (or, capital stock) is the value of shares sold and outstanding to investors. Total capitalization includes capital as well as long-term debt. A company funds its operation through a combination of two sources: equity (capital) and debt (bonds and notes).

The makeup of capitalization varies considerably among companies within a single sector and between stocks that otherwise might look the same, in terms of price per share and annual revenues or profit. The debt capitalization ratio (the percentage of debt to total capitalization) can and does vary widely. A high debt capitalization ratio demands a higher level of interest payments in future periods. In analysis of a company's balance sheet, the trend in the debt capitalization ratio is equally important. When the debt capitalization ratio rises over a period of years, it is a serious warning. For example, the trend shown Wal-Mart, Sears and J.C. Penney earlier in this chapter makes the point: when debt increases over time as a percentage of total capitalization, it is a highly negative indicator for equity investors.

A related indicator is the *dividend payout ratio* (also called "dividend cover"). This ratio compares dividends actually paid to earnings per share. As an investor, you hope to see a steady growth both in earnings and dividends over several years. This does not necessarily mean the dividend payout ratio has to increase each year; but as earnings grow, the percentage of dividend payout per share ideally should remain the same. When you see this slipping over several years, it is a negative sign.

However, there is a direct relationship in the trend toward lower payout ratios and increased organizational activity in buying their own shares of stock. When this occurs, the stock is retired permanently and becomes classified as "treasury stock" on the company's balance sheet. The observation about this trend reveals that:

> ... repurchases have not only become an important form of payout for U.S. corporations, but also that firms finance their share repurchases with funds that otherwise would have been used to increase dividends... young firms have a higher propensity to pay cash through repurchases than they did in the past and ... repurchases have become the preferred form of initiating a cash payout. Although large, established firms have generally not cut their dividends, they also show a higher propensity to pay out cash through repurchases. These findings indicate that firms have gradually substituted repurchases for dividends. [viii]

Consequently, an observed decline in dividend yield might correspond with increased stock buy-back programs. Because this trend is not observed easily across the entire market, focus on the payout ratio remains a reliable means for testing organizational policy for applying earnings in the form of dividends. The formula for dividend payout ratio is:

Formula: dividend payout ratio

$$D \div E = R$$

D = dividend per share
E = earnings per share (EPS)
R = dividend payout ratio

Excel program

A1 dividend per share
B1 earnings per share (EPS)
C1 =SUM(A1/B1)

For example, dividend per share is $1.31 per year and the latest reported earnings per share was $2.03. The dividend payout ratio is:

$$\$1.31 \div \$2.03 = 64.5\%$$

This reveals that the company paid out 64.5% of its annual net earnings, in the form of dividends. The actual payout ratio may be erratic from one year to the next, making it difficult to analyze as party of a trend.

An alternative method yielding the same result is to divide the entire amount of dividends paid, by the total of net income. The per-share dividend compares to is used most of the time.

The dividend payout ratio provides a snapshot of a company's growth (positive or negative) over time. A summary of dividend payout ratio for three companies is shown in Table 6.6.

Table 6.6: Payout Ratio Comparisons

Year	MSFT	IBM	INTU
2016	66%	55%	39%
2015	82	37	69
2014	41	27	26
2013	34	25	25
2012	38	23	24

Source: *CFRA Stock Reports*

The interesting thing to observe in this side-by-side summary of the payout ratio is how the two companies differ. In all three cases, no clear trend is easily identified. The dividend is declared in advance and paid during the year; however, the changes in stock price and earning affect the ratio without regard to corporate policies.

The dividend payout ratio is an important test, not only of capitalization and cash flow, but also of real growth. Even when a company's earnings per share grows over many years, if the dividend payout ratio slips and fails to keep pace, that is a very negative indicator. It is revealing to make comparisons within a market sector in order to make sound judgments about companies.

A final capitalization ratio worth checking is market capitalization, which is the overall value of stock on the market. It summarizes the actual market value based on what investors are willing to pay for stock. It has nothing to do with market value per share. For example, a company with one million shares, selling for $40 per share is worth exactly the same as another company with two million shares, selling for $20 per share. So you cannot rely on the share price to compare one company to another. When you perform side-by-side comparisons of companies, you need to look at the total *market capitalization* to make a valid analysis. The formula:

Formula: market capitalization

$$S * P = C$$

S = shares issued and outstanding
P = price per share
C = market capitalization

Excel program

A1   shares issued and outstanding
B1   price per share
C1   =SUM (A1*B1)

For example, a corporation currently has 120 million shares, and the price per share is $41.15. Market capitalization is:

*120 * $41.15 = $4,938 (in millions)*

In this example, market capitalization was $4.938 billion. The distinctions in the market regarding market capitalization are important because they define risk levels, price volatility, and investment desirability. Some investors diversify their portfolios based on market capitalization, for example. The largest corporations (mega cap) report market capitalization of $200 billion or more; while exact size of different levels is not precise, large cap generally covers a range between $10–200 billion; mid-cap $2–10 billion; and small cap any company with market capitalization under $2 billion.

The study of capitalization and "size" of the company is easily misunderstood. Many investors make quick decisions based on stock price alone, believing that an $80 stock is more valuable than a $70 stock, without regard to market capitalization. Actually, the value of a company combines both price per share and the number of shares. An $80 with 16 million shares outstanding is valued at $1.28 million and a $70 stock with 18 million shares is worth $1.26 billion. The two companies are very close to one another in market capitalization.

A test worth making to further quantify the value of a company is the *common stock ratio*, or the percentage of total capitalization represented by common stock. This is the offset of the debt capitalization ratio if there is no preferred stock or other components to total capitalization. You can track the stock value of a company over time, which reflects not only the book value of common equity, but also the market success of the stock. If a company's stock has risen in value over time, its common stock ratio will rise as well. The formula:

Formula: common stock ratio

$$S \div C = R$$

S = common stock issued and outstanding
C = total capitalization
R = common stock ratio

Excel program

A1   common stock issued and outstanding
B1   total capitalization
C1   =SUM(A1/B1)

For example, common stock of a company was $120 million and total capitalization was $185 million. The common stock ratio is:

$$\$120 \div \$185 = 64.9\%$$

The comparison between common stock and debt will be revealing over a period of years. When the common stock ratio declines over time, it is negative, in the same way as seeing the debt capitalization ratio climb. When you see a consistent record over time, that indicates capital strength. The consistency of the ratio is reassuring to investors.

Tangible and Total Book Value

A final area worth testing-and often overlooked entirely-is the test of accurate book value of a company. Three tests are important. First is the basic *book value per share*. This is a calculation of the per-share value of what the company reports. The net worth of a company is supposed to represent real value, although important adjustments often need to be made. The formula for book value per share is:

Formula: book value per share

$(N-P) \div S = B$

N = net worth
P = preferred stock
S = average shares issued and outstanding
B = book value per share

Excel program

A1   net worth
B1   preferred stock
C1   average shares issued and outstanding
D1   =SUM (A1-B1)/C1

The preferred stock value is removed from total equity because the usual calculation of book value is understood on a "per common share" basis. When preferred stock value is substantial, it would distort the calculation. Calculating "average" shares outstanding requires an averaging between beginning and end of the year and weighting that average to reflect a true average. For example, if a new issue occurred near the beginning of the fiscal year, it would have to be weighted to reflect a true overall average for the entire year.

For example, net worth was $475 million, and preferred stock was valued at $875,000. Average shares issued and outstanding were 15,000,500:

$(\$475,000,000 - \$875,000) \div 15,000,500 = \$31.60$

It often is the case that the current market value per share is a different value than book value. For example, if current market value per share was $45.50, it means shares were traded at a premium of $13.90 per share above book value.

A variation on this formula is *tangible book value per share*, which is isolated to include only tangible assets. Many corporations assign substantial value to goodwill and other intangible assets, distorting the value of the company's real book value. In comparing one company to another, variation in the value on intangible assets will make comparisons invalid. For this reason, tangible book value is more popularly used. The formula:

Formula: tangible book value per share

$(N - P{-}I) \div S = B$

N = net worth
P = preferred stock
I = intangible assets
S = average shares of common stock issued and outstanding
B = tangible book value per share

Excel program

A1 net worth
B1 preferred stock
C1 intangible assets
D1 average shares of common stock issued and outstanding
E1 =SUM(A1-B1-C1)/D1

For example, net worth was $475 million, and preferred stock was valued at $875,000. Intangible assets were reported as $87,525,000. Average shares issued and outstanding were 15,000,500:

$(\$475,000,000{-}\$875,000{-}\$87,525,000) \div 15,000,500 = \$25.77$

This is significantly lower than the book value per share, including intangibles.

Finally, the *core tangible book value per share* tells the real story. But information is not easy to find because core net worth is not normally reported in research reports or in company annual reports. The formula:

Formula: core tangible book value per share

$(N{-}P{-}I \pm C) \div S = B$
N = net worth
P = preferred stock
I = intangible assets
C = core net worth adjustments
S = average shares issued and outstanding
B = core tangible book value per share

Excel program

A1 net worth
B1 preferred stock
C1 intangible assets
D1 core net worth adjustments
E1 average shares issued and outstanding
F1 =SUM(A1-B1-C1-D1)/E1

In this version of the program, the assumption is that core net worth adjustments should be deducted. It is also possible that these adjustments will add to the calculation. Based on the program as displayed, assume net worth was $475 million, and preferred stock was valued at $875,000. Intangible assets were reported as $87,525,000, and core net worth adjustments were ($125,000,423). Average shares issued and outstanding were 15,000,500:

$$(\$475,000,000 - \$875,000 - \$87,525,000 - \$125,000,423) \div 15,000,500 = \$17.44$$

In this example, the significant size of core net worth adjustments drastically reduced the core tangible book value per share. This series of adjustments and reports of "book value" demonstrates not only that the numbers are not always easily comprehended, but also that corporate reporting of outcomes is flexible and easily manipulated.

The core net worth can be significantly changed based on unreported liabilities. This is one of the most troubling aspects of GAAP reporting. For example, GE filed for bankruptcy protection in 2009. Four years earlier, the company was insolvent based on core earnings adjustments due to its unrecorded pension liabilities. GM owed $37 billion, and this showed up only buried in the footnotes to GM's annual report. The liability section did not record this liability. Based on GM's own financial statements, the unrecorded liability did not change between 2004 and 2005; and the reported net worth was not positive, as reported, but negative:

2004:
Net worth as reported (in $millions)	$ 14,597
Core adjustment for unrecorded liabilities	37,000
Core net worth	$(22,403)

2005:
Net worth as reported (in $millions)	$ 27,726
Core adjustment for unrecorded liabilities	37,000
Core net worth	$(9,274) [ix]

Based on this simplified analysis of reported versus core tangible earnings, GM has a negative core earnings per share. This is an extreme case; but it points out the glaring flaws in the accepted reporting standards and rules. The reality of a situation, as reflected by the core tangible net worth, is that a company may have a *negative* value but the accounting rules allowed GM to report positive value.

There are many valuable to be performed based on the balance sheet. Many change valuation of assets, liabilities and net worth based on application of the core earnings principles to affected valuation. The next chapter looks at the most valuable ratios to perform on the operating statement, where comparisons focus on revenue and earnings.

---

[i] Fama, E. F. (January-February 1995). Random walks in stock market prices. *Financial Analysts Journal*, 75

[ii] *CFRA Stock Reports*, Wal-Mart, Sears and J. C. Penney

[iii] Annual reports, Wal-Mart and J. C. Penney and *CFRA Stock Reports*

[iv] *Business Week online*, 2002 index as reported by Standard & Poor's Corporation

[v] VIDRAȘCU, P. (March 2013). The complexity classification of intangible assets. *Hyperion Economic Journal*, Year I, No. 1 (1)

[vi] Annual reports, General Motors, Ford and Lucent Technologies

[vii] Annual reports, Altria and Merck

[viii] Grullon, G. & Michaely, R. (2002), Dividends, Share Repurchases, and the Substitution Hypothesis. *The Journal of Finance*, 57: 1649–1684

[ix] Annual reports, General Motors

Chapter 7
Fundamentals:
Operating Statement Tests You Need to Know

The previous chapter explained analysis of balance sheet accounts. That statement reports on the balances of asset, liability, and capital accounts as of a fixed date, usually the end of a quarter or year. The operating statement is a summary of a series of transactions over a period of time, ending on a specific date. The period covered by the published operating statement reports on transactions through the same date on which the balance sheet is prepared, usually the end of the quarter or fiscal year.

These two statements represent what most people are familiar with in terms of financial reporting. The balance sheet (ending date balances) and the operating statement (summary of transactions for a period of time) are supposed to reveal to you all that you need to know in order to make an informed opinion and to develop comparative value judgments about companies. For this, fundamental analysis is based on a series of ratios and formulas intended to produce a shorthand version of the transactions (by way of percentages, ratio values, and trends). These representations are best reviewed under the following guidelines:

1. *Every ratio is best viewed as part of a long-term trend.* The ratio by itself can be compared to a universally accepted standard, your own goals, or looked at as the latest entry in a long-term trend. The longer the trend, the easier it is to understand the significance of the ratio. Even a two-year comparison has limited value compared to a five-year or a ten-year historical record.
2. *The analyst or investor should ensure that comparisons are valid and accurate.* The problem with the fundamentals is their very complexity and variation. Validity is not as easily found as every investor would like. If one company has significant core earnings adjustments and another does not, it makes little sense to compare the reported numbers without adjusting them to the same basis (core earnings).
3. *Ratios and formulas should reveal meaningful facts about risk and potential growth.* Any number of ratios can be used, but you should be sure you know how to interpret the results. What does a ratio reveal about the company? How can you equate a specific ratio in terms of income potential and risk? These are the key questions to ask about every ratio and every trend.
4. *A program of fundamental analysis should employ a range of tests and never rely on a single indicator by itself.* Analysis becomes valuable when you review an entire series of trends, each developed from ratio tests. This does not mean you need to get an accounting education. In fact, using a handful of well-selected ratios is easy and much of the work may be done for you already. Using a well-structured analytical service like the *CFRA Stock Reports* provides a 10-year summary and includes most of the ratios you are likely to want in your program.

DOI 10.1515/9781501507427-007

5. *A set of conclusions for one industry may not be comparable to the same conclusions in another industry.* One of the most common errors is to develop a series of assumptions about what outcomes should be, and then apply those assumptions to all companies. The truth is that every sector and sub-sector involves companies in particular industry groups, and these are, by definition, different from the companies in other sectors. Once you have decided which set of ratios to use, it makes sense to go through a review of an entire industry; develop a working idea of the standards; and adjust your expectations based on those standards. Even the most basic ratios, such as the percentage of earnings, gross profit, expense levels, and other well-known tests are going to be different between industries.

6. *The value judgments developed are best employed as part of a larger investment goal.* When you begin to invest, you need to set goals for yourself. Most people understand this in terms of price appreciation, and they set goals based on that: "If the stock doubles in value, I will sell" or "If I lose 25% I will cut my losses" are common price-based goal statements. The same strategic approach works with the fundamentals as well, and may be based on the ratios themselves, involving tests of working capital, capitalization ratios, revenue and earnings growth, or— in the best approach of all—a combination of all of these critical areas of analysis.

However, an assumption that income and earnings as reported is by default an accurate report may be wrong. The motivations for accurate reporting are not always as strong as the alternative of reporting earnings in as favorable a light as possible, even if that means exaggerating outcomes: "Powerful incentives to reach elusive earnings expectations can create serious conflicts of interest among corporate executives eager to meet these expectations."[i]

A former chairman of the Securities and Exchange Commission (SEC), Arthur Levitt Jr., explained this problem as one of combined incentive among analysts, management, and auditors:

> Companies try to meet or beat Wall Street earnings projections in order to grow market capitalization and increase the value of stock options. Their ability to do this depends on achieving the earnings expectations of analysts. And analysts seek constant guidance from companies to frame those expectations. Auditors, who want to retain their clients, are under pressure not to stand in the way.[ii]

This problem is nothing new. In fact, the preference in "the market" (referring to a collective Wall Street insider, investors in general and institutional investors specifically, and the journalists and analysts reporting on corporate profit and loss) prefer a predictable year-to-year outcome in earnings over volatile or erratic outcomes. As a result, some organizations have practiced "cookie jar" accounting in which some earnings in exceptionally positive years are deferred until later years to smooth out results. This occurs to the extent that some estimates are reported at lower than accurate levels to avoid future negative outcomes:

Wall Street disapproves of earnings volatility in general, and frequently seeks incremental earnings growth rather than unexpected changes. Companies that have outperformed analysts' growth expectations in the current year, will frequently fear successive years' growth expectations, and will seek to modify those expectations by lowering current year earnings through these charges.[iii]

With this widespread qualifier in mind, reviews of revue and earnings are best performed as part of a long-term trend and not in a single year by itself. A single year's outcome may not be typical, so a trend-based review of revenue and earnings is a wise process.

The Basics of the Operating Statement

The operating statement summarizes revenues, costs and expenses, and earnings for a specified period of time. That time is usually a fiscal quarter or year; and the report normally includes the current period and the previous period, so that comparisons are readily made. In corporate financial statements, the major expenses are summarized in a single line, so detailed analysis requires further investigation (this often means contacting the company's Shareholder Relations Department and requesting breakdowns beyond what is shown on the published financial statement).

The components of the operating statement are summarized in Figure 7.1.

```
            Company Name
          Operating Statement

       For the period January 1,  20xx
          through December 31, 20xx

       Revenues                   xxx
       Less: Cost of goods sold  -xxx

       Gross Profit               xxx
       Less: Expenses            -xxx

       Operating Profit           xxx
       Plus (minus) Other
           Income and Expenses    xxx

       Pre-Tax Profit             xxx
       Less: Provision for
           Income Taxes          -xxx

       After-Tax Profit           xxx
```

Figure 7.1: Operating Statement

Because there are so many divisions to the operating statement, it is imperative to understand which line is being discussed and compared. "Earnings" should mean the same thing when comparing one company to another. The operating profit is normally used to report earnings per share, but important distinctions have to be made between the various kinds of *margins* found on the operating statement. These distinctions are shown later in this chapter. Below is a brief summary of operating statement divisions and terms:

— *Revenue* – The top line is revenue (sales) and is perhaps the best-known line and most often watched indicator on the operating statement. As a general observation, many people believe that as long as revenues are rising each year, all is well. But in reality, you are also likely to see rising revenue accompanied by falling earnings (net profits). That indicates that growth in terms of rising revenues is not always a positive attribute; it is always better when revenues *and* earnings both rise.

— *Cost of goods sold* – This segment of the operating statement is the sum of several accounts. These include merchandise purchased for sale (or manufacture); freight; direct labor (salaries and wages paid to employees directly generating revenues); and a change in inventory levels from beginning to end of the period. A distinction is made between costs and expenses. Costs are expected to track revenues closely, and the percentage of costs should remain about the same even when revenue levels change. In comparison, expenses are assumed to be unresponsive to revenues. In situations where companies expand into new markets or product areas or merge with other companies, expense levels will naturally change as well. But expenses can and should be controlled so that ever-greater profits can be achieved in periods of revenue growth.

— *Gross profit* – This sub-total is the dollar amount of revenues minus costs. The percentage of gross profit is called gross margin. Just as direct costs should track sales closely, the gross profit should do the same. When you see a widely fluctuating gross margin from one period to the next, further analysis is required. Possible reasons include seasonal change, merger or acquisition, development of new product line, sale of an operating unit, changes in inventory valuation method, or lack of internal controls.

— *Expenses* – This category is the most varied and complex. It includes all money going out of the company as well as debts owed at the end of the period, that are not *direct* in relation to revenue production. The distinction between direct costs and expenses is quite important in financial statement analysis because you expect, as a general rule, to see actual internal controls having the greatest impact in this portion of the operating statement. This relationship is demonstrated in Figure 7.2. Note how the changes occur as revenue and costs increase or decrease. First, revenue and costs track on the same trend, as you would expect. Skip to the bottom and you see the area of expenses, which is flat as you would expect. If this trend continues, the profit margin grows when revenues grow, and shrinks when revenues shrink.

Operating Statement relationships – with controlled expenses

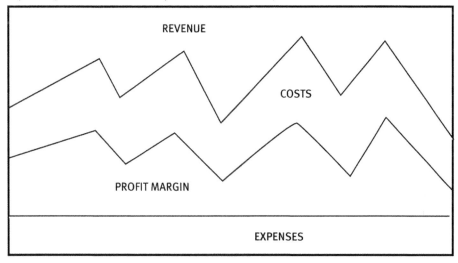

Figure 7.2: Operating Statement Relationships – with Controlled Expenses

Consider what happens when expenses are not controlled. In that situation, the level of expenses tends to rise over time and does not retreat if and when revenues decline. As a consequence, the profit margin shrinks even when revenues rise, and shrinks severely when revenues fall. This relationship is summarized in Figure 7.3. Note how much difference gradually increasing expenses makes. Expenses rise regardless of revenue and cost trends. At the end of the chart, revenues decline so that the profit margin shrinks considerably. Finally, it ends up in the territory of net losses. When a company experiences a net loss, it is usually due to a combination of events, including reduced revenues, non-recurring adjustments or non-core losses, and—most severe of all—uncontrolled expenses.

The level of expenses can also be further subdivided, although the published annual reports and financial statements do not always provide these details. For example, two major sub-divisions are selling expenses (those expenses related to generation of sales but not as directly as direct costs) and general and administrative expenses, also called overhead. These expenses recur each year regardless of revenue levels, and include administrative salaries and wages, rent, office telephone and office supplies, for example.

Operating Statement relationships -- with uncontrolled expenses

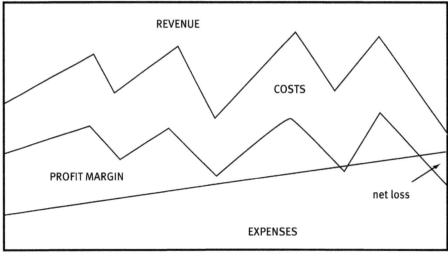

Figure 7.3: Operating Statement Relationships – with Uncontrolled Expenses

– *Operating Profit* – This is the profit from operations which, in most instances, will be the same as (or close to) S&P-defined core earnings. If the company has done a good job of isolating non-operating expenses below this line, then it is a reliable number; but companies do not always make these matters clear. In fact, they may be obscured by application of inconsistent standards, even with the blessing of the GAAP system. Another problem arises in the fact that published earnings are usually computed on the bottom line (net profit) which is likely to include an array of non-operational items. To gauge the significance of this distortion, compare the earnings reported for IBM over five years, both pre-tax and net. This is shown on Table 7.1.[iv]

Table 7.1: Earnings History, IBM

Year	In $ millions Pre-tax	% of Revenue	In $ millions Net profit	% of Revenue
2016	$12,330	15.4%	$11,881	14.9%
2015	15,945	19.5	13,364	16.3
2014	19,985	21.5	15,571	17.0
2013	19,524	19.6	16,483	16.5
2012	21,902	21.0	16,604	15.9

Source: CFRA Stock Reports

This comparison reveals the actual trend. Pre-tax and net earnings both declined during the five-year period. And whereas the pre-tax percentage of revenues declined, the net profit percentage remained more consistent, between 14.9% and 17.0%. This is a reflection of a lower set of adjustments, for tax liabilities as well as non-operating items. However, the pre-tax outcome was disturbing because of the overall decline in both dollars and net yield.

- *Other Income and Expenses* – Following the operating profit are a series of additional adjustments, all part of the non-core or non-operational section. In an ideal world, *all* core earnings adjustments would show up here so that the operating profit could be a universally understood, consistent number. But because so many core earnings adjustments involve expenses not listed on the operating statement, this is not likely to occur any time in the near future. Other income includes profits from the sale of capital assets, currency exchange adjustments, interest income, and the sale of operating units. Other expenses include losses from the sale of capital assets, currency exchange losses, interest expenses, and other non-core forms of income.

- *Pre-Tax Profit* – When you add or subtract the net difference between other income and other expenses from operating profit, you find the pre-tax net profit. This is the value often used in analysis to report net earnings, but because it includes the effect of other income and expenses, this is less than accurate; and when comparing return on sales among different companies, there will be a lot of variation in the pre-tax profit.

- *Provision for Income Taxes* – Companies set up reserves to pay income taxes, and this provision appears here as the second-to-last line of the operating statement. This value can change considerably and for a number of reasons. First, a company may be reducing its tax liability with carryover losses. Second, tax reporting is not always the same as GAAP reporting, so differences in the taxable net income or loss will affect the provision. Third, companies operating in foreign countries may pay a higher or lower overall tax rate depending on their mix of profits. Fourth, companies based in states that do not tax corporate profits will pay lower taxes than those in states with state-level income tax laws on the books.

- *After-Tax Profit* – This is the "net net" profit or loss, the bottom line most often used to calculate earnings per share. The problem with this is that, as the previous explanations demonstrated, the after-tax profit is subject to many accounting interpretations, non-recurring and non-core adjustments, and other factors that make a true comparison between companies less than reliable. Only the operating profit provides an approximation of outcome that can be treated as comparable; but EPS is usually reported on the basis of the bottom line, so investors get a distorted view of a company and its value and profitability.

Revenue Trends

Beginning at the top line of the operating statement, analysis begins by tracking revenue trends. Just about every analyst wants to see revenues grow each year. However, each sector involves competing companies and finite markets, so it is not realistic to expect every well-managed company to increase its revenue every year without fail.

Even when corporate revenues do grow, investors and analysts may place unrealistic expectations about the rate of growth. In other words, if a company increased revenues by 5% the first year, 10% percent the second year, and 15% last year, should you expect a 20% growth rate this year? All statistics tend to level off over time, but that does not mean a slow-down in the rate of growth is bad news; it is simply reality.

The most popular method for tracking revenue is by year-to-year percentage of change (up or down) in revenues. This is a reasonable method for tracking revenues, because it ignores the dollar amount and reduces growth to a simple percentage. If a company's annual growth *rate* remains consistent or shows little change, that is far more positive in the long term than the less realistic demand for ever-higher rates of growth. To calculate the *rate of growth in revenue*, the formula is:

Formula: rate of growth in revenue

$$(C - P) \div P = R$$

C = current year revenue
P = past year revenue
R = rate of growth in revenue

Excel program

A1 current year revenue
B1 past year revenue
C1 =SUM(A1-B1)/B1

For example, current year revenue was $93,580 (in millions of dollars) and past year's was $86,833. The formula for rate of growth:

$$(\$93{,}580 - \$86{,}833) \div \$86{,}833 = 7.8\%$$

It is more revealing to compare *rate* of growth (plus or minus) than to review the dollar values of revenue from year to year. To demonstrate this, consider the case of three companies over a five-year period. This is summarized in Table 7.2.[v]

Table 7.2: Rate of Revenue Growth

Year	IBM In $ millions Revenue	IBM % Of Growth	MSFT In $ millions Revenue	MSFT % Of Growth	ADBE In $ millions Revenue	ADBE % Of Growth
2016	$ 79,919	- 2.2%	$ 85,320	- 8.8%	$ 37,047	- 3.1%
2015	81,741	-11.9	93,580	7.8	38,226	- 0.1
2014	92,793	- 7.0	86,833	11.5	38,275	2.9
2013	99,751	- 4.6	77,949	5.7	37,180	0.1
2012	104,507	–	73,723	–	37,211	–

Source: *CFRA Stock Reports*

In spite of the significant differences in dollar levels of revenue, the three companies had vastly different rates of growth (positive or negative). IBM declined each year, as reflected in both dollar amount and rate of growth. In fact, of the three, IBM's rate was the largest decline reported. Adobe showed very little change from year to year, in a period of weakness in the sector. In that regard, their rate of growth was far better than that of IBM. And although Microsoft reported a decline in 2016, its overall rate of change in revenue was far stronger than its two competitors.

An analyst looking at the dollar values of revenue might conclude that as candidates for long-term growth, Adobe has a relatively small dollar level of revenue, and IBM has the strongest overall level; however, this would be a misleading conclusion. When dollar values are accompanied by an analysis of trends in the rate of growth, a more accurate picture emerges.

Earnings Trends

Trends in growth should not be restricted to revenue, but should include earnings as well. Only in this way can the importance of revenue growth by appreciated. If a company reports increases in revenue but losses in the same years, that is far from a positive outcome. At the same time, a decline in revenue accompanied by growth in earnings is a promising trend.

The study of earnings can be done on a percentage basis just as revenues can be; and you will gain greater insight into the trend by performing an analysis on this basis. Two formulas are involved in the analysis of earnings. The traditional *rate of growth in earnings* is calculated with this formula:

Formula: rate of growth in net earnings

$$(C - P) \div P = R$$

C = current year net earnings
P = past year net earnings
R = rate of growth in net earnings

Excel program

A1 current year net earnings
B1 past year net earnings
C1 =SUM(A1-B1)/B1

For example, current year earnings were reported at $16,798 million; past year was $12,193. The rate of change is:

$$(\$16,798 - \$12,193) \div \$12,193 = 37.8\%$$

Using the same companies as those in the revenue example, the dollar value of traditional earnings is summarized in Table 7.3.

Table 7.3: Rate of Net Earnings Growth

Year	IBM In $ millions Net Earnings	IBM % Of Growth	MSFT In $ millions Net Earnings	MSFT % Of Growth	ADBE In $ millions Net Earnings	ADBE % Of Growth
2016	$ 11,881	- 11.1%	$ 16,798	- 37.8%	$ 1,169	85.6%
2015	13,364	- 15.2	12,193	- 44.8	630	135.1
2014	15,751	- 4.4	22,074	1.0	268	– 7.6
2013	16,483	- 0.7	21,863	28.8	290	– 65.2
2012	16,604	–	16,978	–	833	–

Source: *CFRA Stock Reports*

The tracking of earnings presents a more volatile result that revenues. IBM reported a negative rate each year and Microsoft's results were in double digits in three of the four years. However, the dollar value of earnings was nearly identical from the beginning to the end of the period. Adobe's results point out a flaw in this type of analysis. The dollar values of earnings were so low that year-to-year changes were large on a percentage basis.

A more accurate rendition of earnings requires analysis of core earnings rather than reported net earnings. The formula for *rate of growth in core earnings* is:

Formula: rate of growth in core earnings

$$(CC - PC) \div PC = CE$$

CC = current year core earnings
PC = past year core earnings
CE = rate of growth in core earnings

Excel program

A1 current year core earnings
B1 past year core earnings
C1 =SUM(A1-B1)/B1

For example, current and past year earnings were reported as $16,798 million and $12,193 million. However, with core earnings adjustments, the core net earnings changed to $12,044 and $9,427. The result:

$$(\$12,044 - \$9,427) \div \$9,427 = 27.8\%$$

There are substantial differences between reported earnings and core earnings in this example, a reduction of 10%. These types of analysis—using percentage changes and comparing reported revenues and earnings rather than changes in dollar amounts—provide the most meaningful conclusions of top-line and bottom-line change over time. This is the most reliable operating statement trend analysis, especially when the flaws in GAAP reporting are understood, and how those flaws distort the fundamental analysis itself.

Revenue Compared to Direct Costs and Expenses

Within the operating statement, you will find additional valuable information for selecting companies. To better understand the causes of trends in revenue and earnings, begin with an analysis of the relationship between revenue and gross profit. If the gross profit is inconsistent from year to year, you can expect to see a corresponding inconsistency in reported profits or losses.

Direct costs—expenditures that are relating specifically to generation of revenues—should remain a constant from year to year. The costs—including merchandise as the primary element—will change only due to changes in valuation methods for inventory; catastrophic inventory losses; or changes in the mix of business. A change can be brought about through mergers or as a consequence of selling off an operating segment. But assuming that none of those unusual events occur, you should be able to track direct costs and gross profit and see consistency from year to year.

When you deduct direct costs from revenue, you find the gross profit. The percentage of gross profit to revenue is called *gross margin*. The formula for checking the gross margin is:

Formula: gross margin

$$G \div R = M$$

G =gross profit
R = revenue
M = gross margin

Excel program

A1 gross profit
B1 revenue
C1 =SUM(A1/B1)

For example, IBM reported revenues, direct costs and gross profit for three years as shown on Table 7.4.[vi]

Table 7.4: IBM Annual Gross Margin

Year	Revenue	Direct Costs	Gross Profit	Gross Margin
2016	$ 79,919	$41,625	$38,294	47.9%
2015	81,741	41,057	40,684	49.8
2014	92,793	46,386	46,407	50.0
2013	99,751	49,683	49,683	50.2
2012	104,507	52,513	52,513	49.8

Source: *IBM annual reports*

The consistency of gross margin in this example makes the point that direct costs should not vary greatly from year to year. During this five-year period, revenue and gross profit changed significantly; but gross margin changed by just over 2% during the period.

The analysis becomes even more revealing when expenses are studied in relation to revenue, and when changes in expenses are reviewed on a percentage basis. The formula for *rate of growth in expenses* is:

Formula: rate of growth in expenses

$(C - P) \div P = E$

C = current year expenses
P = past year expenses
E = rate of growth in expenses

Excel program

A1   current year expenses
B1   past year expenses
C1   =SUM(A1-B1)/B1
     For example, current expenses were $21,069 (million), and the past year's expenses were $20,430. The formula:

$(\$21,069 - \$20,430) \div \$20,430 = 3.1\%$

A five-year summary for IBM's rate of growth in expenses is summarized in Table 7.5. [vii]

Table 7.5: IBM Annual Rate of Growth in Expenses

Year	Selling, G&A Expenses	Change
2016	$21,069	3.1%
2015	20,430	−11.9
2014	23,180	− 0.1
2013	23,451	− 0.0
2012	23,463	--

Source: *IBM annual reports*

The change between 2015 and 2014 was substantial, but otherwise it did move in a discernable trend. This leads to a conclusion that other than the one spike, expenses did not change much during the period, even when revenue and gross profit declined considerably. Gross profit fell from 2012 levels of $51,994 (million) to $38,294, a decrease of $13,700 (million). However, selling and general & administrative expenses declined in the same period from $23,463 (million) to $21,069, a decline of only $2,394 (million). The disparity in decline of gross profit versus the decline in expenses reveals a negative trend that would not be obvious other than through an analysis of expense trends.

The picture is not, complete, however. Expenses need to be further reviewed in comparison to revenue levels. This is likely to shed more light on the expenses trend. For this reason, expenses may be further analyzed through the formula for *ratio of expenses to revenue*, which is:

Formula: ratio of expenses to revenue

$$E \div R = P$$

E = expenses
R = revenue
P = ratio (percentage)

Excel program

A1   expenses
B1   revenue
C1   =SUM(A1/B1)

For example, with annual expenses at $21,069 (million) and revenue at $79,919, the ratio of expenses to revenue is:

$21,069 ÷ $79,919 = 26.4%

In the case of IBM, this ratio for the five-year period is summarized in Table 7.6.[viii]

Table 7.6: IBM Ratio of Expenses to Revenue

Year	Selling, G&A Expenses	Revenue	Ratio
2016	$21,069	$ 79,919	26.4%
2015	20,430	81,741	25.0
2014	23,180	92,793	25.0
2013	23,451	99,751	23.5
2012	23,463	104,507	22.5

Source: *IBM annual reports*

Here, the negative trend in expenses is confirmed. The ratio rose from 22.5% in 2012 to 26.4% in 2016, revealing that as revenues declined through the period, expenses (which also declined on the basis of dollars) actually rose as a percentage of revenue.

A final level of analysis is based on the operating profit. The previous formulas show how the items between top and bottom are studied, and how they affect the overall results. The operating profit—assumed to be the profit from all continuing operations—is the number to watch when trying to quantify growth potential. The first of two formulas to study is the *rate of growth in operating profit*, which is not the same as the previously introduced rate of growth in net earnings. That formula includes all other income and expenses and is normally based on the after-tax profit. Operating profit (also called profit from continuing operations before income taxes) is limited to earnings from operations and is computed by the following formula:

Formula: rate of growth in operating profit

$$(C - P) \div P = R$$

C = current year operating profit
P = past year operating profit
R = rate of growth in operating profit

Excel program

A1 current year operating profit
B1 past year operating profit
C   =SUM(A1-B1)/B1

For example, current year operating profit was \$12,330 (million) and past year's was \$15,945. The negative rate of growth was:

(\$12,330 – \$15,945) ÷ \$15,945 = –22.7%

IBM's operating profit over a five-year period is summarized in Table 7.7.[ix]

Table 7.7: IBM Annual Growth in Operating Profit

Year	Operating Profit	Annual Growth
2016	$12,330	-22.7%
2015	15,945	-20.2
2014	19,986	- 1.3
2013	20,244	-10.2
2012	22,540	--

Source: *IBM annual reports*

The annual declines, in double digits for three of the four years between 2013 and 2016, further confirms the negative long-term trend in earnings.

An additional formula is equally important for long-term trend watching. This is the *operating profit margin*, which is computed as:

Formula: operating profit margin

$E \div R = M$

E = expenses
R = revenue
M = operating profit margin

Excel program

A1 expenses
B1 revenue
C1 =SUM(A1/B1)

For example, the latest year's operating profit was $12,330 (million) versus revenue of $79,919 (million). The profit margin was:

$\$12,330 \div \$79,919 = 15.4\%$

IBM's five-year operating profit margin is summarized in Table 7.8.[x]

Table 7.8: IBM Annual Operating Profit Margin

Year	Operating Profit	Revenue	Profit Margin
2016	$12,330	$ 79,919	15.4%
2015	15,945	81,741	19.5
2014	19,986	92,793	21.5
2013	20,244	99,751	20.3
2012	22,540	104,507	21.6

Source: *IBM annual reports*

The consistent annual decline in margin further reveals the weakness in the profit trend reported by IBM. Only through calculating the ratios over a period of time can the direction of the trend be recognized.

The evaluation of these many versions of "income," "profits," and "earnings" demonstrates that the many terms only confuse the issue of determining whether the trend is positive or negative. Just reviewing the dollar values is not enough. True insight is possible only with a series of analyses over time. The accounting industry is a passive and reactive culture; it is not in their interests to improve the terminology used in financial reporting, although it should be. Ultimately, it will be up to corporate leaders to achieve true transparency. However, in annual reports, companies rarely disclose the negative trends in clarified, honest language. The tendency is to focus on segments where improvement has taken place and to downplay the negative trends seen only through year-to-year analysis.

As an investor, you ensure that your comparisons are truly valid by following these guidelines:

1. *Study the terminology to ensure that you're using comparable values.* Not every company uses the same phrasing for the various levels on the operating statement. One may refer to net income, another to income from continuing operations. But are these truly comparable? The value used affects not only return on sales, but also PE ratio and EPS, among the important ratios popularly followed.

2. *Remove non-core income and add excluded expenses to reported earnings to ensure accuracy.* The inclusion of non-core income or exclusion of core expenses is a significant problem in the accounting/auditing culture *and* in the corporate reporting culture as well. Unfortunately, the reporting formats considered official and correct are unreliable and misleading. You need to seek out the true core earnings from operations to develop reliable long-term trends.

3. *Pay close attention to the differences between reported and core earnings* You will discover in reviewing the long-term trends for many companies that there is a close relationship between core earnings adjustments and volatility (both in revenues and stock prices). As a general rule, companies with relatively high core

earnings adjustments are also going to experience higher than average stock price volatility. Conversely, those with low core earnings adjustments will be far less volatile. Rather than simply accepting reported net earnings, use the core earnings value as the most reliable indicator of where earnings are leading into the future.

Conclusion

The relationship between the fundamentals and a stock's price volatility is direct. The two camps (fundamental and technical) complement one another, and should not be thought of as different or separate. The next chapter provides you with valuable market trend formulas that can be used, along with fundamental tests, to evaluate risks and to pick stocks.

---

[i] Rodriguez, M.A. (2014), The Numbers Game: Manipulation of Financial Reporting by Corporations and Their Executives, *University of Miami Business Law Review* Vol. 10(2), 451.

[ii] Levitt, A. (December 1998). The Numbers Game: Manipulation of Earnings in Financial Reports, *The CPA Journal*, Vol. 68(12).

[iii] Rubin, S. (March 17, 2000). Market Pushes Many Firms to Paper Over the Cracks. *The National Post*, C9.

[iv] *CFRA Stock Reports s.*

[v] *Ibid.*

[vi] IBM annual reports, at www.ibm.com/annualreport/.

[vii] *Ibid.*

[viii] *Ibid.*

[ix] *Ibid.*

[x] *Ibid.*

Chapter 8
Market Trend Calculations

The two primary forms of analysis in the stock market are fundamental and technical. The fundamentals refer to financial statement trends, including profitability, capitalization and cash flow. Technical analysis, in following chapters, refers to all matters concerning price, volume, momentum, and moving averages. This chapter explains some of the less direct market indicators stock investors and traders use.

These relate to price trends in the overall market, not only for price and its immediate trends, but also for the weighting of indexes, new high and new low statistics, advances and declines, short interest, volatility, mutual fund cash to asset ratio, and the large block ratio.

Unlike fundamental analysis of individual companies and technical analysis affecting price, these indicators apply to the overall market and help investors determine whether the current mood of the market is positive or negative.

Index Weighting

Investors and traders are familiar with the many different indexes used in the market. In fact, as a starting point the rise or fall of index points indicates the overall condition and sentiment of the market from one day to the next.

An index may be either capitalization-weighted or price-weighted. Capitalization weighting calculates index valuation for each component by multiplying the number of shares issued and outstanding, by the current price per share; and then assigning a weight representing the capitalization of each company as a percentage of the overall capitalization of all components in the index.

Indexes may contain hundreds or thousands of individual companies, so the calculation would be time-consuming without the use of automation. However, as a simplified example, assume an index of 8 companies with following shares and market value as summarized in Table 8.1.

As one version of a "composite index," market capitalization provides one form of benchmark for judging the market. The Wilshire 5000 and NASDAQ Composite are examples of this form of index. As the overall capitalization level rises or falls based on changes in market price, the index value also moves. Higher-priced components will have greater influence on the overall index, so as those components rise or fall, an overall greater influence will be witnessed in the market capitalization.

DOI 10.1515/9781501507427-008

Table 8.1: Market Capitalization Weighting

	Number of Shares	Price per Share	Total Cap. ($ mil)	%
1	800,000	$ 82.35	$ 65.88	14.76%
2	600,000	31.00	18.60	4.17
3	250,000	205.00	51.25	11.48
4	700,000	82.00	57.40	12.86
5	400,000	35.50	14.20	3.18
6	2,000,000	42.35	84.70	18.98
7	500,000	110.60	55.30	12.39
8	1,500,000	66.00	99.00	22.18
		Total	$446.33	100.00%

The formula for calculating the individual component weight is:

Formula: component weight, market capitalization

$$S * P = C$$

S = shares issued and outstanding
P = price per share
C = component weight

Excel program

A1 shares issued and outstanding
B1 price per share
C1 =SUM(A1*B1)

The formula for calculating the percentage of each components, to the entire index is:

Formula: component percentage, market capitalization

$$C \div SC = W$$

C = component weight
SC = sum of component weights
W = weight percentage

Excel program

A1   shares issued and outstanding
B1   price per share
C1   =SUM(A1*B1)

The value of cap rated indexing has been questioned, however. Reliance on cap rating would have to assume that investors track the full index precisely, in order to achieve the assumed efficiency it provides. The term "efficiency" refers here to an accurate and reliable overall market. While it does not exist except in theory, "efficiency" provides a form of benchmark all on its own, by which investors can quantify their ability to generate informational efficiency. However, this is a problem because:

> no investor invests in the cap-weighted index; rather all manage risk in the context of their own expectations and take an optimal position on their own perceived efficient frontier. Some might suggest that those who invest in cap-weighted portfolios believe the market to be information-ally efficient. Because of this they are willing to accept the mean-variance efficiency of the cap-weighted index based on consensus market expectations. In an informationally efficient market, however, security prices reflect the views of fully informed investors as opposed to the consensus views of all investors. [i]

This problem is unavoidable in the market. The index itself is a benchmark, not a guide for where and how to invest. The same limitation applies to the second type of index, a price weighted one. The Dow Jones Industrial Average (DJIA) of 30 stocks is an example. Each component is weighted by market price alone, and not by total capitalization. As a consequence, higher-priced components have greater weight on the overall index. The DJIA as of June, 2017 reveals that four companies (Goldman Sachs, 3M, Boeing and United Health Group) represent more than one-fourth of the composite value, the result of price weighting. The problem this raises concerns the comparison between weight of a stock and liquidity or performance tests. The price-weighted index:

> seeks to assign the greatest weights to stocks with high share prices, even though firms with higher share prices do not necessarily make greater contributions to the economy. Therefore, the price-weighted index can be regarded as less adequate to measure market performance. Further, while larger-cap stocks are likely to be more liquid, stocks with higher share prices do not always have greater liquidity. Thus, the price-based weighting system is greatly disadvantageous relative to the cap-weighting system in terms of reducing the price impact of index portfolio transactions. [ii]

Since both capitalization and price weighting create a similar favoritism toward some issues over others, investors may choose to follow one index or another, recognizing that both types weight components unequally.

In the previous example of capitalization weighting, the number of shares influenced the outcome. The same data used to calculate capitalization weighting creates a substantially different result when weighted by price alone, as shown in Table 8.2.

Table 8.2: Price Capitalization Weighting

	Number of Shares	Price per Share	%
1	800,000	$ 82.35	12.58%
2	600,000	31.00	4.73
3	250,000	205.00	31.31
4	700,000	82.00	12.52
5	400,000	35.50	5.42
6	2,000,000	42.35	6.47
7	500,000	110.60	16.89
8	1,500,000	66.00	10.08
	Total	**$ 654.80**	**100.00%**

The formula for calculating the percentage of each components, to the entire index is:

Formula: component percentage, price capitalization

$P \div SC = W$

P = price of each component
SC = sum of components
W = weight percentage

Excel program

A1 price of each component
B1 sum of components
C1 =SUM(A1/B1)

The advantage to generating index benchmarks is that it represents a segment of the market (industrials, stocks on the NASDAQ, etc.), making it easier for investors to draw conclusions about marketwide trends. Tracking more than one index ensures that distortions will be taken in context. For example, the DJIA contains only 30 industrial companies, whereas the NASDAQ and S&P 500 contains a broader representation of market movement.

Breadth of the Market

Among the many marketwide indicators, breadth of the market compares the total number of advancing and declining stocks. This is viewed as a very broad signal of whether market sentiment is positive or negative at the moment. It becomes most significant when one direction (dominance of advances or declining securities) dominates during most sessions over a period of time. Dominance by advancing stocks is bullish, and dominance by declining stocks is considered bearish. Because this is marketwide, it is a generalization of the market and cannot be applied directly to a portfolio or to a specific stock. In fact, breadth may distort actual trend-based outcomes based on how and why investors choose a particular company. In such cases, marketwide breadth provides only limited value as an indicator. This is true in part because:

> ...firms that spend more on advertising, ceteris paribus [all else being equal], have a larger number of both individual and institutional investors. Further, we find that advertising has a stronger effect on individuals than institutions. This result is consistent with recent evidence of a "home bias" among investors and suggests that advertising helps to attract a disproportionate number of investors who, at least in part, make their investment decisions based on familiarity rather than on more fundamental information. [iii]

Breadth provides specific value, however, but it should be analyzed in context. The question is one of how marketwide indicators (like breadth) affect price behavior of individual stocks. Breadth is measured by advance/decline line. This summarizes the net difference between advances and declines. This is used not only to summarize current sentiment, but also to spot times when a current trend is weakening or beginning to turn in the opposite direction. The line is a cumulative indicator, with the latest net change added to or subtracted from the previous index value. This is a confirming indicator used along with other sentiment signals, and reversal may be anticipated when the a/d line diverges from the prevailing trend.

Formula: advance/decline price line

$$P \pm N = C$$

P = previous a/d line
N = net advances (+) or declines (-)
C = current a/d line

Excel program

A1   previous a/d line
B1   net advances or declines
C1   =SUM(A1+B1) or =SUM(A1-B1)

For example, a series of entries to the a/d line are summarized in Table 8.3.

Table 8.3: Advance/Decline Price Line

Advances	Declines	Net	A/D Line
			599
2,314	742	1,572	2,171
765	2,302	-1,537	634
2,365	694	1,671	2,305
438	2,655	-2,217	88
627	2,463	-1,836	-1,748

The rapidly changing a/d line on this table reveals the potential volatility in the a/d line. However, this also reveals a shift from bullish to bearish sentiment, to the point that the a/d line turned negative by the last session reported.

A variation of changes in the a/d line is calculation of the percentage change from one session to the next. In some respects, the percentage of change is easier to comprehend than the net number of advancing or declining issues and changes to the a/d line.

Formula: advance/decline price percentage

$$(A - D) \div (A + D) = P$$

A = advances
D = declines
P = percentage change

Excel program

A1   advances
B1   declines
C1   =SUM(A1-B1)/(A1+B1)

For example, using the same data reported in Table 8.3, the a/d percentage calculation is applied and results are shown in Table 8.4.

Table 8.4: Advance/Decline Price Percentage

Advances	Declines	Net	A/D Line	%
			599	
2,314	742	1,572	2,171	51.4%
765	2,302	−1,537	634	−50.1
2,365	694	1,671	2,305	54.6
438	2,655	−2,217	88	−71.7
627	2,463	−1,836	−1,748	−59.4

This calculation reveals the often highly volatile day-to-day changes in advance/de-cline trends. However, the overall sentiment in these five sessions turned from previ-ous bullish bias to bearish. Due to the volatile daily changes, analysts tend to rely more on moving averages than on the short-term and highly volatile changes in indi-cators such as this.

Another variation of advance/decline analysis focuses on daily volume rather than on the number of advancing and declining issues. Like the a/d line, the net ad-vance/decline of volume is a cumulative index in which each session's net advance is added, or decline subtracted, from the previous volume index value. This is used as a confirming indicator, used in conjunction with other marketwide signals; or as a divergence signal when the prevailing sentiment is contradicted by the volume trend. In that case, the volume a/d may be used as a forecast of a change in price direction. Calculation of the a/d volume line is the same as that for the price-based a/d line, with the volume advances and declines substituted for the number of advancing and declining issues. The advance/decline volume line is summarized for five sessions in Table 8.5.

Table 8.5: Advance/Decline Volume Line

Advances	Declines	Net	A/D Line
			−2,547
1,335	822	513	−2,034
1,688	301	1,387	− 647
1,347	689	658	11

The percentage change is also calculated on the same basis as the advance/decline price formula, with volume advances and declines substituted. The advance/decline volume percentage is shown in Table 8.6.

Table 8.6: Advance/Decline Volume Percentage

Advances	Declines	Net	A/D Line	%
			−2,547	
1,335	822	513	−2,034	20.1%
1,688	301	1,387	− 647	68.2
1,347	689	658	11	101.7

The double-digit changes in a/d volume support what was revealed with a/d of price. Short-term volatility in volume advances and declines makes it difficult to judge markets and their longer-term sentiment. The a/d volume indicator is useful for anticipating trend reversal or for identifying divergence from the prevailing trend itself.

Short Interest Ratio

Another marketwide indicator, the short interest ratio, compares the current number of short shares (short interest) to average daily trading volume. It is calculated for individual stocks, but may serve as a marketwide sentiment indicator when the short interest for a large company changes dramatically. Among the popular application of short interest is one performed for all of the issued traded on the New York Stock Exchange. The NYSE short interest ratio applies the calculation for the entire market over a period of the last 30 trading days.

Short interest is a relatively minor indicator. Because short selling is not widespread in most stocks, its overall value, whether taken as a direct or contrarian signal, is limited:

> The typical stock has very little short interest; most stocks have less than 0.5% of their shares outstanding held short. Thus, while there is substantial cross-sectional variation in short-interest levels, based in part on the determinants discussed in this section, the reader should bear in mind that short selling represents only a small proportion of total transactions in the average stock. [iv]

The short interest ratio is calculated by dividing the number of short shares (short interest) by the average daily volume, usually based on the past 30 trading days.

Formula: short interest ratio

$$S \div (D \div 30) = R$$

S = short interest
D = total monthly volume
R = short interest ratio

Excel program

  A1 short interest
  B1 accumulated daily volume for 30 days
  C1 =SUM(A1/(B1/30))

For example, current short interest is 4,865,000 shares. Daily volume for the past 30 days has added up to 5.66 billion shares. Short interest is:

  4,865,000 ÷ (5.66 ÷ 30) = 2.6%

Because short sellers expect the price of a security (or the entire market) to decline, the level of short interest is bearish when it rises. When short interest is covered, it indicates that short sellers are taking profits, or are concerned about possible losses if and when share prices rise. As a consequence, short cover in large volume appears as buying demand rather than as short cover. This is a deceptive indicator, and those not familiar with the trend of short cover may incorrectly believe that increased buy demand is a bullish signal.

Although changes in short interest imply a change in sentiment, contrarians view short interest in the opposite way. To the contrarian, growth in short interest predicts a bullish trend, not a bearish trend. This approach assumes that with growing short interest, upward pressure eventually overcomes the short strategy.

For contrarians – those investment based on analysis rather than on instinct or emotion – sentiment itself is a questionable cause for making trading decisions. A contrarian view of investor behavior points to the flaws in reliance on the past to identify future performance. In other words:

> some investors tend to get overly excited about stocks that have done very well in the past and buy them up, so that these "glamour" stocks become overpriced. Similarly, they overreact to stocks that have done very badly, oversell them, and these out-of-favor "value" stocks become underpriced. Contrarian investors bet against such naive investors. Because contrarian strategies invest disproportionately in stocks that are underpriced and underinvest in stocks that are overpriced, they outperform the market. [v]

This opposite-leaning bias among contrarians is based on observations that crowd thinking in the market is poorly timed more often than it is well-timed. The short interest ratio is one way to measure the sentiment and to time trades by contrarians.

New Highs and New Lows

New highs and new lows represent statistical ranges, thus the degree of volatility over time in the market, broadly speaking. For calculation of the broader historical volatility, the current trend can be viewed easily be application of other technical indicators with chart overlays. Chapter 11 introduces and explains Bollinger Bands, a moving average based on a simple moving average of price and upper and lower bands, each two standard deviations removed from price. This represents a simplified version and visualization of historical volatility.

Because volatility is a quantified expression of market risk, stock investors track the degree of volatility, in the form of the number of stocks reaching new high or new low prices. As one or both sides expand, volatility also grows; and if the annual number of record new high or new low prices declines, this is one version of declining volatility.

The new high/low index tracks the number of records set over 52 weeks. It is referred to as a breadth indicator because it defines the range of price movement, and several different versions can be calculated. The record-high percentage is calculated by dividing the number of new highs by the sum of new highs and new lows, and the result multiplied by 100, to calculate the index value.

Formula: record-high percentage

$$(H \div (H + L)) * 100 = P$$

H = new highs
L = new lows
P = record-high percentage

Excel program

A1   new highs
B1   new lows
C1   =SUM(A1/(A1+B1))*100

For example, during the past month, new highs were 413 and new lows were 367. The record-high percentage was:

$$(413 \div (413 + 367)) * 100 = 52.9\%$$

A second calculation is the high/low index, which is a simple moving average of the latest 10 days' record-high percentage.

Formula: high/low index

$$(R_1 ... R_{10}) \div 10 = I$$

R = record-high percentage (for days 1 through 10)
I = high/low index

Excel program

A1:A10   record-high percentages
B10   =SUM(A1:A10)/10

For example, the 10-day record-high percentage outcomes were: 52.9, 48.3, 46.6, 54.1, 56.0, 53.1, 49.0, 46.8, 52.7, and 54.3. The high/low index was:

$$(52.9 + 48.3 + 46.6 + 54.1 + 56.0 + 53.1 + 49.0 + 46.8 + 52.7 + 54.3) \div 10 = 51.4$$

The high/low percentage is another variation on this form of analysis. It is the sum of all 52-week highs minus 52-week lows, divided by the total number of issues.

Formula: high/low percentage

$$(H - L) \div T = P$$

H = 52-week highs
L = 52-week lows
T = total issues
P = high/low percentage

Excel program

A1 52-week highs
B1 52-week lows
C1 total issues
D1 =SUM(A1-B1)/C1

For example, the number of new high priced stocks over the last 52 weeks on the S&P 500 was 120, and low lows were 32. With a total of 500 issues, the high/low percentage is:

$$(120 / 32) \div 500 = 17.6\%$$

The overall trend in high/low analysis is expressed as the net new 52-week high. It indicates not only a trend toward bullish or bearish sentiment, but the strength of that trend as well. The indicator could be in the negative in instances when new low issues exceed the number of new high issues.

Formula: net new 52-week high

$$H - L = N$$

H = 52-week new highs
L = 52-week new lows
N = net new highs

Excel program

A1   52-week new highs
B1   52-week new lows
C1   =SUM(A1-B1)

For example, new high issues were 120 and new lows were 32. The net new high was:

$$120 - 32 = 88$$

This can be tracked through a cumulative analysis of the trend, call the high/low line. Each session's net new high is added to (or when negative, subtracted from) the prior net new high.

Formula: high/low line

$$N \pm P = L$$

N = net new high, current
P = net new high, prior
L = high/low line

Excel program

A1   net new high, current
B1   net new high, prior
C1   =SUM(A1+B1)

For ex ample, the current net new high was calculated as 88. The prior net new high line was 62. The high/low line is:

$$88 + 62 = 150$$

The same data are used to track the number of issues trading above a specified moving average. Various MA's can be applied. For example, using a 50MA (50-session moving average), the calculation of the percent trading above is revealing and tracks a bullish or bearish trend over the period studied.

Formula: percent above MA

$$S \div T = P$$

S = number of stocks trading above MA
T = total stocks in the index
P = percent above MA

Excel program

A1   number of stocks trading above MA
B1   total stocks in the index
C1   =SUM(A1/B1)

For example, applying the 50MA to the S&P 500, 42 stocks were currently trading above the 50MA line. The percent above MA is:

$$42 \div 500 = 8.4\%$$

Put/Call Ratio

An overall market indicator is also calculated using the relationship between volume of options. A comparison between puts and calls is believed to track market trends. When the ratio is greater than 1, it is the result of puts having greater volume than calls. A ratio less than '1' results from the opposite. A high ratio is interpreted as bearish, so that a rising ratio tracks a bearish trend.

Formula: put/call ratio

$P \div C = R$

P = put volume
C = call volume
R = put/call ratio

Excel program

A1   put volume
B1   call volume
C1   =SUM(A1/B1)

For example, a day's summary reveals that equity put volume was 492,606 contracts, and equity call volume was 741,190. The put/call ratio was:

492,606 ÷ 741,190 = 0.66

This result is less than 1.0, the result of greater volume in calls. Tracking this relationship over a series of trading sessions reveals the continuation or reversal of the trend.

The overall market may be further judged by a series of ratios concerning trading and profitability in mutual funds. The fund-based trends are significant, as total dollars invested (approximately $15 trillion) represent about 22% of total worldwide stock valuation of $69 trillion. [vi]

Mutual Fund Ratios

With many investors choosing to invest in a variety of mutual funds and rely on the services of professional managers, the question of how to pick a fund has to be raised. Load and no-load funds are a starting point, but an array of fees are also applied. No direct management is required in an exchange-traded fund (ETF), because rather than managing a portfolio of securities, the ETF is based on a predetermined "basket of securities" with something in common (geography, sector, or type, such as equity, debt, currency, or commodity, for example).

For any mutual fund investment, either as an alternative to direct ownership of securities or as a means of diversification, specific calculation help determine the viability and potential of one fund compared to another. The first important calculation is the liquidity ratio.

This is a method for quantifying whether a mutual fund management team is bullish or bearish. It compares the level of total assets invested versus the amount held in the form of liquidity (cash or cash equivalents). If fund management has a larger than average percentage of a portfolio held in cash, it implies that management has difficulty finding investments that meets its standards, or that management is cautious under current market conditions. Conversely, when a fund's management has the minimum amount of the overall portfolio held in the form of cash, it implies a bullish position based on current market conditions.

Formula: mutual fund liquidity ratio

$C \div A = R$

C = cash and cash equivalents
A = total assets
R = liquidity ratio

Excel program

A1   cash and cash equivalents
B1   total assets
C1   =SUM(A1/B1)

For example, a mutual fund reports current cash and cash equivalents of $32,515,800 and a total portfolio value of $107,550,034. The liquidity ratio is:

$\$32,515,800 \div \$107,550,034 = 30.2\%$

A second ratio of importance to mutual fund investors is net asset value (NAV). This is the total value of all a fund's assets, minus its liabilities. It is also termed net book value per share. If NAV rises, it points to increased profits from investments, and conversely, NAV will decline if the portfolio experiences net losses. The calculation takes into account all assets, including securities in the portfolio, plus cash and cash equivalents, accounts received, and accrued income, all calculated at market value (usually at the end of a trading day). From this, all liabilities are subtracted, including accrued expenses and debts owed by the mutual fund. NAV is then expressed per unit, which is the mutual fund's equivalent if a share.

Formula: net asset value

$(A - L) \div U = N$

A = assets
L = liabilities

U = units outstanding
N = net asset value

Excel formula

A1 assets
B1 liabilities
C1 units outstanding
D1 =SUM(A1-B1)/C1

For example, at the end of a trading day, a fund reports total assets of $107,550,034, total liabilities of $3,007,623, and units outstanding of 4,016,660. NAV is:

($107,550,034 - $3,007,623) ÷ 4,016,660 = $26.03

Thus, an investor holding 800 units would have current value in the mutual fund of:

*800 * $26.03 = $20,824*

A third key ratio for mutual fund investors is the expense ratio. Funds, including both load and no-load funds, assess a variety of fees. These include load, management fees, 12b-1 (marketing and distribution fees), and administrative fees. A wide variety of different fees makes reliable comparisons elusive. For this reason, using a fund analyzer and calculator helps make valid and accurate analyses of mutual fund fees.

Valuable Resource: FINRA publishes a free calculator to compare mutual fund fees and expenses. Go to http://apps.finra.org/fundanalyzer/1/fa.aspx

---

The expense ratio calculates total operating expenses as a percentage of average net asset value for the fund, calculated for one full year. Average net asset value is the average of monthly or quarterly NAV over a year, or the average of the beginning and ending NAV reported for a year.

Formula: mutual fund expense ratio

$E \div (A * U) = R$

E = total operating expenses
A = average NAV
U = outstanding units
R = expense ratio

Excel formula

    A1 total operating expenses
    B1 average NAV
    C1 outstanding units
    D1 =SUM(A1/(B1*C1))

For example, a fund's operating expenses are $2,660,583. Average NAV is $28.15, and outstanding units are 5,004,551. The expense ratio is:

    *$2,660,583 ÷ ($28.15 * 5,004,551) = 1.9%*

The expense ratio will vary considerably between funds, even those appearing to contain similar levels of fees. This occurs because there are so many different types of fees as well as methods for assessing them. For example, some funds charge no sales load at the time of investment, but do assess a load when funds are withdrawn. This back-end load affects the calculation of expense ratio.

    Also significant in assessing funds in the calculation is the yield. This is calculated as the yield earned over a one-year period, divided by the price per share as of yearend. If this calculation is performed for a period of less than one yea, the income should be annualized to ensure comparable yields between different investments.

Formula: mutual fund yield

    $I \div N = Y$

    I = income distribution per share
    N = NAV
    Y = yield

Excel program

    A1 income distribution per share
    B1 NAV
    C1 =SUM(A1/B1)

For example, a mutual fund's income distribution per share is $108.16 for the full year. NAV is $26.03. Yield is:

    $108.16 ÷ $26.03 = 4.2%

The yield is perhaps the true "bottom line" for mutual fund investors. A means for comparison is the mutual fund yield to the dividend yield on a portfolio of directly owned stocks. Without having to pay the mutual fund expenses, direct ownership may improve overall net yield. The comparison is not precise, however. Variations of market risk in both the mutual fund and a directly held portfolio of stocks, makes this exercise an estimate only.

A final calculation for mutual fund investing is total return. This is the current value of the account plus cash distributions, minus the initial investment. The "return" is a dollar value and not the *rate* of return.

Formula: mutual fund total return

$$V + C - I = R$$

V = value of the account
C = cash distributions received
I = initial investment
R = total return

Excel formula

A1   value of the account
B1   cash distributions received
C1   initial investment
D1 =SUM(A1+B1-C1)

For example, an investment made one year ago currently is valued at $5,100. The original amount placed into the fund was $5,000. At the end of one year, $975 was received in distributions. Total return is:

$5,100 + $975 - $5,000 = $1,075

From this calculation, total *yield* can be calculated.

Formula: mutual fund total yield

$$(V + C - I) \div I = TR$$

V = value of the account
C = cash distributions received
I = initial investment
TR = total yield

Excel formula

A1 value of the account
B1 cash distributions received
C1 initial investment
D1 =SUM(A1+B1-C1)/C1

In the preceding example, total return was set at the dollar value of $1.075. Total yield is:

($5,100 + $975 - $5,000) ÷ $5,000 = 21.5%

The most accurate expression of total yield depends on whether distributions are taken in the form of cash payments, or reinvested to purchase additional shares. Reinvestment creates a compounding effect of the total yield, so the outcome would be different, especially over a period of many years.

---

[i] Haugen, R. A. & Baker, N. L. (Spring 1991). The efficient market inefficiency of capitalization-weighted stock portfolios. *The Journal of Portfolio Management*, 35–40

[ii] Miwaa, K. & Uedab, K. (2015). Price Distortion Induced by a Flawed Stock Market Index. *Journal of Behavioral Economics and Finance*, Vol. 8, 55–61

[iii] Grullon, G., Kanatas, G. & Weston, J. P. (2004). *The Review of Financial Studies*, Vol. 17, No. 2, pp. 439–461

[iv] Arnold, T.; Butler, A.W.; Crack, T. F.; & Zhang, Y. (July, 2005). The Information Content of Short Interest: A Natural Experiment. *The Journal of Business* 78, no. 4: 1307–336

[v] Lakonishok, A. S. & Vishny, R. W. (December 1994). Contrarian investment, extrapolation, and risk. *Journal of Finance*, Vol. XLIV, No. 5

[vi] www.ici.org/research/stats

Chapter 9
Price Indicators

The fundamentals include financial statements, earnings reports, dividend declarations and payments, and other financially-based information. Fundamental analysis involves looking backward to the historical facts in order to develop a sense of the trends and estimate where the future is heading. In comparison, technical analysis is based on today's price and volume facts and is focused on how trading trends affect price.

In using technical factors, a few guidelines to keep in mind:

1. *Technical and fundamental analysis can be used together for cross-confirmation.* The various indicators you track in a fundamental program often work well when augmented with specific technical indicators and ratios. Neither point of view has an exclusive on being right more than the other; all analysis involves estimates. The more valid information you employ, the better. Looking to historical information exclusively and ignoring current price trends is a mistake; and restricting your analysis to price without also checking profitability and capital strength is equally misguided.

2. *Technical trends are valuable for identifying risk levels.* Even when a company has adequate capitalization, a strong and consistent record of managing debt, creating higher revenue and earnings, and paying dividends, it does not tell the whole story. If you check price volatility, you discover that many companies that are equal in terms of fundamental strength often have far different volatility levels. This defines market risk and is a factor you cannot afford to ignore. Based on your individual risk profile, you might prefer low-volatility stocks, or be willing to accept greater volatility in order to also expose yourself to greater profit potential.

3. *Many technical trends signal changes in fundamental trends.* Many investors believe that the fundamentals and technicals operate distinctly and differently from one another. But you cannot ignore either side because they work interchangeably. A change in stock price volatility often foreshadows surprises in earnings reports, for example. The tendency is to think that earnings news creates reaction in price, which may be true; but the action-reaction cycle works in the other direction as well.

The Basics of Technical Analysis

Technical analysis is premised on one feature: The stock's price moves in trends. A related feature, volume, is also considered in interpreting stock price movement. A primary aspect of technical analysis anticipation of the next direction a stock's price

DOI 10.1515/9781501507427-009

is likely to move, and to invest either long or short accordingly; to time not only purchase decisions, for sale or hold decisions as well; and to improve the percentage of correct timing estimates based on techniques such as chart-watching, price and volume formulas, and observation of price trading ranges. Whether such prediction can be made accurately has been a source of debate for some time. Some belief that it is impossible to predict price movement, and others rely on technical analysis in the belief that price patterns, indicators, and reaction to fundamental news and events, all create price movement that is predictable in the short term. Believers in the technical side rely on price and related indicators for all of the information they require:

> Technical analysis has one core tenet: The market is right. Technicians believe that the most important source of information is the market itself and will thus comb through price structure and price histories, relative-strength rankings, volume analysis, and increasingly, analysis of investor behavior. [i]

The underlying philosophy of technical analysis is found in the Dow Theory. Although this theory is most often applied to marketwide indices like the Dow Jones Industrial Average, its precepts can also be used to technically analyze individual stocks.

Charles Dow, co-founder of the Dow Jones & Company, developed the initial theory in the 1880's and 1890's. Originally, Dow intended his theories to be applied to business models in predicting revenue and other financial trends. Dow was also interested in tracking his theories to predict market movements, and he developed the concept of using an index of typical stocks to track and develop trends. Dow himself did not develop what is today known as the Dow Theory. After his death in 1902, Samuel Nelson, an associate, published a book called *The ABCs of Stock Speculation*. In this book Nelson referred to many of Charles Dow's essays as a premise for predicting market change. This has become known as the Dow Theory.

The premise of this theory is that stock prices tend to act in concert; so when the trend is upward, the overall market trends in that direction, and vice versa. A limited number of market leaders can be identified and most other stocks will follow the lead established by those influential companies. This led to identification of 30 stocks that today make up the best-known average, the DJIA. Taken together, these 30 companies represent about 25% of the total value of all companies listed on the New York Stock Exchange (NYSE). [ii]

Under the Dow Theory, specific concepts mandate how trend analysis takes place. Technicians track three types of trends. First is the daily trend, also called the market's tertiary movement, which is not reliable for the purposes of developing actual longer-term trends. Second is a 20-to-60-day trend, also called a secondary movement and reflecting current sentiment. Finally, a primary movement represents the overall long-term market sentiment and may last between several months and several years. The primary trend underway at any moment is usually described as a bull market (upward moving) or a bear market (downward moving).

In addition to distinguishing the types of trends from one another, the Dow Theory requires that any indicated change in a trend be confirmed. Under the beliefs of the Dow Theory, the Dow Jones Transportation Average has to change in the same way as the Dow Jones Industrial Average, in order to establish as fact that a change in direction has occurred. So if and when one of the two averages falls below previous lows in successive declines, or above previously established highs in successive rallies, it does not signal a change in the primary trend until the second, confirming indicator follows suit. Figure 9.1 provides a one-year comparison between the DJIA and the DJTA, which demonstrates the tendency for both to move in a similar fashion.

Comparison, market indices

Figure 9.1: Comparison, market indices

The rules found in the Dow Theory are important because they form the basic beliefs among technicians, or at least among those technicians who swear by the Dow Theory. Without a precise requirement in pace to set and confirm a new trend direction, there would be no certainty as to whether a current trend had ended, or merely paused. The DJIA serves an important function in the market, by enabling investors to make judgments about the overall market at any time, based on the recent point changes, volume, and volatility of the market. But even the most faithful technicians are aware of a few additional points:

1. *The index does not affect individual stocks.* The DJIA is a barometer of the entire market, but it should not be assumed as an indicator of when to buy or sell individual stocks. Every stock changes in price due to numerous causes, including sector-wide trends, cyclical business changes, overall economic influences, activity among large institutional investors, competitive changes, and earnings reports. So any one of these or a combination of all of them will affect a stock's price from day to day, apart from what the index of 30 industrial stocks is doing at the same time.

2. *Every index is an average of several stocks, some advancing and some declining.* A strong point movement in the DJIA does not represent the entire market. In fact, every day's point change is the *net* difference between advancing and declining issues within the index. With this in mind, only market-wide composite indices can be expected to represent the real activity in the market. The DJIA is a valuable tool for gauging market sentiment, but not for making decisions within a portfolio.

3. *The DJIA, like all indices, is a useful tool but not the final word.* All indicators add something to a body of knowledge about the market, whether in the moment or with a broader view. It is always a mistake to rely on any one indicator, however. The DJIA sets a tone and tells you what investment professionals, institutions, and other individuals are thinking. It summarizes degrees of optimism or pessimism. But in evaluating how to act for your own portfolio, you need to use the DJIA as one of several useful indicators, and not as the last word.

The Random Walk Hypothesis and the Efficient Market Theory

The Dow Theory forms the basis for technical analysis of the stock market. There are additional theories about how and why prices change and what influences are at work in the market. The random walk hypothesis, for example, is a belief that all price change is arbitrary. This is based on the idea that current prices result from agreement among buyers and sellers in a complex understanding of stock share value. The random walk hypothesis is troubling to an army of well-paid insiders. If the hypothesis is correct, then those thousands of experts – analysts, managers, stockbrokers, and researchers – are of no real value. Cynically speaking, all price change is random:

The theory of random walks implies that a series of stock price changes has no memory--the past history of the series cannot be used to predict the future in any meaningful way. The future path of the price level of a security is no more predictable than the path of a series of cumulated random numbers ... for investment purposes, the independence assumption of the random walk model is an adequate description of reality as long as the actual degree of dependence in series of price changes is not sufficient to make the expected profits of any more "sophisticated" mechanical trading rule or chartist technique greater than the expected profits under a naïve buy-and-hold policy. [iii]

If the random walk hypothesis is applicable, it also means that any stock you buy is going to be a 50-50 proposition. It will have an equal chance of rising or falling, according to the hypothesis. But like most theories, this one is flawed and it can be demonstrably disproved. An analysis of long-term price trends reveals that well-managed companies produce profits; and that consistent growth in profits directly causes long-term increases in value. Many well-managed companies can be studied to make this point, just as poorly managed companies' stock falls on hard times. But it is not just poor management that causes these problems. For example, economic changes have affected the airline and auto industries. These same industries have competed over many years by creating attractive employee and retirement benefit programs, and these same programs have bankrupted many of the companies in those industries. Technology also affects corporate profitability and competitiveness. A few decades ago, Polaroid introduces the instant camera and revolutionized that industry; but with the emergence of the digital camera technology, the relatively expensive Land Camera was no longer appealing and Polaroid filed bankruptcy. [iv]

A similar trend can be seen even in large, well-capitalized corporations. Eastman Kodak has experienced several years of declining stock price levels *and* key fundamental indicators. In 1996, Kodak's stock (at the time trading under the symbol EK) ranged between $65 and $85 per share; in 2005, the range was between $21 and $35. The slide in prices reflects not only the problems of Kodak's continued dependence on old-style film products and a late entry into the digital camera market; it also reflects declining earnings along with increased debt levels. [v]

The company filed for bankruptcy protection in 2012, after operations spanning 131 years. Reorganizing and trading under the new symbol KODK, the company continued experiencing declining revenue and profits, and falling stock prices. The stock trend, far from random, is shown in Figure 9.2. As revenues fell, the stock price followed. This sort of connection between fundamental trends and technical response disputes the random walk theory, and supports the belief in predictability of price trends.

Eastman Kodak, price chart

Chart courtesy of StockCharts.com

Figure 9.2: Eastman Kodak, price chart

It would be difficult to find a company with declining fundamentals (revenue and earnings, debt ratio, etc.) that also experienced *rising* stock prices. It would be equally difficult to find a company with declining fundamentals whose stock price randomly changed from one year to another. The trend in prices tends to follow the bad news in the financial reports.

By the same argument, it would be unusual to see long-term good news in the financial statement accompanied by a declining stock price (or one moving randomly). In those cases where revenue and earnings rise consistently over time, when debt levels are kept low, and where other fundamental indicators remain strong, you also see rising stock values. These realities disprove the random walk hypothesis in the long term. However, most market theories, including the Dow Theory, discount the value of any short-term trends; so the random walk hypothesis may be applicable to price movement from one day to the next, regardless of long-term fundamental and technical trends.

A second market theory worth study is the efficient market theory. This theory simply states that the current prices of all stocks reflect all known information about a company:

> Technical analysis involves making investment decisions based on past trading data. It aims to establish buying and selling rules that maximize profits and still control risks of loss. Unfortunately, according to the efficient market hypothesis (EMH), this endeavor is ultimately futile. The EMH states that all available and relevant information are already incorporated in security prices. As technical analysis uses only current and past trading data, it is not possible to obtain abnormal positive returns by applying these technical trading rules. If investors could make money from applying these trading rules, this would indicate that the market is inefficient.

Therefore, the question of whether technical trading rules can consistently generate profits becomes an empirical issue concerning efficiency of actual markets. [vi]

Bad news is already discounted in the price, and good news is already factored in. The efficient market theory is tidy and reassuring but, like the random walk hypothesis, it is flawed. Short-term price movement is caused by an unknown variety of factors and tends to be over-reactive to virtually all news and information. The efficiency market theory refers to the efficiency in which information is taken into account in price response. However, this does not mean the price response is rational. Exaggeration is predictably experienced after earnings surprises and other unexpected news, for example. Secondly, no distinction is made between factual news and unproven rumor. Accordingly, the efficient market theory cannot be reliably used to track price movement. The random short-term chaos experienced in price behavior makes it mathematically challenging to track or predict. For this reason, reliance on technical signals and confirmation has proven to be the best alternative to assumptions of efficiency or randomness.

Even with its flaws, the efficient market theory – and efficiency in general – cannot be discounted or ignored. Perceptions have impact on investor behavior:

> The debates over market efficiency, exciting as they are, would not be important if the stock market did not affect real economic activity. If the stock market were a sideshow, market inefficiencies would merely redistribute wealth between smart investors and naïve traders. But if the stock market influences real economic activity, then the investor sentiment that affects stock prices could also indirectly affect real activity. [vii]

Basic Price Calculations

Because technical analysis focuses on price, it is also the most common form of information available today. To the extent that the stock market news is covered in the television and online media, there are usually only three types of reports. First is specific company news, often only local in nature (for example, if a major employer lands a new long-term contract, issues earnings reports, or lays off a large number of employees). Second is the daily change in the indices, especially the DJIA, which for most observers is "the market." Third and most popular is the day's change in a stock's price.

The changing stock price is almost always reported by the number of points. You will hear, for example, that a particular stock "lost two points in active trading" or that another stock rose "five points on positive earnings news." But what does this really mean? When you consider that the stock's price varies, a point change does not always mean the same thing. For example, what happens when two stocks both rise three points in a single day? One stock opened the day at $27 per share and the other opened at $81:

Stock	open	close	change	%
A	$ 27	$ 29	+ 2	7.4%
B	81	83	+ 2	2.5%

To compute the relevant *percentage price change*, the formula is:

Formula: percentage price change

$$C \div O = P$$

C = change
O = opening price
P = percentage price change

Excel program

A1 change
B1 opening price
C1 =SUM(A1/B1)

Applied to the previous example of tow stocks with a two-point change for each:

$$\$2 \div \$27 = 7.4\%$$
$$\$2 \div \$81 = 2.5\%$$

This is an important distinction. The percentage of change rather than points is what really counts. Consider the outcome when one stock opens at $27 and rises two points; and another stock opens at $81 and rises five points. On a percentage basis:

Stock	open	close	change	%
A	$ 27	$ 29	+ 2	7.4%
B	81	86	+ 5	6.2%

If you had the same amount of money invested in both of these issues, the $27 stock would have outperformed the higher-priced $81 stock:

300 shares @ $27	=	$8,100
2 points	=	600
increased value		$8,700 7.4%

100 shares @ $87	=	$8,100
5 points	=	500
increased value		$8,600 6.2%

Because the lower-priced stock rose at a greater percentage, the increase in dollar value and percentage is greater as well. The difference in points – two versus five – is not as significant when you consider that the percentage change is more relevant.

Chart Patterns and Interpretations

Even when focusing on the formulas and ratios of technical analysis, you cannot avoid the price trends showing up in chart patterns. The premise of technical analysis is the study of price and price patterns. A limited number of classic technical patterns and concepts form the basis for a rudimentary appreciation of this effort.

The purpose in computing market mood and directions of trends is not only to time purchase and sale decisions, but also to judge risk. Viewing price trends and patterns demonstrates the unavoidable risk/reward relationship. When price movement is highly volatile, opportunity is greater but so is risk. Conservative investors prefer low-volatility stocks and in exchange accept the probability that prices will not move upward (or downward) rapidly.

A distinction has to be made between volatility and breadth. Volatility is the tendency of price to move within its current high-to-low range. The greater the movement, the higher the volatility. As a range of movement (breadth) grows, so does volatility (risk).

Beginning with breadth, the venue of analysis is the trading range. Stocks tend to establish a limited number of points in which they trade. If and when price breaks through above or below this established range, it is a significant event, signaling a new rally or decline in the stock's price level. Technicians also observe that when price approaches the upper or lower limits on two or more consecutive attempts to break through, it is likely to predict a price movement in the opposite direction. This price behavior is one of breadth rather than strictly of volatility, but the two aspects also work together.

The upper trading limit is also called resistance level. It is the highest price in the current trading range that buyers are willing to pay. The lower price limit is called support level, which is the lower price that sellers are willing to accept upon sale of their stock. Once these well-defined lines are crossed, the trading range is likely to become more volatile, at least in the short term, until a new trading range has been set.

The trading range, resistance, and support are summarized in Figure 9.3.

Deere & Co., Trading range

Figure 9.3: Deere & Co., Trading range

The area of resistance and support is clearly marked. During the period this range remained in effect, price did not move outside of the range, although it tested the resistance and support price levels many times. The point of breakout is clearly identified because price did move above resistance *and* continued trading in a higher range. When price gapped even higher it was accompanied by a volume spike, which confirmed the strength of the upward price move.

Technicians are continually looking for revealing patterns in price trends. For example, a classic charting pattern is called head and shoulders, so named because it involves three high prices with the middle price (the head) higher than the first and third price peaks (the shoulders). The head and shoulders is seen as an attempt to break out above resistance. Upon retreat without successfully breaking through, the pattern indicates a pending price retreat. An inverse head and shoulders pattern (one in which low price levels are seen in place of high levels) indicates the opposite: After three unsuccessful attempts to move price below support level, the inverse head and shoulders is a signal that prices are about to move upward. Both of these patterns are summarized in Figure 9.4.

head and shoulders

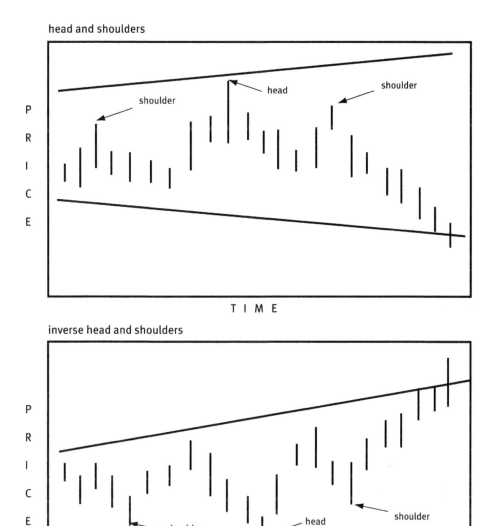

Figure 9.4: head and shoulders

When price moves above resistance or below support, it is called a breakout. A similar aberration in price patterns occurs through gaps. A gap occurs whenever the price closes on one day and opens above or below the trading range of the previous day (creating a visible price gap between the high and low range of each day).

The gap is important because it implies significant changes in trading range and interest among buyers (or the loss of interest among sellers). Four kinds of gaps are worth comparing: the *common gap* occurs as part of routine trading and does not signify big changes by itself. A *breakaway gap* moves price into new territory and does not retreat to fill in the gap in subsequent trading. A *runaway rap* is actually a series of gaps over several days, with price moving in the same direction. Finally, an *exhaustion gap* is likely to be quite large and signals the end of the runaway pattern, followed by price movement in the opposite direction.

The various types of gaps are summarized in Figure 9.5.

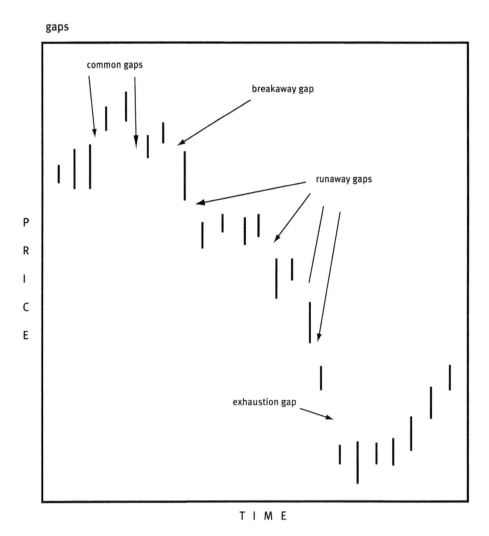

Figure 9.5: gaps

Many additional technical patterns are used by technicians, but these represent the major and most important signals. Tracking a stock's trading range reveals the degree of price volatility and, thus, market risk in a particular stock. The trading range – and its stability – is the best measure of this risk.

Technical Tests of Market Sentiment

Many additional technical indicators have been used by traders and analysts over many years to judge market sentiment and anticipate the direction of price movement. A word of caution: In the quickly changing market environment, many historical indicators may be less significant today than in the past. In addition, the actual meaning of some indicators could be different today due to widespread use of the Internet and improved information resources.

Useful resource: To find current market and trading statistics, check the New York Stock Exchange (NYSE) historical records site, at https://www.nyse.com/data/transactions-statistics-data-library

---

Sentiment indicators are not as precise as many other formulas and ratios. A lot of time may be spent checking economic indicators and other trends outside of the immediate market issues. The question on everyone's mind is: What are price levels today and what will they be tomorrow? To answer this question, sentiment indicators, economic trends, and other indirect influences on the market are less reliable that the tried and true technical signs: Emerging changes in trading range, price volatility and volume.

Checking degrees of insider trading, tracking cyclical changes, and equating fundamental trends with technical reaction are all valid and useful indicators. But in the venue of technical analysis, focus is going to be more likely to remain on price and price trends.

Breadth of Trading

The trend in price volatility is a central issue to the technician. Trading range that remains within a few points – low trading breadth – is a symptom of low volatility. So even as price levels evolve, the trading range may remain relatively narrow. In other words, price levels may be inching upward or downward over time but the breadth of the trading range remains small. If and when a broadening formation emerges, that is a sign of coming change. Greater price volatility is best understood in terms of emerging changes in trading range.

The formula for breadth of trading, when expressed as a percentage, provides a means for comparison between two or more stocks, or for one stock as breadth changes over time.

Formula: Breadth of trading

$$(H - L) \div L = B$$

H = high price in the range
L = low price in the range
B = breadth of trading

Excel program

A1 high price in the range
B1 low price in the range
C1 =SUM(A1-B1)/B1

For example, consider the 52-week price history for three stocks:
Stock A 22 – 28
Stock B 42 – 48
Stock C 62 – 68

Each of these stocks experienced a six-point spread through a 52-week period. But breadth of treading is different for each based on the formula:

Stock A $(28 - 22) \div 22 = 27.3\%$
Stock B $(48 - 42) \div 42 = 14.3\%$
Stock C $(68 - 62) \div 62 = 9.7\%$

An analyst be inclined to think of a six-point trading range as low breadth, especially over an entire 52-week period. And that is true; but the traditional method of calculating breadth is flawed in one sense. All of these stocks experienced a six-point trading range for the year. For this reason, a more reliable method for judging breadth could involve a rather simple comparison of the point spread itself. With this alternative method, all of these stocks would have a breadth of trading of '6' – six points over a 52-week period. However, because the price range was different for each, '6' does not reveal much about the scale of price behavior in the stock.

Another flaw in the traditional method of calculating breadth is that it does not allow for spikes in price. In most statistical analyses, a spike is considered out of the range, so it would be excluded. By definition, a spike in a stock's price occurs when the following conditions are met:

1. The price spike is substantially above or below established trading range.
2. The price trading immediately returns to previously established levels.
3. The spike trading level is not repeated.

For example, consider the trading history of a stock trading between $22 and $28 per share for the entire year, with one exception. Based on a rumor that the company was about to be taken over by a competitor, the price jumped in a single day to $37 per share. The rumor proved to be unfounded and price retreated over the next two days to the established $22-28 range. Under the traditional measurement of breadth, the outcome is:

$$(37 - 22) \div 22 = 68\%$$

Removing the spike returns the volatility to a more typical level:

$$(28 - 22) \div 22 = 27\%$$

If you use the proposed point-based alternative, the 52-week range extends over 15 points, but the removal of the spike in price returns it to the more typical level of 6 points.

The problem with the traditional method of calculating price breadth comes from two issues. First, the analysis is based on a percentage of variation, so that higher-price stocks appear to have lower breadth of trading, even when the point spread is identical to lower-priced stocks. Second, the method ignores the ramifications of untypical price spikes outside of an established trading range. These may be caused by rumors, earnings surprises, and institutional investor activity; but as long as the spike is not permanent, it should be taken out of the equation.

An *adjusted breadth of trading* formula that removes spikes also improves accuracy.

Formula: Adjusted breadth of trading

$$((H - S) - L)) \div L = B$$

H = high price in the range
S = spike (above price range)
L = low price in the range
B = adjusted breadth of trading

Excel program

> A1 high price in the range
> B1 spike above price range
> C1 low price in the range
> D1 =SUM((A1-B1)-C1)/C1

This formula is based on a spike *above* the established breadth. If a spike occurs below that level, the formula would have to discount the lower price in order to calculate adjusted volatility.

Application of this formula would be to adjust the 52-week range and adjust to a realistic range without spikes; and then employing the standard volatility formula based on the adjusted levels. However, this method still provides only a percentage comparison, distorting the issue. A comparison at various price levels makes this point clearly. The higher the trading range, the lower the volatility.

---

[i] Bollinger, J., CFA (2005). Combining technical and fundamental analysis. *CFA Institute*, institute conference proceedings, p. 61

[ii] Dow Jones & Company website, http://djindexes.com/mdsidx/index.cfm?event=show-AvgStats#cmc

[iii] Fama, E. F. (January-February 1995). Random Walks in Stock Market Prices. *Financial Analysts Journal*, 75–80

[iv] Polaroid filed for Chapter 11 bankruptcy protection in 2001 after years of ever-higher long-term debt on its books. The company could not meet its nearly $1 billion in bond and note liabilities.

[v] Eastman Kodak (EK) annual reports

[vi] Tharavanij, P., Siraprapasiri, V., & Rajchamaha, K. (2015). Performance of technical trading rules: evidence from Southeast Asian stock markets. *SpringerPlus*, 4, 552

[vii] Morck, R., Shleifer, A., Vishny, R., Shapiro, M., & Poterba, J. (1990). The Stock Market and Investment: Is the Market a Sideshow? *Brookings Papers on Economic Activity*, 157–215

Chapter 10
Volume Indicators

According to the Dow Theory, volume leads price. In an ideal application of this theory, this would mean price movement could be anticipated simply by tracking volume. In practice, however, this is not quite as easy as it sounds. Volume might lead price over longer-term trends, but short-term volume and price changes remain chaotic.

Even so, using a series of volume-based indicators, it is possible to confirm price signals and to identify opportunities to time trades. However, trend movement does not always confirm continuation of a current trend. It may also serve as a warning of a coming reversal. When volume acts as a form of divergence, seek confirmation in order to anticipate a change. A volume spike, for example, may signal the end of a trend, especially if confirmed by a price gap. However, changes in volume may be confusing because they result from either bullish or bearish news, events, and announcements. So both good news and bad news can have the same impact on price action and reaction.[i]

Chart watchers tend to see the volume spike as a signal of reversal; however, this reliance requires confirmation since the spike, by itself, implies chaos but not always reversal.

This uncertainty extends to the varying expectations among buyers and sellers, which often are not the same. So a volume spike's meaning is subject to not only the incentives of market participants, but also on their levels of knowledge and experience:

> Information diffuses gradually and has varying effect on valuation through the population of investors, because investors have differing investment objectives and differing degrees of access to information and different levels of expertise, attention, and time with which to interpret that news and apply its import to their situation.[ii]

Spikes often do act as significant reversal signals or confirmation, and are defined as exceptionally large volume days, followed by a return to more typical levels. When accompanied by price gaps, spikes mark a substantial change in the price pattern. Figure 10.1 has an example of this.

DOI 10.1515/9781501507427-010

the role of volume spikes

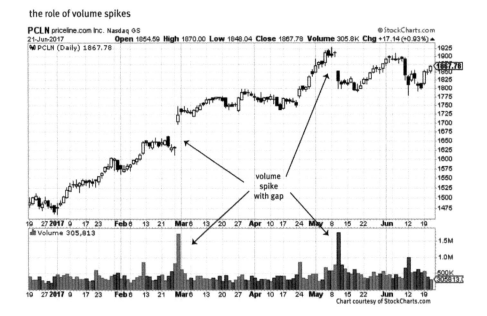

Figure 10.1: The Role of Volume Spikes

A spike often marks the point of price breakout; however, that alone does not guarantee the success of the breakout. Many of these price patterns fail, regardless of how exceptionally large a volume spike may occur. As a result, volume spikes are best viewed prudently, as one of many indicators of what might occur in the next price pattern.

The spike, in fact, might mislead chart analysts. As a general rule, low volume following breakout is a sign of weakness and likely reversal; and high volume is a sign of strength and likely success. However, reliance on volume alone to determine success or failure of a breakout is not advisable. The volume spike, accompanied by gaps, may further act as a marker of a trend climax and coming change in price direction, to move in the opposite direction or to plateau and move sideways in a consolidation pattern.

Change in Volume

The most basic volume signal is its change from one day to the next. This is especially worth following when a dynamic price trend—bullish or bearish—is underway. In consolidation periods, when price is range-bound, tracking volume is useful only when anticipating a breakthrough. At such times, movement above resistance or below support serves as an initial signal of breakout. An increase in volume is strong confirmation.

Because technicians study not only price, but trading volume as well, the two sets of indicators work well together as signal and confirmation. While price is easily comprehended, volume is not. You can see a price change and immediately grasp its implications. Stock value rises and it falls. But volume is a combination of activity by buyers and sellers. Exceptionally high volume may occur in a single day, but what does it mean?

One factor creating changes in volume is the extent of coverage about a company in the print and Internet media. One study based on mentions of companies on the Dow Jones Industrial Average (DJIA) in the *Financial Times*, for a six-year period from January 2007 through December 2012. The result of this study revealed that:

> ... a greater number of mentions of a company in the news on a given morning corresponds to a greater volume of trading for that company during a given day, as well as a greater change in price for a company's stocks. Our analyses also uncover a link between the volume of trading for a company and the number of mentions of company in the news on the next day ... movements in the news and movements in the markets may exert a mutual influence upon each other.[iii]

This correlation should not be surprising, because market activity tends to be reactive in many respects. When traders and investors (both institutional and individual) begin the day by discovering news items concerning a specific company, a natural response is to consider trading in that company's stock. This naturally creates the raw material for a volume-based analysis called *change in volume*, which tracks shares traded from day to day or from week to week. The formula:

Formula: change in volume

$$(C - P) \div P = V$$

C = current period volume
P = past period volume
V = change in volume

Excel program

A1 current period volume
B1 past period volume
C1 =SUM(A1-B1)/B1

For example, past period volume was 14.66 million, and the current is 17.91 million. The change is:

$$(17.91 - 14.66) \div 14.66 = 22.2\%$$

This formula is useful in tracking change when calculated using a moving average. In other words, rather than using a single day for analysis, a series of days is expressed as a simple moving average in order to track the change from period to period. Many websites providing charting service include price or volume moving average totals as part of the chart. However, this does not tell you much about the underlying causes of volume changes. For that, you must rely on a series of other volume-based calculations.

On Balance Volume (OBV)

Among the signals traders may add to online charts, one of the most popular is *on balance volume (OBV)*. This indicator is of the greatest value when the indicator diverges from price. This indicates a likely coming price reversal. The value of OBV as a technical signal is in its combination of trend direction and investor sentiment:

> The on-balance-volume (OBV) indicator incorporates a measure of market psychology and participation in a trend by weighing price action with its volume. The OBV can confirm the quality of the current price trend by moving in the same direction as price or warn of an impending reversal by diverging from the price action. The OBV above its long-term moving average indicates an up-trend and the OBV below its long-term moving average indicates a down-trend.[iv]

OBV is thus a combination of price with volume accumulation and distribution. An upward-moving price day causes volume to be added to a cumulative index; and when prices move down, volume is subtracted. A problem with OBV is that it makes no distinction between a slight move favoring one direction or another, versus a very large move. Big moves and little moves are treated in the same way.

Formula: on balance volume (OBV)

Higher closing price: $P + C = O$
   or
Lower closing price: $P - C = O$

P = previous OBV cumulative value
C = current volume
O = revised OBV

Excel program

Higher closing price:
A1 previous OBV
B1 current volume
C1 =SUM(A1+B1)

Lower closing price:
A1   previous OBV
B1   current volume
C1   =SUM(A1-B1)

For example, the previous OBV was 16,400. If price moved up in the latest day with volume of 7,250, revised OBV would be:

16,400 + 7,250 = 23,650

The following day, price declined and volume was 11,400. The revised OBV value reflecting this change would be:

23,650 – 11,400 = 12,250

An example of OBV is shown in Figure 10.2, the chart of McDonald's:

Figure 10.2: Rising On Balance Volume

In this case, OBV rose as a reflection of price gaining in most of the period reported. The positive move in price caused the addition of volume to the cumulative total of OBV. In cases where price is erratic, OBV tends to rise and fall as well. An example of this is shown in Figure 10.3.

erratic on balance volume

Figure 10.3: Erratic On Balance Volume

OBV provides a worthwhile device for tracking price movement. In the first example, as expected, as the stock price advances most days in a period, OBV follows suit. With a more erratic case, as in the second chart, OBV also tracks. The degree of movement helps confirm the price behavior through volume movement.

Accumulation/Distribution (A/D)

The calculation of OBV also points out its flaw. No distinction is made between large and small movement in either direction. As a result, an explosive price move in either direction will not show up as a matching trend in the volume indicator. This flaw is adjusted for and corrected with another volume indicator, accumulation/distribution (A/D).

A/D takes the range of price into account during each session, so that greater price volatility is reflected in what A/D reports. This volume indicator is a more accurate tracking device than OBV because it adjusts the volume trend for degrees of volatility in price. A/D is used to forecast price reversals likely to occur in the near future. Some analysts use divergence between price and A/D as a means for predicting reversal and confirming other signals.

The calculation requires three steps, all based on price and volume. First, the *money flow multiplier* is calculated. This is a factor varying between +1 and −1. Second, *money flow volume* is calculated by multiplying the first step by volume. Third, the cumulative total of money flow volume creates the A/D line.

Formula: money flow multiplier

$$((C - L) - (H - C)) \div (H - L) = M$$

C = close
L = low
H = high
M = money flow multiplier

Excel formula

A1 close
B1 low
C1 high
D1 =SUM((A1-B1)−(C1-A1))/(C1-B1)

For example, the current closing price was $58.50, low was $57.90 and high was $59.15:

$$((58.50 - 57.90) - (59.15 - 58.50)) \div (59.15 - 57.90) = -0.04$$

The next step is to multiply by volume for the period to arrive at the current A/D line; and to then add this to the previous A/D line.

Formula: A/D line

$$(M * V) + P = N$$

M = money flow multiplier

V = current volume
P = prior A/D
N = new A/D

Excel formula

A1 money flow multiplier
B1 volume
C1 prior A/D
D1 =SUM(A1*B1)+C1

For example, current volume was 11,450 and the prior A/D line was 18,009:

$(-0.04 * 11,450) + 18,009 = 17,551$

An example of A/D and its forecasting value is shown in Figure 10.4.

Figure 10.4: A/D Line with Price Trend

One particular segment is highlighted on this chart. As price moved toward the large gap occurring at the time of a positive earnings surprise, A/D anticipated a big move by advancing to the high point in its index. This is one example of how A/D can be used along with price to predict potential price behavior in the near future.

Money Flow Index (MFI)

The *money flow index (MFI)* calculates daily volume and its relationship to momentum. In this application, momentum is measured by *relative strength index* (RSI). This is described in Chapter 11. The MFI calculation sets up an index intended to demonstrate when a particular stock is overbought or oversold, an indication similar to RSI. Like RSI, the index for MFI ranges between zero and 100 and identifies 80 as the overbought level and 20 as the undersold level. In this respect, MFI and RSI are similar. However, RSI is based strictly on averages of price, whereas MFI combines price with volume. This adds a dimension to the analysis of momentum.

One element of MFI, similar to that of A/D, is divergence. A bullish divergence is found where MFI advances but price declines; and a bearish is the opposite. More often, however, MFI acts as a confirming indicator, tracking the price trend; and as MFI weakens, it may serve as an early signal that the current trend will plateau or reverse. Three steps are required in calculating MFI. First, the *raw money flow (RMF)* is a simple average of high, low, and closing price, multiplied by volume.

Formula: raw money flow

$$((H + L + C) \div 3) * V = R$$

H = high price
L = low price
C = closing price
V = volume
R = raw money flow

Excel program

A1 high price
B1 low price
C1 closing price
D1 volume
E1 =SUM((A1+B1+C1)/3)*D1

For example, the latest high price was $88.42, low was $81.07, and closing price was $83.50. Volume for the session was 142,800:

$$((88.42 + 81.07 + 83.50) \div 3) * 142{,}800 = 12{,}042{,}324$$

Second is calculation of a *money flow ratio (MFR)*. This represents the net positive money flow (MF) sessions within the most recent 14 trading days, divided by the negative sessions in the same period.

Formula: money flow ratio

$$P \div N = R$$

P = positive MF sessions (out of 14)
N = negative MF sessions (out of 14)
R = money flow ratio

Excel program

A1 positive MF sessions
B1 negative MF sessions
C1 =SUM(A1/B1)

For example, over the past 14 days, eight sessions were positive, totaling 2,883,401; and six sessions were negative, totaling 2,300,102:

$$2{,}883{,}401 \div 2{,}300{,}102 = 1.25$$

Note that the two sides—8 and 6 sessions—must equal a total of 14 within this range of calculations. The result of this calculation is a ratio of 1.25. Third, the money flow index, which always ranges between zero and 100, is calculated, by applying the money flow ratio.

Formula: money flow index

$$100 - ((100 \div (1 + M)) = I$$

M = money flow ratio
I = money flow index

Excel program

A1   money flow ratio
B1   =SUM(100-(100/(1+A1)))

For example, with a money flow ratio of 1.25, the calculation of MFI is:

100 − ((100 ÷ (1 + 1.25)) = 55.6

Online charting services provide the calculations automatically. An example of a chart with MFI is shown in Figure 10.5.

Figure 10.5: Money Flow Index

There were three instances of movement by MFI into the overbought range. Each corresponded with a short-term bullish move in the price. However, price continued advancing throughout the period. In this instance, MFI served as a test of volume-based money flow. The trend and occurrence of overbought conditions would not be evident in a study of volume alone, as the chart proves. The indicator provides value in the same way that momentum oscillators such as RSI do, by tracking the status of over-bought or oversold price levels.

Large Block Ratio

One volume-based test of institutional trading is the *large block ratio*. A large block (10,000 shares or more) summarizes institutional activity. Financial publications such as *The Wall Street Journal* publish daily summaries of large block trading and total volume. The level of large block trading indicates the level of volume attributed to institutional traders. The formula:

Formula: large block ratio

$$B \div V = R$$

B = large block volume in shares
V = total volume in shares
R = large block ratio

Excel program:

A1   large block volume
B1   total volume
C1   =SUM(A1/B1)

For example, the current session's large block shares traded was 2,413,500 shares. Total shares traded was 18,609,551 shares. The large block ratio was:

$$2,413,500 \div 18,609,551 = 13.0\%$$

The large block ratio is popular among contrarian investors. This is based on the belief that mutual funds and other institutional investors are more often wrong about their opinion of market direction. When the large block ratio begins to increase—meaning more activity among institutions—that implies that the market is likely to move in the opposite direction.

A deceptive aspect to this assumption is that large block trading may occur when institutions *buy* as well as when they *sell*. Volume itself is a net total of all large block activity. A more revealing trend is a study of advance/decline and new high/new low accompanied by a large block ratio analysis. In this way, you can judge mutual fund volume along with the trend toward issues rising or falling in market value. This potential distortion due to imbalances created through large block trading provides insights beyond the implied bullish or bearish sentiment often assumed as part of changing volume at these levels:

> Intuition suggests that prices and liquidity should be more strongly affected by more extreme order imbalances, regardless of volume, for two reasons. First, order imbalances sometimes signal private information, which should reduce liquidity at least temporarily and could also move the market price permanently . . . Second, even a random large order imbalance exacerbates the inventory problem faced by the market maker, who can be expected to respond by changing bid–ask spreads and revising price quotations. Hence, order imbalances should be important influences on stock returns and liquidity, conceivably even more important than volume.[v]

Large block trading, like so many indicators, should be viewed through the lens of its effect on the overall market. Because institutional trading represents a majority of trading volume, retail investors will invariably follow the volume trends this sort of indicator provides. However, the implications often move beyond the most obvious aspects of the indicator itself.

Several additional volume-based indicators may also be performed, but all are variations of the analysis presented here. By combining and averaging both price and volume, and determining whether buyers or sellers dominate a current trend, the analysis of price is augmented through volume signals. This represents one of several methods for forecasting price direction and reversal.

Conclusion

The next chapter explores the role of two additional types of technical indicators, the momentum oscillator and the moving average. When used to confirm other signals from price, volume, or moving averages, both of these indicator signals round out a technical program, combining information from an array of sources.

---

[i] Pritamani, M., and Singal, V. (2001). Return predictability following large price changes and information releases. *Journal of Banking & Finance*, 25, pp. 631–656.

[ii] Leigh, W. and Purvis, R. (2008). Implementation and validation of an opportunistic stock market timing heuristic: One-day share volume spike as buy signal. *ScienceDirect, Expert Systems with Applications*, 35, pp. 1628– 1637.

[iii] Alanyali, M., Moat, H.S., and Preis, T. (2013). Quantifying the Relationship Between Financial News and the Stock Market. *Scientific Reports 3*, Article number 3578.

[iv] Zeigenbein, S. (2011). A Fuzzy Logic Stock Trading System Based on Technical Analysis. *Regis University Theses*. Paper 474.

[v] Chordia, T., Roll, R. & Subrahmanyam, A. (2002). Order imbalance, liquidity, and market returns. *Journal of Financial Economics 65*, pp. 111–130.

Chapter 11
Momentum Oscillators and Moving Averages

Augmenting the value of price indicators, several additional sources for price prediction may be used by technicians. The last chapter introduced volume indicators; this chapter focuses on momentum oscillators and moving averages.

Movement in cannot be predicted. For others, the markets are considered to be *efficient*, meaning all known information is accounted for in the price immediately. Both of these theories contain flaws when applied in "real world" situations and to price behavior. Some specific events (earnings surprises, mergers and acquisitions, product announcements, for example) have a direct and immediate effect on price. These news items demonstrate that randomness is only one attribute of short-term price behavior. Many price indicators, notably candlesticks and traditional gapping activity, reliably predict the next move in price.

The assumption that the trend is a random walk, calls this system into question, especially by anyone who has observed the strength of price, volume, and momentum-based reversal signals and confirmation. Random activity tends to apply in short-term and highly volatile conditions, but for the longer-term, price behavior appears to be less random than many traders assume.

The assumption may also rely on market efficiency, even though that theory is also questionable as a valid means for price testing. The "efficient" market refers only to the way in which publicly known information is immediately taken into account. It does not ensure that price behavior will react appropriately. Price may easily overreact and does so many times. For example, a positive earnings surprise may cause price to gap higher in a single session (just as a negative surprise often causes price to gap lower). This immediate reaction often leads to a corrective, opposite-move within one to three days. Thus, while news is efficiently reflected in price, it does not result in an accurate level of price movement. An additional problem is that this efficiency makes no distinction between true information and rumor. It also does not separate price reaction between known matters (such as an earnings report) and speculation (changes in price targets or guidance, for example). For all of these reasons, chartists rely on an array of indicators that may be used to round out the efficiency of information and its outcome in price movement or trend continuation and reversal. Among the valued indicators to achieve this balancing out, is a range of tests for momentum.

Overview, Momentum Oscillators

By definition, "momentum" means the strength and speed of price change. However, this measurement is not concerned with the direction of price movement. The more

DOI 10.1515/9781501507427-011

rapidly price advances or declines, the greater its momentum; however, momentum applies equally in either direction.

Momentum oscillators help traders to better understand the nature of price behavior and, equally, to better manage volatility. In fact, even selection of a random set of signals by an experienced and diligent investor may yield better results than the alternative of paying for professional financial advice:

> Financial markets are often taken as example for complex dynamics and dangerous volatility. This somehow suggests the idea of unpredictability. Nonetheless, due to the relevant role of those markets in the economic system, a wide body of literature has been developed to obtain some reliable predictions. As a matter of fact, forecasting is the key point of financial markets ... for the individual trader, a purely random strategy represents a costless alternative to expensive professional financial consulting, being at the same time also much less risky, if compared to the other trading strategies.[i]

One such set of strategies may include analysis of oscillators, although using these as singular indicators is not advisable. The most effective means for developing a strategy to predict price movement is through combinations of price, volume, and momentum, in order to accomplish the desired signal *and* confirmation.

Momentum can be viewed on a price chart in two ways, by visual attribute and by indicator. The visual attribute is the slope of a price move. A steep slope is a symptom of strong momentum. For example, in Figure 11.1, high momentum is visually apparent by the slope of the two downtrend periods.

high momentum

chart courtesy of StockCharts.com

Figure 11.1: High Momentum

In comparison, relatively low momentum is visually apparent in the chart in Figure 11.2, where the slope of the uptrend is much more gradual.

low momentum

Figure 11.2: Low Momentum

A second method for judging momentum and its effect on price predictability, is through the application of a *momentum oscillator*. This is a signal based on averaging of price over a finite period of time, calculated to reflect movement in an index and location of several elements: overbought or oversold conditions, convergence and divergence, and the rapidity of change in the index as a reflection of strength or weakness in price movement.

Oscillators, because they represent an averaging of price, are lagging indicators. They reveal how the recent past price trend is reflected in momentum. However, some oscillators begin to slow down or speed up in advance of actual price reversal. This appears as a leading indicator, but actually is not. It is a change in the lag of the oscillator itself. Arguments have been put forth to make a case for oscillators as leading indicators. The debate ultimately is settled by awareness of how the oscillator is constructed. It represents an average of past closing price levels.

Relative Strength Index (RSI)

Among popular momentum oscillators, *relative strength index (RSI)* is the most basic, and is easy to interpret. However, its value is not absolute. Because it represents an average of recent closing prices, some of the signals generated can be misleading.

The calculation sets up an index between zero and 100. As long as the index value remains between 30 and 70, no warnings appear. However, if RSI moves above 70 it is classified as overbought; and below 30, it is oversold. In both cases, the initial indication is for reversal, so those using RSI look for these moves outside of the midrange to enter a trade. Because reliance on any one indicator is never advisable, RSI should serve as a confirming indicator for other reversal signals, such as price patterns or volume changes.

To calculate RSI, the first step is to determine *relative strength*. This is the average of the number of gaining sessions in the most recent 14, divided by the average of the number of losses.

Formula: relative strength

$$AG \div AL = RS$$

AG = average gains (of the most recent 14 sessions)
AL = average losses (of the most recent 14 sessions)
RS = relative strength

Excel program

A1   average gains (of the most recent 14 sessions)
B1   average losses (of the most recent 14 sessions)
RS =SUM(A1/B1)

For example, in the last 14 sessions, eight gained an average of 4.35 points; and six lost an average of 2.70 points. RS is:

$$4.35 \div 2.70 = 1.61$$

RS is used as part of the formula for the index representing "normal" versus overbought or oversold conditions.

Formula: relative strength index (RSI)

$$100 - ((100 \div (1 + RS)) = RSI$$

RS = relative strength
RSI = relative strength index

Excel program

A1 RS
B1 =SUM(100-(100/(1+A1)))

For example, RS was previously calculated as 1.61. Applying the formula:

$$100 - ((100 \div (1 + 1.61)) = 61.69$$

In this example, RSI was 61.69, which is within the "normal" range between 70 and 30.

RSI is normally based on 14 consecutive and most recent sessions, and it changes each day as the oldest session is dropped and replaced by the most recent one. Since this averaging of 14 sessions (some gains and some losses) involves daily recalculation, RSI would be labor-intensive to calculate every day. Fortunately, online charting services include RSI automatically as part of the chart if RSI is selected. For example, the chart of Chipotle (Chipotle Mexican Grill, Inc.) in Figure 11.3 demonstrates instances of overbought and oversold conditions. The overbought condition, accompanied by a volume spike, accurately predicted the reversal and downtrend that followed after a delay. Because the RSI signal was confirmed by volume, it was a strong forecast.

Some chartists like to adjust the default settings of many signals to increase the instances of reversal signals. This is not necessarily a positive change in what the indicator reveals. For example, in the case of Chipotle, notice that two previous volume spikes were not confirmed by any move in RSI outside of the 70-30 range. However, if the default of 14 sessions is changed to 8 sessions, the signal takes on a different appearance, as shown in Figure 11.4.

RSI as a forecasting signal

Figure 11.3: RSI as a Forecasting Signal

RSI as a forecasting signal

Figure 11.4: RSI with Adjusted Settings

This chart, with the use of six sessions instead of 14, generates many more over-bought and oversold signals. However, all of the additional signals were mislead-ing and did not accurately forecast actual price reversal. The desire for more sig-nals is misguided in many instances. In fact, the lack of movement by RSI above 70 or below 30 is itself a type of signal, indicating that no extreme price behavior is underway.

Moving Average Convergence Divergence (MACD)

A second momentum oscillator is MACD, which calculates the interaction between three separate averages. These are 12-day, 26-day, and 9-day exponential moving av-erages (EMA). There are three parts:

1. MACD line is the net of the 12-EMA minus the 26-EMA.
2. Signal line is the 9-EMA.
3. Histogram is the net of MACD minus the signal line.

The three are placed together to form the rather complex appearance of MACD, as shown in Figure 11.5.

Figure 11.5: MACD

As the MACD and signal lines cross over one another, a coming reversal in price may be signaled. Convergence occurs as the MACD and signal lines move closer together, and divergence is identified when these lines move apart. Analysts use these trends to confirm reversal signals seen elsewhere, in price and volume. The three calculations are relatively simple, but used together, they represent the complex appearance of MACD.

Formula: MACD calculations

12-EMA – 26-EMA = M
9-EMA = S
M – S = H

12-EMA = 12-day EMA
26-EMA = 26-day EMA
M = MACD line
9-EMA = 9-day average of MACD line
S = signal line
H – histogram

Excel program

MACD line:
A1 12-EMA
B1 26-EMA
C1 =SUM(A1-B1)

Signal line:
A1 MACD, 9 days
A2 =SUM(A1/9)
Histogram:

A1 MACD line
B1 signal line
C1 =SUM(A1-B1)

The *exponential moving average* (EMA) is a form of moving average that weighs the latest period more than the earlier periods. The first step is to calculate the exponent. This is a weighting step consisting of dividing 2 by the number of fields being averaged:

Formula: Exponent

$2 \div N = W$

N = number of fields
W = weight (exponent)

Excel program

A1: =SUM(2/N)

Next calculate the exponential moving average (EMA using the weighted exponent:

Exponential moving average (EMA)

$[(L*W)+O]*(1-W)=A$

L = latest value
W = weight (exponent)
O = old average
A = new average

Excel program

A1: latest value
A2: weight
A3: old average
A4 =SUM((A1*A2)+A3)*(1-A2)

The value of MACD as a momentum oscillator is in identification of likely reversal confirming patterns (convergence and divergence) as well as crossover of the lines to one another. A potential problem in the use of MACD is confusion arising from the complexity in the use of multiple averages, leading to divergent interpretations or false signals.

Stochastic Oscillator

A signal very similar to RSI is the *stochastic oscillator*. The word "stochastic" means an outcome randomly determined, or having a random distribution. This may be analyzed statistically but cannot lead to accurate prediction. However, by identifying levels of overbought or oversold, the stochastic oscillator provides a similar value as RSI, but with the use of two separate averages.

The indicator has two signal lines, known as %K and %D. Calculations are performed over 14 consecutive periods. This default setting can be changed to generate a higher number of signals, but as pointed out with RSI, many of the increased number of signals are likely to be false.

Formula: stochastic oscillator

$(C - L) \div (H - L) * 100 = \%K$
$3\text{-}SMA \ of \ \%K = \%D$

C = closing price, current
L = lowest low, last 14 periods
H = highest high, last 14 periods
%K = %K average
3-SMA = simple moving average, last 3 %K
%D = %D average

Excel program

%K:
A1 closing price, current
B1 lowest low, last 14 periods
C1 highest high, last 14 periods
D1 =SUM(A1-B1)/(C1-B1)*100

% D:
A2 %K, latest day
B2 %K, second latest day
C2 %K, third latest day
D2 =SUM(A1+B1+C1)/3

An example of the stochastic oscillator is found in Figure 11.6.

Stochastic oscillator

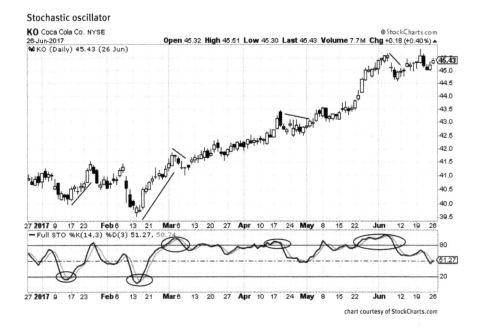

chart courtesy of StockCharts.com

Figure 11.6: Stochastic Oscillator

The highlighted areas show when the oscillator has identified overbought or oversold conditions. Only those times when both %K and %D moved above 80 or below 20 are shown. These index values—80 and 20—are the default marks for highlighting the price moves outside of the middle zone. Also marked are the short-term trendlines revealing price activity immediately after the move of the stochastic oscillator out of range. In the example, it is evident that this oscillator is a short-term signal, which often leads to a short-term price reversal or retracement.

Moving Averages

The use of moving averages as overlays to stock charts is popular; however, traders may use moving averages most effectively as confirming indicators, never as primary ones. This is because moving averages are always lagging indicators. They summarize the movement of price over a defined period of time (commonly used are the 50-day moving average (50-MA) and the 200-day moving average (200-MA)).

The value in a moving average is in the way it summarizes the trend currently underway. As the MA approaches price or crosses above or below, it serves as one of many signals that a direction might be about to change. There is no certainty to this; but when MA movement confirms what other signals reveal—for example, reversal signals in price or volume—they provide one more confirming signal of what price forecasting reveals.

Simple moving averages, previously introduced, are the result of adding together the values in a field, and dividing by the number of values. For example, a 50-MA is the sum of 50 sessions of closing prices divided by 50. An exponential moving average (EMA) gives greater weight to the latest entry in the field, on the theory that most recent information has greater validity and application than older information. This is why some calculations, such as the momentum oscillator MACD, rely more heavily on EMA.

Moving average signaling takes several forms. Using 50-MA and 200-MA together enables traders to analyze the interaction between price and averages, as well as between one MA and the other. Shorter MA lines move faster than longer ones, so using the two together generates signals that chartists use to confirm trends. When a shorter MA crosses above a longer MA, it is a bullish crossover. A bearish crossover is the opposite, when the shorter MA crosses below the longer MA.

A second form of crossover is movement of the MA with price. A price crossover is of greater interest to swing traders, so using a shorter-term MA usually generates greater interest. When the 50-MA moves above price, it is a bullish signal. Some crossovers are very brief, revealing or confirming price retracement.

When the two MA lines move closer to one another, creating convergence, it may confirm a developing price reversal signal. If, for example, price begins forming a wedge as convergence occurs, it can confirm price-based signals. The opposite, when MA lines move apart, creates divergence, which may signal increasing volatility or continuation of the prevailing trend. When price crosses both a 50-MA and a 200-MA, it is an exceptionally strong directional signal.

MA lines can also provide dynamic forms of resistance or support. Rather than the straight line often used to denote these borders of the trading range, MA tends to track moves in price direction. Because the 50-MA is the more responsive of the two, it is most likely to closely track price during a strong bullish or bearish trend.

The greater the price volatility, the more signals will be found on the chart. For example, Figure 11-7 highlights six specific MA-based reversal signals.

The first and third signals are examples of convergence. In both cases, the movement is brief, and quickly evolves to other signals. The first turns into a bearish crossover, when the 50-MA moved below the 200-MA. The second convergence moved into a bullish crossover, which led to significant divergence. Finally, as price gapped lower, the 50-MA moved above price, setting up a bullish signal.

In the last three months of the chart, the 50-MA tracked price as a form of support, moving five points below the price as it trended higher. Because the MA lines change as rapidly as they do in this case, they are not as effective in tracking resistance or support as some other signals, specifically Bollinger Bands.

moving average signals

Figure 11.7: Moving Average Signals

Bollinger Bands (BB)

One form of moving average employs three separate ones. Even so, it is among the easiest to use and to understand. Bollinger Bands (BB) establish a likely trading range based on a simple moving average of 20 days; and an upper band and lower band two standard deviations from that middle band.

This sets up many different methods for identifying continuation and reversal of price. The range of standard deviations also defines historical volatility of the current price, making it easy to spot expanding or contracting levels of change. When price moves outside of the standard deviation lines, it is highly likely that a retracement will follow, returning price into range. In fact, retracement is made highly visible using this signal.

For example, Figure 11.8 highlights the three bands as well as seven instances of price moving outside of the band ranges. In every case, price quickly retreats back into range, demonstrating the value of BB as a method for locating retracements and timing short-term trades.

Bollinger Band retracements

Chart courtesy of StockCharts.com

Figure 11.8: Bollinger Band Retracements

The BB signals also identify likely reversals through a series of specific signals worth researching further. These include the M top, W bottom, Bollinger squeeze, and island cluster. All of these provide exceptional signaling strength and reliability. In specific situations, such as earnings surprises, product announcements, or merger and acquisition news, observing BB behavior is of great value. The default of two standard deviations can be adjusted to reflect three standard deviations, and in extreme price movement, price may also violate these levels. The higher degree of standard deviation adds to confidence of a quick reversal back into range.

Although BB is added automatically as a selection in free online charting services, it is instructive to trace the process for developing this signal. It requires several steps:

1. Enter closing prices for the number of days in the analysis. Since BB is based on 20 sessions, this would be a likely starting point.
2. Find the change from each day to the average of the entire field, the "deviation."
3. Finds each deviation's square.
4. Add the squared deviations.
5. Find the square root of the squared deviations.
6. Annualize using 252 days (the average number of trading days per year), to arrive at the standard deviation.

The formulas for these steps follow:

Formula: Bollinger Band 20-day average

$(V_1 ... V_{20}) \div 10 = A$
V_1 = first value
V_{20} = final value
A = average

Formula: Bollinger Band deviation per period

$V_X - A = D$

V_X = value
A = average of the field
D = deviation

Formula: Bollinger Band square of deviation

$D^2 = S$

D^2 = deviation squared
S = square of the deviation

Formula: Bollinger Band sum of squared deviation

$S_1 + ... S_{20} = SD$
S_1 = squared deviation, first value
S_{20} = squared deviation, final value
SD = sum of squared deviations

Formula: Bollinger Band sum of squared deviation average

$\sqrt{SD}$

$\sqrt{SD}$ = square root of the average of squared deviations

Formula: standard deviation

$$\sigma = \sqrt{\frac{1}{N} \sum_{i=1}^{N} (x_i - \mu)^2}$$

σ = standard deviation
N = addition of values

Σ = range of values from 1 to n
χ_1 = individual values
μ = average

Excel program

A1 ... A20 each session's closing price
B2 ... B20each session's net change
C2 ... C20=SUM(B2*100) *(copy and paste for each cell in 'B')*
D20 =STDEV(C2:C20)
E20 =SQRT(252)*E20

The complexity of figuring out standard deviation points out why Bollinger Bands and similar technical signals were difficult to employ before the advent of free online charting services. These calculations are automatic once BB is selected as a chart overlay. Including this in a chart is simply a matter of selection, without manual calculations required.

Momentum oscillators and moving averages are lagging indicators, which limits their usefulness in predicting price behavior. The exception to this general rule is what can be discovered though analysis of patterns. For momentum oscillators, movement outside of a defined range and location of overbought and oversold conditions, may confirm what is observed in other signals, notably price-based signals pointing to continuation or reversal. For moving averages, convergence and divergence are predictive, as are crossover between averages and price. In the case of Bollinger Bands, the patterns generated by movement outside of the range between upper and lower bands are reliable and strongly correlated with price and the retracement most likely to occur as a next step.

Conclusion

These signals – oscillators and moving averages – often are elusive in what they reveal and what it means in terms of signals. For this reason, this range of indicators should be used only when confirming indicators or other types are also visible. Price and volume as well as traditional technical signals may provide greater certainty in trying to time trades.

---

[i] Biondo, A.E., Pluchino, A., Rapisarda, A. and Helbing, D. (2013). Are Random Trading Strategies More Successful than Technical Ones? *PLoS ONE* 8(7).

Chapter 12
Combined Testing:
Merging Price and Financial Tests

The debate about whether fundamental or technical analysis is better or more reliable often polarizes opinions. But the choice between one over the other is only one possible decision. The best strategy combines both fundamental and technical tests, for several reasons:

1. *Both approaches offer something of value.* It is not fair to assume that one approach is "correct" and the other is "wrong." Both offer useful information that you need to make good decisions and to time your buy, hold or sell actions. It is impossible to ignore price trends, even if you are a dedicated fundamental "true believer." And even the most focused technician understands that financial trends and reports directly affect price. The two cannot be separated and this indicates that you need to employ both fundamental and technical indicators in managing your portfolio.

2. *Each side is valuable for confirming trends seen in the other.* One valuable use of indicators often ignored in the debate between fundamental and technical proponents, is the importance of confirmation. Each side can be used to confirm trends seen emerging in the other. For example, when you see a lot of variation between reported earnings and core earnings, it implies that you cannot rely on the numbers as much as you'd like. When you see price volatility occurring, it confirms your suspicion. As a trading range broadens and stock price trends begin to look more volatile, you are likely to see a confirming change in reported revenue and earnings.

3. *The two approaches are really different aspects of the same grouping of trends.* Fundamental and technical really come down to degrees of value in a company and its stock. A long-term investor is more likely to ignore short-term price trends and focus primarily on financial information; and a speculator is just as likely to focus only on chart patterns and price-based trends. Realistically, however, these are simply different timeframes for the same pricing and valuation issues. Short-term trends are known to be unreliable for long-term forecasting, and speculators accept this as a risk. But those same trends, as chaotic as they are, represent segments of the longer-term trend; and you can begin to understand how those trends evolve by tracking both fundamental and technical indicators.

4. *Some of the most valuable indicators combine fundamental and technical information.* Finally, you cannot avoid using both fundamental and technical indicators. Two of the most popular and valuable indicators already combine both sides. Earnings per share (EPS) compares the fundamental earnings to the technical price per share; and the price/earnings ratio (PE) represents price as a

DOI 10.1515/9781501507427-012

multiple of earnings. In fact, there are several additional indicators combining price per share with fundamental indicators, and these are explained later in this chapter.

Effective Use of Combined Analysis

The process of *confirmation* is a crucial process for every investor and trader, no matter whether the individual leans toward speculative or conservative thinking. To effectively time your decisions, you can make good use of combined analysis. You can confirm any apparent trend by checking relevant information on the other side (fundamental versus technical and vice versa).

The technical side will invariably involve comparisons of price; so you may find valuable information comparing prices to the following fundamental indicators:

1. *Changes in revenue and earnings.* The levels of revenue and earnings are reported quarterly. The great "game" on Wall Street is prediction. Analysts consult with corporate management and examine the financial trends, and then publish their estimates of earnings, usually expressed in earnings per share. Remembering that the analyst's opinion is only an estimate, it is disturbing that so much weight is given to it. For example, if a corporation's quarterly earnings exceed their own internal expectations, you would expect the stock value to rise. But if actual reported results are a penny or two per share less than an analyst predicted, that causes the stock to fall.

    Ignoring the game of prediction and reaction, how can you use revenue and earnings information to confirm (or contradict) what you see in the stock's price? As revenue grows, you have every reason to expect net earnings to improve as well. But this does not always occur. So if earnings remain flat or even decline in a period of higher revenue, it is a negative signal. It may explain why a stock's price performance has been weak as well.

    Changes in trading range may also foreshadow disappointments is earnings or, in many cases, positive earnings surprises. For example, if reported earnings are higher than the analysts predicted (or, more importantly, higher than the corporation estimated) that is very positive. And you might see a positive trend in the stock's price, confirming the good news.

2. *Earnings surprises.* The differences of a few pennies between expected earnings and actual earnings is part of the expectation on the market. And when these small adjustments occur, a stock's price may fall or rise for one or two days, usually returning to "normal" levels quickly. But an earnings surprise is somewhat different. For example, if a corporation booked a large downward adjustment in the latest quarter, earnings may be reported substantially lower than expected. Even an announcement that future revenue and earnings are expected to be

lower than previously announced, a drop in the stock's price confirms the earnings surprise, often months in advance.

This works in the opposite direction as well. A surprise may be a reported higher than predicted level of revenue and earnings, usually based on exceptionally strong sales in the last portion of the quarter. The inevitable result will be higher stock prices, sometimes temporarily and at other times as part of a breakout leading to a higher trading range. The identification of cause and effect is difficult because with every price movement, some stockholders take profits (at the top) or cut losses (at the bottom). So short-term speculation in trading obscures what is going on with long-term investors who follow the fundamentals. On a day-to-day basis, price movement is likely to be chaotic and involving a series of offsetting over-reactions to virtually everything. So confirming earnings surprises with observation of trading range adjustments is a valuable step.

3. *Rumors or news reports concerning mergers and acquisitions.* Wall Street loves rumors and thrives on them. The culture of the market prefers rumor over fact, and investors often make snap decisions on the basis of rumor, without even knowing whether the information is true or false. At the same time, those enthusiasts who encourage rumor also worry constantly about whether their information is reliable. The expression, "Stocks climb a wall of worry" is based not only on realities of supply and demand, but also on the popularity of the rumor.

One of the favorite rumors is that a particular company is going to be taken over by a competitor. This "merger mania" comes and goes in various times, but the course of the rumor is always the same. The fact that the rumor exists makes it more likely than not that it is true; and traders react accordingly. This gives way to one of the favorite (but illegal) tactics used by some traders, the "pump and dump." An individual buys a large number of shares in a company and then spreads a rumor (on investment chat lines, for example) that the company is about to be acquired by a larger competitor. This rumor drives up the stock's price (pump) and then the instigator sells (dumps) the stock.

4. *News announcements concerning lawsuits, tax matters, and more.* A bit more tangible than the rumor concerning mergers or acquisitions is the reality of contingent liabilities. In recent years, two very large companies have been named as defendants in literally thousands of lawsuits. Altria (MO), the world's largest tobacco company, has been and remains a defendant in lawsuits filed by smokers, states, and the federal government. These suits will not be settled for many years and could end up costing the company billions of dollars. But because outcome is not known, the problem is only a *contingent* liability. The second company is Merck (MRK), whose Vioxx problems also led to thousands of lawsuits when it was revealed that the prescription drug was far from safe. As in the case of Altria, Merck's actual future liability cannot be known until the thousands of lawsuits run their course.

Merck suffered another contingent problem in 2006 when it was revealed the company might face as much as a $5.58 billion additional tax liability with the U.S. and Canada. As a result of this story (accompanied by November, 2006 election results) the company's stock fell several points. The liability itself – like the lawsuit liabilities – is contingent and final outcome may be far lower; but the contingency itself is enough to cause the stock's price to fall several points.

Valid Versus Invalid Forms of Testing

One of the important assumptions about any form of analysis is that it will yield information that is valuable as well as revealing. For example, there are valid justifications for comparing revenue and expenses or dividends and price; but there is no logical reason to compare accounts receivable to depreciation, or to track a developing trend in fixed overhead compared to intangible assets.

This issue is an important one because, in order for your own program to make sense, you need to be able to achieve the following:

1. *You have to limit the number of indicators you follow.* It would be impossible to track every possible form of analysis. With thousands of possible methods you could use, the sheer weight of information would make it impossible to draw useful conclusions. The greater the number of indicators, the higher the chance you will find contradictory outcomes. You are much better off identifying a very limited number of indicators and tracking them together.

2. *The information has to be readily available.* Another problem with some theories is that the raw information itself is not readily available. For example, even a simple balance sheet item such as inventory level is not likely to be published by companies every month, so you will need to use quarterly levels. Physical counts of inventory are not performed routinely either, so the information may not be accessible. This means that a detailed month-to-month average of inventory cannot be part of your program of analysis.

3. *The data you employ has to be current.* Some data are simply outdated by the time you get the information. If you are referring to published financial statements from six months in the past, matters are likely to have changed due to emerging earnings, cyclical realities, and changed markets. Finding current data may rely on estimates and unaudited results, but there is a trade-off between timing and accuracy. This doesn't mean certain ratios should not be performed; it does mean that current information is not always available, and whatever is published might be modified later.

4. *Data in related sets of information should be comparable, in terms of valuation and time.* A ratio should involve two or more sets of information that are directly related. This applies in two specific ways. The first is valuation; second is timing.

For example, the inventory turnover ratio should be performed comparing inventory to the cost of goods sold, because both of these are reported on a cost basis. (Inventory statistics used should be an average for the period in which costs of goods sold is derived.) However, some analysts prefer comparing inventory values to revenue. The reported revenue total is marked up, so inventory is at cost and revenue is at retail. This makes the comparison less reliable, because the valuation base is not the same. Proponents of using revenue argue that the mix of cost mark-up is one feature in tracking turnover; and while this is true, the outcome can be distorted when one line of business is marked up more than another.

Timing is also a crucial factor influencing comparability of data. For example, if you use the traditional price/earnings (PE) ratio, you will be comparing price (current value) to latest-reported earnings, which may be several months old. Invariably, this gap in time makes PE less reliable than analysts would like. With that in mind, PE makes sense when compared as a matter of period-specific ending price and earnings (so that PE can be tracked from quarter to quarter over time). Or current price should be representative of average prices for the last period of time extending back to through the earnings period (quarter or year). As an alternative, average mid-trading range price may be compared to estimated current-period earnings. This is an unreliable method because it includes data that are not specific. However, the current-period PE is always going to be unreliable because it uses information from two different time periods.

5. *You need to be able to act on the information revealed.* Finally, the ratios and formulas you use must be valuable in some way. The outcome of indicated trends must provide you with a conforming or contradicting set of circumstances. For example, if a company's revenues have been rising and earnings keeping pace, this is a positive trend. But if the latest quarter's results show continuing increased revenue but *declining* earnings, this is an indication that something has changed. It warrants further investigation and may signal that a previously positive trend has turned negative.

Identifying Important Combined Tests

The major indicator using a combination of fundamental and technical information is the price/earnings (PE) ratio. The price is shown as a multiple of earnings. So when the PE is 10, that means that the *current* price is 10 times greater than the *latest* earnings per share.

The problem in relying heavily on this popular ratio is its potentially inaccurate outcome. The problem of distortion is especially severe if and when the interim cycles of an industry have changed since the latest earnings report. For example, in the retail sector, the quarter ending December 31 is usually the highest volume for revenue and earnings; and the March 31 quarter is often the lowest. So if your PE calculation takes place in March or early April, it could be unreliable. If the current price is compared to the latest reported earnings as of December 31, the entire latter has been distorted. In fact, if the price itself has remained within a narrow trading range but actual current revenue and earnings levels have fallen off, the PE cannot be assumed to be accurate at all.

Even with the obvious distortion between price and earnings, current PE remains a popular litmus test of stock values. The historical quarterly and annual PE are much more revealing, in which a year-end price is compared to that year's earnings. However, even this test makes PE outdated throughout most of the year.

A solution involves tracking the price of a stock throughout the year. You can calculate and estimate a trend in both stock price and earnings and avoid the inaccuracy of time distortions. However, this only works in those companies with relatively stable price movement and predictable earnings.

For example, a test of Wal-Mart's annual revenue shows that top-line growth has been remarkably consistent. This is summarized in Table 12.01.

Table 12.1: Annual Revenue, Five Years

Wal-Mart: Year	$ Millions
2012	$446,950
2013	469,162
2014	476,294
2015	485,651
2016	482,130

Source: *CFRA Stock Reports*

Earnings were also fairly reliable during this same period, averaging between 3.05% and 3.62%. But when this record is compared to other retail corporations, the consistency is not always found. In the case of Wal-Mart, tracking year-to-year PE is an easy matter and because revenue and earnings are so consistent, it is easy to rely on estimates during the year. The same suggestion does not apply to every company in the sector, however.

When you are trying to track PE but recognize that price or earnings volatility makes the outcome less than reliable, you have some alternatives. These include:

1. *Use PE along with related and confirming indicators.* All indicators and trends should be confirmed or tested through alternatives. Never rely on any single indicator to make a decision about a stock, recognizing that it is the combination of many different indicators that really points out the relative strength of a company and its stock. So when the apparent PE seems consistent with the historical

trend, confirm this with a check of current quarter revenue, estimated earnings, and other tests. The same applies when the PE seems off from the average: Why is price more volatile than usual? Are cyclical forces at work? What else has changed?

2. *Compare price volatility to reported versus core earnings.* If the trading range of a stock has broadened since the previous year's range, what does that mean? One way to confirm greater volatility is to track the spread between reported earnings and core earnings. You are likely to see a correlation between price volatility and inconsistency in earnings. As core earnings increase, price volatility is likely to increase as well; and when there is very little adjustment between reported and core earnings, it is more likely that the stock's trading range will be narrow and consistent. While these are generalizations, the indicators may serve as confirming data for the current PE.

3. *Evaluate historical year-end PE and price range next to current quarter data.* Does the current PE seem in line with the historical trend? This is always an important test. If you discover that the current PE is far out of line with the year-end historical level for PE, it could be that your information is flawed (comparing old earnings with current price levels). If price has spiked above or below historical trading ranges, this could explain who the change has occurred, also indicating that the PE developed currently is not reliable. If earnings estimates are also unusual compared to historical levels for the same quarter (or based on typical year-end) then the PE should not be assumed as a conclusive sign of change in the trend.

4. *Confirm PE changes by comparing price to revenue, book value per share, and cash.* The next section (below) provides additional ratios for comparison of price data. By using these as well as the traditional PE analysis, you improve the reliability of your information. For example, if all of the indicators wander from established levels, you can conclude that the current price is not typical; current earnings are not typical (or perhaps cyclical and distorting the year-long outcome); or that both sides of the ratio are less than reliable. In that case, the information gained from fundamental/technical analysis is not reliable. But when these additional price-based tests provide confirming information about the historical consistency in price-based trends, that strengthens the reliability of the current PE.

Additional Price-Based Combined Tests

The importance of the PE ratio in evaluating stocks includes the following points:

1. *It is an efficient method for deciding whether a stock is priced at bargain levels.* The higher the PE, the more chance a stock is overpriced. Over many years, studies have concluded that lower-PE stocks out-perform higher-PE stocks. When enthusiasm for a stock drives the price up, the PE follows so the multiple above earnings rises as well. An efficient method for narrowing down a field of potential

investments is to eliminate stocks above a specific PE level. For example, you might seek stocks with low price volatility (measured by trading range), dividend yield, revenue and earnings, *and* moderate to low PE. In this simplified variation of analysis, your rule might be to not even consider stocks whose current PE is greater than 25, for example. (This assumes, of course, that you are also able to eliminate the timing disparities inherent in the PE.) A more conservative investor may set the bar lower; for example, this investor might not care to look at stocks with PE above 15.

2. *The ratio is easily understood.* Most people can easily comprehend the significance of earnings multiples. The PE is popular largely because it is simple, easily computed and tracked, and reliable as a comparable indicator. Many other ratios have to be evaluated based on the industry. For example, profitability in the construction sector is expected to be much lower than information technology or finance. But the PE tends to be more universal, so it is an excellent test of pricing across the board.

3. *The PE can help you to set standards for stocks.* The PE can also be used to set decision points for buy, hold or sell decisions. A *range* for PE is useful for investors, because in the ideal circumstances you want some strong market interest (thus, you don't want the PE to fall too low) while wanting to avoid unjustified price run-up (so the PE should not rise too high). Another version of this is a comparison of PE and core PE (based on core earnings rather than on reported earnings). The greater the gap between these two, the less reliable the historical PE. As an alternative test of fundamental volatility (and price volatility), core PE serves as a way for confirming other emerging trends in price as well as in earnings.

Some additional tests between technical (price) and fundamental results can help to both confirm PE and expand its significance. The first of these is the *price to revenue ratio*. This test, sometimes called the revenue multiplier, is less popular than the PE ratio, but can provide depth in the all-important comparison between price and fundamentals. The current price per share is divided by revenue per share:

Formula: price to revenue ratio

$(P \div S) * 100 = R$

P = price per share
S = revenue per share
R = price to revenue ratio

Excel program

A1 price per share
B2 revenue per share
C1 =SUM(A1/B1)*100

For example, current price per share is $75.93. Latest reported revenue per share is 156.89. The price to revenue ratio is:

($75.93÷$156.89)*100 = 48.4%

In situations where earnings are flat as a percentage of revenue, but represent a growing dollar value each year, the PE ratio can become less revealing. As a measurement, PE has always been assumed as a positive indicator when it remains within a narrow band. However, as long as the number of outstanding shares remaining stationery, you would expect the PR revenue to change as revenue levels expand.

A second of the alternative price-based tests is the *price to book value per share*. This compares price at the end of a quarter or year to the reported book value:

Formula: price to book value per share

(P ÷ B)*100 = R

P = price per share
B = book value per share
R = price to book value per share

Excel program

A1 price per share
B2 book value per share
C1 =SUM(A1/B1)*100

For example, price per share was $75.93 and book value per share was $40.53. The ratio:

$75.93 ÷ $40.53 = 187.3%

A problem with book value is what it includes and excludes. Under GAAP, companies are not required to report pension liabilities even when they are huge. At the same time, numerous inflated intangible assets such as goodwill distort book value, and market value of real estate may be far greater than the acquisition price minus depreciation. The price-to-book by itself is not meaningful; but if you track is as a trend over time, you may discover that a company is being perceived as more valuable or less valuable (based on this ratio). Most analysts agree that market value is a factor of revenue and earnings more than book value; but this serves as a good confirming test.

A more reliable version of this is the *price to tangible book value per share*, in which intangible assets are removed from the equation. This formula at least is more likely to approximate a "liquidation value" of a company, since goodwill and other intangibles cannot be given a sales value. The tangible book value per share is more widely used by analysts than the unadjusted book value; but under GAAP it continues to present problems with accuracy. The formula:

Formula: price to tangible book value per share

$$[P \div (B - I)]*100 = R$$

P = price per share
B = book value per share
I = intangible assets per share
R = price to tangible book value per share

Excel program

A1 price per share
B1 book value per share
C1 intangible assets per share
D1 =SUM((A1/(B1-C1))*100

For example, price per share was $75.93; book value was $40.53; and intangible assets per share was $20.46. The formula:

$$\$75.93 \div (\$40.53 - \$20.46) = 378.3\%$$

One final price-based ratio is the *price to cash ratio*. This is a comparison between current price per share and current cash per share. Included in cash are other liquid assets such as marketable securities – in other words, cash plus assets immediately convertible to cash. The formula:

Formula: price to cash ratio

$$P \div (C + L) = R$$

P = price per share
C = cash on hand per share
L = liquid assets per share
R = price to cash ratio

Excel program

A1   price per share
B1   cash on hand per share
C1   liquid assets per share
D1   =SUM(A1/(B1+C1))

For example, price per share is $75.93. Cash on hand is $2.83 per share and liquid assets total $19.60 per share. The ratio:

$$\$75.93 \div (\$2.83 + \$19.60) = 3.39$$

Use of cash within a company is going to vary greatly by sector; so this ratio is useful only in tracking a trend within one company, or for comparing companies within a single sector. It is also a valuable confirming test when companies allow their long-term debt to rise while creating an offsetting increase in cash balances. (This keeps current ratio at desired levels while creating long-term problems for the company.) The price to cash ratio is also a test of how efficiently a company manages its working capital while avoiding inefficient use of cash balances. Thus the ratio may be tied to a calculation of return on equity and return on invested capital.

The Oddities of Hybrid Analysis

The traditional ratios such as PE are hybrids; this term is used because fundamental and technical analysis are so dissimilar that many people don't consider the viability of combining both. Beyond the PE, little discussion takes place about combining fundamental and technical analysis. This is true because the two sides are based on different influences and forces:

1. *Price is the result of auction bidding; earnings are not.* The dynamic changes in the price of stock can be describing in simple terms. For example, a supply and demand argument tells you that increased supply drives prices down and increased

demand drives prices up. But within the realm of supply and demand, an unknown number of forces are at work: knowledge about earnings strength or weakness, changes in management, insider buy or sell decisions, labor disputes, institutional acquisition or disposal or large blocks, good or bad news among a company's competitors, unrest in some part of the world, election results ... the list can go on endlessly. Price and the influences around it are highly chaotic and unpredictable.

The fundamentals are far more predictable, gives a range of possible outcomes. Compared to prices, the fundamentals usually offer very few surprises. You probably know the likely range of earnings per share for a company you are tracking; revenue and earnings growth is probably going to occur within a known range as well. In companies with volatility in levels of revenue and earnings, investors become uncertain because predictions are difficult if not impossible to make. But compared to price uncertainty, the fundamental tests – especially over many years – reveal trends more dependable than price trends.

2. *The number of causes of movement in revenue and earnings are finite.* It is reassuring to a fundamental analyst that specific trends need to be tracked and interpreted. The set of potential cause and effect is smaller than the technical (price-based) cause and effect. Fundamental change in corporate valuation involves capitalization and working capital. Fundamental change in profitability involves study of revenue trends, costs and expenses. Within that, an analyst considers capitalization, competition, sector strength or weakness, management, and other fundamental realities. The difference between reported and core earnings also affects the analyst's judgment about a company. This does not mean that volatility is always bad news; it does mean that prediction is more difficult when volatility is greater.

3. *Price potentially changes rapidly in either direction based on perceived value; earnings and valuation tend to be more stable and rational.* The changes in price levels can be studied and quantified in many ways. Traditional but overly simplified analyses of price volatility ignore price spikes. A more insightful analysis of typical breadth in trading range is more dependable for identifying price volatility. Combined with a study of the direction the trading range is moving (prices trending up, down, or flat) is also more revealing than traditional volatility studies. When trading range broadens or narrows, that may also signal changes in the near future. Technical analysis is complex because it requires interpretation without any specific, limited standards.

Fundamental analysis is more likely to be based on a universally understood standard. A current ratio of 2 or better is good; when it slips down below 1 or into negative territory, that is bad. In a particular sector, companies usually report net earnings of 4 to 6%. If a company's profits fall below that, it is negative. Virtually any company wants to report a profit, which is always better than reporting a net loss (in spite of what some annual reports claim to the contrary). Most ratios are the latest entry in a trend. Thus, you can quickly and easily determine whether a trend is positive or negative, or whether the results are reasonable predictable or highly volatile.

With these comparisons and differences in mind, it makes sense to combine both sides of the analytical model. The fundamentals can be more easily interpreted and trends established and followed; but financial reports are historical and out of date by the time you have final data. To find out what is taking place today in a highly erratic and dynamic market, you also need to track the technical trends. Specifically, trading range and its emerging trend, price volatility itself, volume, and the hybrid ratios comparing price to fundamentals, are all valuable in confirming fundamental trends, establishing and spotting new trends in price and risk, or setting up an apparent trend for additional confirmation through other tests.

To the text that you identify useful and insightful forms of hybrid analysis, your overall program is going to improve in the process. For the most part, all analysis is going to improve your estimates; but remember, decisions you make based on analysis are at best informed guesses. Good analysis improves your profits, but there are no guarantees, except one: If you make a profit, the government is going to want its share of your profits.

The mathematics applied to stock investing and trading can enlighten or mislead. This depends on whether adequate weight and importance are assigned to calculations, and also whether less relevant calculations are given excess weight. For every investor and trader, the purpose to this mathematical exercise should be to make valid comparisons, quantify risk, and gain insight into the positive or negative choices – both fundamentally and technically – that ultimately have to be made. It's a practical matter. The math is only as good as the relevance of the calculation, and to the extent that it helps improve the rate of profitable outcomes in the individual's portfolio.

Appendix A
Stock Market Formulas:
Summarizing the Essentials

accounts receivable turnover

$$S \div A = T$$

S = credit sales
A = average accounts receivable
T = accounts receivable turnover

accumulated value of 1 per period

$$[D [(1 + R)^n - 1] \div R] \times P = A$$

D = periodic deposit amount
R = periodic interest rate
n = number of periods
P = principal
A = accumulated value of 1 per period

A/D line

$$(M * V) + P = N$$

M = money flow multiplier
V = current volume
P = prior A/D
N = new A/D

Adjusted breadth of trading

$$((H - S) - L)) \div L = B$$

H = high price in the range
S = spike (above price range)
L = low price in the range
B = adjusted breadth of trading

DOI 10.1515/9781501507427-013

adjusted debt ratio

$$(D + S) \div C = R$$

D = long-term debt
S = mandatorily redeemable preferred stock
C = total capitalization
R = adjusted debt ratio

advance/decline price line

$$P \pm N = C$$
P = previous a/d line
N = net advances (+) or declines (-)
C = current a/d line

advance/decline price percentage

$$(A - D) \div (A + D) = P$$
A = advances
D = declines
P = percentage change

after-tax income

$$I * [(100 - R) \div 100] = A$$

I = income before taxes
R = effective tax rate
A = after-tax income

annualized rate (days)

$$(R \div D) * 365 = A$$

R = net return
M = days the position was open
A = annualized yield

annualized rate (months)

$(R \div M) * 12 = A$

R = net return
M = months the position was open
A = annualized yield

average

$(O_1 + O_2 + \ldots O_n) \div E = A$

O = outcomes
E = number of entries $(_n)$
A = average

average collection period

$365 \div T = A$

T = accounts receivable turnover
A = average collection period

average inventory

$(I_a + I_b + \ldots I_n) \div n = A$

I = inventory value
a, b = period used in calculation
n = total number of periods
A = average inventory

bad debts to accounts receivable ratio

$B \div A = R$

B = bad debts reserve
A = accounts receivable
R = bad debts to accounts receivable ratio

Bollinger Band 20-day average

$(V_1 \ldots V_{20}) \div 10 = A$
V_1 = first value
V_{20} = final value
A = average

Bollinger Band deviation per period

$V_X - A = D$

V_X = value
A = average of the field
D = deviation

Bollinger Band square of deviation

$D^2 = S$

D^2 = deviation squared
S = square of the deviation

Bollinger Band sum of squared deviation

$S_1 + \ldots S_{20} = SD$
S_1 = squared deviation, first value
S_{20} = squared deviation, final value
SD = sum of squared deviations

Bollinger Band sum of squared deviation average

$\sqrt{SD}$

$\sqrt{SD}$ = square root of the average of squared deviations

book value per share

$(N - P) \div S = B$

N = net worth
P = preferred stock
S = average shares of common stock issued and outstanding

B = book value per share

breadth of trading

$(H - L) \div L = B$

H = high price in the range
L = low price in the range
B = breadth of trading

breakeven return

$I \div (100 - R) = B$

I = rate of inflation
R = effective tax rate (federal and state)
B = breakeven return

cash-on-cash return

$C \div I = R$
C = annual cash flow
    I = cash investment
    R = cash-on-cash return

cash ratio

$(C + M) \div L = R$

C = cash
M = marketable securities
L = current liabilities
R = cash ratio

change in volume

$(C - P) \div P = V$

C = current period volume
P = past period volume
V = change in volume

common stock ratio

$$S \div C = R$$

S = common stock issued and outstanding
C = total capitalization
R = common stock ratio

component percentage, market capitalization

$$C \div SC = W$$

C = component weight
SC = sum of component weights
W = weight percentage

component percentage, price capitalization

$$P \div SC = W$$

P = price of each component
SC = sum of components
W = weight percentage

component weight, market capitalization

$$S * P = C$$

S = shares issued and outstanding
P = price per share
C = component weight

core debt to capitalization ratio

$$L \div (T \pm A) = C$$

L = long-term debt
T = total capitalization
A = core valuation adjustments
C = core debt to capitalization ratio

core earnings per share

$$(N \pm A) \div S = C$$

N = net earnings
A = core earnings adjustments
S = shares outstanding
C = core earnings per share

core net worth

$$N \pm A \pm L = C$$

N = net worth as reported
A = adjustments to reported value of assets
L = adjustments to reported value of liabilities
C = core net worth

core PE ratio

$$P \div (E \pm A) = C$$

P = price per share
E = earnings per share as reported
A = core earnings adjustments
C = core P/E ratio

core return on equity

$$C \div E = R$$

C = core earnings (profit) for a one-year period
E = shareholders' equity
R = core return on equity

core return on total capitalization

$$(C + I) \div (E + B) = R$$

C = core earnings (profit) for a one-year period
I = interest paid on long-term bonds
E = shareholders' equity

B = par value of long-term bonds
R = core return on total capitalization

core tangible book value per share

$$(N - P - I \pm C) \div S = B$$

N = net worth
P = preferred stock
I = intangible assets
C = core net worth adjustments
S = average shares issued and outstanding
B = core tangible book value per share

cumulative return

$$(C - I) \div I = R$$

C = current value
I = initial value
R = cumulative return

current ratio

$$A \div L = R$$

A = current assets
L = current liabilities
R = current ratio

current yield (bond)

$$A \div P = Y$$

A = annual interest
P = price of the bond
Y = current yield

debt capitalization ratio

$D \div C = R$

D = long-term debt
C = total capital
R = debt capitalization ratio

debt equity ratio

$L \div E = R$

L = total liabilities
E = total equity
R = debt equity ratio

debt ratio

$L \div A = R$

L = total liabilities
A = total assets
D = debt ratio

declining balance depreciation

$((B - P) \div R) * A = D$

B = basis of asset
P = prior depreciation deducted
R = recovery period
A = acceleration percentage
D = annual depreciation

dividend payout ratio

$D \div E = R$

D = dividend per share
E = earnings per share (EPS)
R = dividend payout ratio

dividend yield

$$D \div P = Y$$

D = dividend per share
P = current price per share
Y = dividend yield

earnings per share

$$N \div S = E$$

N = net earnings
S = shares outstanding
E = earnings per share

effective tax rate (federal)

$$L \div T = R$$

L = liability for taxes
T = taxable income
R – effective tax rate

effective tax rate (total)

$$(FL + SL + LL) \div T = R$$

FL = liability for taxes, federal
FT = liability for taxes, state
LL = liability for taxes, local
T = taxable income (on federal return)
R = effective tax rate, total

equity dividend yield

$$C \div N = Y$$

C = net cash flow
N = net cash paid
Y = equity dividend yield

Exponent

$2 \div N = W$
N = number of fields
W = weight (exponent)

exponential moving average (EMA)

$[(L*W) + O]*(1-W)=A$

L = latest value
W = weight (exponent)
O = old average
A = new average

gross margin

$G \div R = M$

G =gross profit
R = revenue
M = gross margin

high/low index

$(R_1... R_{10}) \div 10 = I$

R = record-high percentage (for days 1 through 10)
I = high/low index

high/low line

$N \pm P = L$

N = net new high, current
P = net new high, prior
L = high/low line

high/low percentage

$$(H - L) \div T = P$$

H = 52-week highs
L = 52-week lows
T = total issues
P = high/low percentage

interest

$$P * R * T = I$$

P = principal
R = interest rate
T = time
I = interest

inventory turnover

$$C \div A = T$$

C = cost of goods sold (annual)
A = average inventory
T = turnover

large block ratio

$$B \div V = R$$

B = large block volume in shares
V = total volume in shares
R = large block ratio

MACD calculations

$$12\text{-}EMA - 26\text{-}EMA = M$$
$$9\text{-}EMA = S$$
$$M - S = H$$

12-EMA = 12-day EMA
26-EMA = 26-day EMA

M = MACD line
9-EMA = 9-day average of MACD line
S = signal line
H – histogram

market capitalization

$$S * P = C$$

S = shares issued and outstanding
P = price per share
C = market capitalization

money flow index

$$100 - ((100 \div (1 + M)) = I$$

M = money flow ratio
I = money flow index

money flow multiplier

$$((C - L) - (H - C)) \div (H - L) = M$$

C = close
L = low
H = high
M = money flow multiplier

money flow ratio

$$P \div N = R$$

P = positive MF sessions (out of 14)
N = negative MF sessions (out of 14)
R = money flow ratio

mutual fund expense ratio

$$E \div (A * U) = R$$

E = total operating expenses

A = average NAV
U = outstanding units
R = expense ratio

mutual fund liquidity ratio

$$C \div A = R$$

C = cash and cash equivalents
A = total assets
R = liquidity ratio

mutual fund total return

$$V + C - I = R$$

V = value of the account
C = cash distributions received
I = initial investment
R = total return

mutual fund total yield

$$(V + C - I) \div I = TR$$

V = value of the account
C = cash distributions received
I = initial investment
TR = total yield

mutual fund yield

$$I \div N = Y$$

I = income distribution per share
N = NAV
Y = yield

net after-tax annualized return

$$I\,((100 - R) \div 100)\,(\div M * 12) = A$$

I = income from investments
R = effective tax rate (federal and state)
M = months held
A = net after-tax annualized return

net asset value

$$(A - L) \div U = N$$

A = assets
L = liabilities
U = units outstanding
N = net asset value

net new 52-week high

$$H - L = N$$

H = 52-week new highs
L = 52-week new lows
N = net new highs

net return on equity

$$P \div (E - S) = R$$

P = profit for a one-year period
E = shareholders' equity
S = mandatorily redeemable preferred stock
R = net return on equity

nominal yield (bond)

$$A \div F = N$$

A = annual interest
F = face value of the bond
N = nominal yield

on balance volume (OBV)

Higher closing price: $P + C = O$
   or
Lower closing price: $P - C = O$

P = previous OBV cumulative value
C = current volume
O = revised OBV

operating profit margin

$E \div R = M$

E = expenses
R = revenue
M = operating profit margin

payback ratio

$I \div C = R$

I = cash invested
C = net cash flow
R = ratio

percent above MA

$S \div T = P$

S = number of stocks trading above MA
T = total stocks in the index
P = percent above MA

percentage price change

$C \div O = P$

C = change
O = opening price
P = percentage price change

preferred stock dividend coverage

$$N \div P = R$$

N = net income
P = preferred dividend
R = ratio

preferred stock ratio

$$P \div C = R$$

P = preferred stock
C = total capitalization
R = preferred stock ratio

present value of 1

$$1 \div (1 + R)^n = P$$

R = periodic interest rate
n = periods
P = present value factor

price/earnings ratio

$$P \div E = R$$

P = price per share
E = earnings per share
R = p/e ratio

price to book value per share

$$(P \div B) * 100 = R$$

P = price per share
B = book value per share
R = price to book value per share

price to cash ratio

$$P \div (C + L) = R$$

P = price per share
C = cash on hand per share
L = liquid assets per share
R = price to cash ratio

price to revenue ratio

$$(P \div S) * 100 = R$$

P = price per share
S = revenue per share
R = price to revenue ratio

price to tangible book value per share

$$[P \div (B - I)] * 100 = R$$

P = price per share
B = book value per share
I = intangible assets per share
R = price to tangible book value per share

put/call ratio

$$P \div C = R$$

P = put volume
C = call volume
R = put/call ratio

quick assets ratio

$$(A - I) \div L = R$$

A = current assets
I = inventory
L = current liabilities
R = quick assets ratio

rate of growth in core earnings

$$(CC - PC) \div PC = CE$$

CC = current year core earnings
PC = past year core earnings
CE = rate of growth in core earnings

rate of growth in expenses

$$(C - P) \div P = E$$

C = current year expenses
P = past year expenses
E = rate of growth in expenses

rate of growth in net earnings

$$(C - P) \div P = R$$

C = current year net earnings
P = past year net earnings
R = rate of growth in net earnings

rate of growth in operating profit

$$(C - P) \div P = R$$

C = current year operating profit
P = past year operating profit
R = rate of growth in operating profit

rate of growth in revenue

$$(C - P) \div P = R$$

C = current year revenue
P = past year revenue
R = rate of growth in revenue

rate of return

$$(C - B) \div B = R$$

C = current value (or sales price)
B = original cost or basis
R = rate of return

ratio of expenses to revenue

$$E \div R = P$$

E = expenses
R = revenue
P = ratio (percentage)

raw money flow

$$((H + L + C) \div 3) * V = R$$

H = high price
L = low price
C = closing price
V = volume
R = raw money flow

record-high percentage

$$(H \div (H + L)) * 100 = P$$

H = new highs
L = new lows
P = record-high percentage

relative strength

$$AG \div AL = RS$$
AG = average gains (of the most recent 14 sessions)
AL = average losses (of the most recent 14 sessions)
RS = relative strength

relative strength index (RSI)

$100 - ((100 \div (1 + RS)) = RSI$

RS = relative strength
RSI = relative strength index

return if exercised

$(S - I) \div (I - O) = R$

S = sales price of stock
I = invested capital
O = option premium received
R = return

return on book value of capital

$(P - T) \div C = R$

P = net operating profit
T = taxes
C = invested capital
R = return on invested capital

return on covered calls

$(S - B) + P = R$

S = strike of the option (* 100)
B = basis in underlying stock
P = premium received for option
R = return

return on equity

$P \div E = R$

P = profit for a one-year period
E = shareholders' equity
R = return on equity

return on invested capital

$$(S - I) \div I = R$$

S = sales price
I = invested capital
R = return

return on investment net of margin

$$(V - B - I) \div C = R$$

    V = current market value
        B = basis (including leveraged portion)
    I = interest cost
    C = cash invested net of margin
    R = return on investment net of margin

return on long options

$$(S - P) \div P = R$$

S = closing net sales price
P = opening net purchase price
R = net return

return on net investment

$$(S - I - C) \div I = R$$

S = sales price
I = invested capital
C = costs
R = return

return on net investment with net cost basis

$$(S - I) \div (I + C) = R$$

S = sales price
I = invested capital
C = costs
R = return

return on purchase price

$$[(S - I) \div I] * 100 = R$$

S = sales price
P = purchase price
R = return

return on total capitalization

$$(P + I) \div (E + B) = R$$

P = profit for a one-year period
I = interest paid on long-term bonds
E = shareholders' equity
B = par value of long-term bonds
R = return on equity

return on uncovered calls

$$P - C - S = R$$

P = premium received
C = current market value of stock
S = strike price of call
R = return (profit or loss)

rule of 113

$$113 \div i = Y$$

i = interest rate
Y = years required to triple

rule of 69

$$(69 \div i) + 0.35 = Y$$

i = interest rate
Y = years required to double

rule of 72

$$72 \div i = Y$$

i = interest rate
Y = years required to double

short interest ratio

$$S \div (D \div 30) = R$$

S = short interest
D = total monthly volume
R = short interest ratio

Simple interest

$$P \times R = I$$

P = principal amount
R = annual rate
I = interest (per year)

standard deviation

$$\sigma = \sqrt{\frac{1}{N} \sum_{i=1}^{N} (x_i - \mu)^2}$$

σ = standard deviation
N = addition of values
Σ = range of values from 1 to n
χ_1 = individual values
μ = average

stochastic oscillator

$$(C - L) \div (H - L) * 100 = \%K$$
$$3\text{-}SMA \text{ of } \%K = \%D$$

C = closing price, current
L = lowest low, last 14 periods
H = highest high, last 14 periods

%K = % K average
3-SMA – simple moving average, last 3 %K
%D = %D average

straight-line depreciation

$A \div R = D$

A = basis of asset
R = recovery period
D = annual depreciation

tangible book value per share

$(N - P - I) \div S = B$

N = net worth
P = preferred stock
I = intangible assets
S = average shares of common stock issued and outstanding
B = tangible book value per share

taxable income

1) $I - A = G$
2) $G - E - D = T$

I = total income, all sources
A = adjustments
G = adjusted gross income
E = exemptions
D = deductions (itemized or standard)
T = taxable income

total return per year

$(C + I - B) \div B \div Y = R$

C = capital gains
I = total net income
B = basis
Y = years held
R = total return

total return with dividends

$$(S - I - C + D) \div I = R$$

S = sales price
I = invested capital
C = costs
D = dividends earned
R = return

weighted average capital, half-months

$$[(P_1 * v) + (P_2 * v) + (P_3 * v)] \div 24 = W$$

P_1 = period 1 (number of months)
P_2 = period 2 (number of months)
P_3 = period 3 (number of months)
v = value
P_t = 24 half-months per year
W – weighted average capital

weighted average capital, months

$$[(P_1 * v) + (P_2 * v)] \div 12 = W$$

P_1 = period 1 (number of months)
P_2 = period 2 (number of months)
v = value
W – weighted average capital

weighted average interest rate

$$[(L_1 \times R_1) + (L_2 \times R_2)] \div L_t = A$$

L_1 = balance, investment 1
L_2 = balance, investment 2
L_t = total balances of investments
R_1 = rate on investment 1
R_2 = rate on investment 2
A = average rate

working capital turnover

$$R \div (A - L) = T$$

R = one year's revenue
A = current assets
L = current liabilities
T = working capital turnover

Appendix B
Excel Program Entries:
Automating the Formulas

accounts receivable turnover

    A1 credit sales
    B1 average accounts receivable
    C1 =SUM(A1/B1)

accumulated value of 1 per period

    A1: $FV(r/n, y*d)$
    r = interest rate
    n = number of periods per year
    y = number of years
    d = amount of periodic deposits

A/D line

    A1 money flow multiplier
    B1 volume
    C1 prior A/D
    D1 =SUM(A1*B1)+C1

Adjusted breadth of trading

    A1 high price in the range
    B1 spike above price range
    C1 low price in the range
    D1 =SUM((A1-B1)-C1)/C1

adjusted debt ratio

    A1 long-term debt
    B1 mandatorily redeemable preferred stock
    C1 total capitalization
    D1 =SUM(A1+B1)/C1

DOI 10.1515/9781501507427-014

advance/decline price line

A1 previous a/d line
B1 net advances or declines
C1 =SUM(A1+B1) or =SUM(A1-B1)

advance/decline price percentage

A1 advances
B1 declines
C1 =SUM(A1-B1)/(A1+B1)

after-tax income

A1 income before taxes
B1 effective tax rate
C1 =SUM(A1*(100-B1)/100)

annualized rate (days)

A1 net return
B1 = days the position was open
C1 =SUM(A1/B1)*365

annualized rate (months)

A1 net return
B1 = months the position was open
C1 =SUM(A1/B1)*12

average

A1 entry 1
B1 entry 2
C1 entry 3
D1 entry 4
D2 =AVERAGE(A1:D1)

average collection period

A1 accounts receivable turnover
B1 =SUM(365/A1)

average inventory

A1   inventory value a
B1   inventory value b
C1 ... inventory value n
C2   =SUM(A1+B1+C1)/n

bad debts to accounts receivable ratio

A1   bad debt reserve
B1   accounts receivable
C1   =SUM(A1/B1)

book value per share

A1   net worth
B1   preferred stock
C1   average shares of common stock issued and outstanding
D1   =SUM (A1-B1)/C1

Breadth of trading

A1   high price in the range
B1   low price in the range
C1   =SUM(A1-B1)/B1

breakeven return

A1   rate of inflation
B1   effective tax rate
C1   =-SUM(A1/(100-B1))

cash-on-cash return

A1: annual cash flow
B1: cash investment
C1: =SUM(A1/B1)

cash ratio

A1   current assets
B1   marketable securities

    C1 current liabilities
    D1 =SUM(A1+B1)/C1

change in volume

    A1 current period volume
    B1 past period volume
    C1 =SUM(A1-B1)/B1

common stock ratio

    A1 common stock issued and outstanding
    B1 total capitalization
    C1 =SUM(A1/B1)

component percentage, market capitalization

    A1 shares issued and outstanding
    B1 price per share
    C1 =SUM(A1*B1)

component percentage, price capitalization

    A1 price of each component
    B1 sum of components
    C1 =SUM(A1/B1)

component weight, market capitalization

    A1 shares issued and outstanding
    B1 price per share
    C1 =SUM(A1*B1)

core debt to capitalization ratio

    A1 long-term debt
    B1 total capitalization
    C1 core valuation adjustments
    D1 =SUM(A1/((B1-C1))

core earnings per share

A1 net earnings
B1 core earnings adjustments
C1 shares outstanding
D1 =SUM(A1-B1)/C1

core net worth

A1 net worth
B1 adjustments to assets
C1 adjustments to liabilities
D1 =SUM(A1+B1-C1)

core PE ratio

A1 price per share
B1 earnings per share
C1 core earnings adjustments per share
D1 =SUM(A1/(B1-C1))

core return on equity

A1 core earnings
B1 shareholders' equity
C1 =SUM(A1/B1)

core return on total capitalization

A1 core earnings, one year
B1 interest paid
C1 shareholders' equity
D1 par value, long-term bonds
E1 =SUM((A1+B1)/(C1+D1))

core tangible book value per share

A1 net worth
B1 preferred stock
C1 intangible assets
D1 core net worth adjustments
E1 average shares issued and outstanding

F1 =SUM(A1-B1-C1-D1)/E1

cumulative return

A1 current value
B1 initial value
C1 =SUM(A1-B1)/B1

current ratio

A1 current assets
B1 current liabilities
C1 =SUM(A1/B1)

current yield (bond)

A1: annual yield
B1: price of the bond
C1: =SUM(A1/B1)

debt capitalization ratio

A1 long-term debt
B1 total capital
C1 =SUM(A1/B1)*100

debt equity ratio

A1 total liabilities
B1 total equity
C1 =SUM(A1/B1)

debt ratio

A1 total liabilities
B1 total assets
C1 =SUM(A1/B1)*100

declining balance depreciation

A1 basis of asset
B1 prior depreciation deducted

C1   recovery period
D1   acceleration percentage
E1   =SUM((A1-B1)/C1)*D1

dividend payout ratio

A1   dividend per share
B1   earnings per share (EPS)
C1   =SUM(A1/B1)

dividend yield

A1   dividend per share
B1   current price per share
C1   =SUM(A1/B1)

earnings per share

A1   net earnings
B1   shares outstanding
C1   =SUM(A1/B1)

effective tax rate (federal)

A1   liability for taxes
B1   taxable income
C1   =SUM(A1/B1)

effective tax rate (total)

A1   liability for taxes, federal
B1   liability for taxes, state
C1   liability for taxes, local
D1   taxable income
E1   =SUM(A1+B1+C1)/D1

equity dividend yield

A1: net cash flow
B1: down payment
C1: =SUM(A1/B1)

exponent

A1: =SUM(2/N)

exponential moving average (EMA)

A1: latest value
A2: weight
A3: old average
A4 =SUM((A1*A2)+A3)*(1-A2)

gross margin

A1 gross profit
B1 revenue
C1 =SUM(A1/B1)

high/low index

A1:A10 record-high percentages
B10   =SUM(A1:A10)/10

high/low line

A1 net new high, current
B1 net new high, prior
C1 =SUM(A1+B1)

high/low percentage

A1 52-week highs
B1 52-week lows
C1 total issues
D1 =SUM(A1-B1)/C1

interest

A1 principal
B1 interest rate
C1 time
D1 =SUM(A1*B1*C1)

inventory turnover

A1   cost of goods sold (annual)
B1   average inventory
C1   =SUM(A1/B1)

large block ratio

A1   large block volume
B1   total volume
C1   =SUM(A1/B1)

MACD calculations

MACD line:
   A1   12-EMA
   B1   26-EMA
   C1   =SUM(A1-B1)
Signal line:
   A1   MACD, 9 days
   A2   =SUM(A1/9)
Histogram:
   A1   MACD line
   B1   signal line
   C1   =SUM(A1-B1)

market capitalization

A1   shares issued and outstanding
B1   price per share
C1   =SUM (A1*B1)

money flow index

A1   money flow ratio
B1   =SUM(100-(100/(1+A1)))

money flow multiplier

A1   close
B1   low
C1   high

    D1 =SUM((A1-B1)-(C1-A1))/(C1-B1)

money flow ratio

    A1 positive MF sessions
    B1 negative MF sessions
    C1 =SUM(A1/B1)

mutual fund expense ratio

    A1 total operating expenses
    B1 average NAV
    C1 outstanding units
    D1 =SUM(A1/(B1*C1))

mutual fund liquidity ratio

    A1 cash and cash equivalents
    B1 total assets
    C1 =SUM(A1/B1)

mutual fund total return

    A1 value of the account
    B1 cash distributions received
    C1 initial investment
    D1 =SUM(A1+B1-C1)

mutual fund total yield

    A1 value of the account
    B1 cash distributions received
    C1 initial investment
    D1 =SUM(A1+B1-C1)/C1

mutual fund yield

    A1 income distribution per share
    B1 NAV
    C1 =SUM(A1/B1)

net after-tax annualized return

A1   income from investments
B1   effective tax rate
C1   months held
D1   =SUM(A1*(100-B1)/100)
E1   =SUM(D1/C1*12)

net asset value

A1   assets
B1   liabilities
C1   units outstanding
D1   =SUM(A1-B1)/C1

net new 52-week high

A1   52-week new highs
B1   52-week new lows
C1   =SUM(A1-B1)

net return on equity

A1   net profit
B1   shareholders' equity
C1   mandatorily redeemable preferred stock
D1   =SUM(A1)/(B1-C1)

nominal yield (bond)

A1:   annual interest
B1:   face value of the bond
C1:   =SUM(A1/B1)

on balance volume (OBV)

Higher closing price:
    A1   previous OBV
    B1   current volume
    C1   =SUM(A1+B1)
Lower closing price:
    A1   previous OBV

B1 current volume

C1 =SUM(A1-B1)

operating profit margin

A1 expenses

B1 revenue

C1 =SUM(A1/B1)

payback ratio

A1 cash invested

B1 net cash flow

C1==SUM(A1/B1)

percent above MA

A1 number of stocks trading above MA

B1 total stocks in the index

C1 =SUM(A1/B1)

percentage price change

A1 change

B1 opening price

C1 =SUM(A1/B1)

preferred stock dividend coverage

A1 net income

B1 preferred dividend

C1 =SUM(A1/B1)

preferred stock ratio

A1 Preferred stock

B1 total capitalization

C1 =SUM(A1/B1)

present value of 1

A1: =PV(r,p,0,FV)

r = interest rate
P = number of periods
0 = starting point (beginning of period)
FV = future value

price/earnings ratio

A1 price per share
B1 = earnings per share
C1 =SUM(A1/B1)

price to book value per share

A1 price per share
B2 book value per share
C1 =SUM(A1/B1)*100

price to cash ratio

A1 price per share
B1 cash on hand per share
C1 liquid assets per share
D1 =SUM(A1/(B1+C1)

price to revenue ratio

A1 price per share
B2 revenue per share
C1 =SUM(A1/B1)*100

price to tangible book value per share

A1 price per share
B1 book value per share
C1 intangible assets per share
D1 =SUM((A1/(B1-C1))*100

put/call ratio

A1 put volume
B1 call volume
C1 =SUM(A1/B1)

quick assets ratio

A1 current assets
B1 inventory
C1 current liabilities
D1 =SUM(A1-B1)/C1

rate of growth in core earnings

A1 current year core earnings
B1 past year core earnings
C1 =SUM(A1-B1)/B1

rate of growth in expenses

A1 current year expenses
B1 past year expenses
C1 =SUM(A1-B1)/B1

rate of growth in net earnings

A1 current year net earnings
B1 past year net earnings
C1 =SUM(A1-B1)/B1

rate of growth in operating profit

A1 current year operating profit
B1 past year operating profit
C   =SUM(A1-B1)/B1

rate of growth in revenue

A1 current year revenue
B1 past year revenue
C1 =SUM(A1-B1)/B1

rate of return

A1: current value
B1: original cost or basis
C1: =SUM(A1-B1)/B1

ratio of expenses to revenue

A1 expenses
B1 revenue
C1 =SUM(A1/B1)

raw money flow

A1 high price
B1 low price
C1 closing price
D1 volume
E1 =SUM((A1+B1+C1)/3)*D1

record-high percentage

A1 new highs
B1 new lows
C1 =SUM(A1/(A1+B1))*100

relative strength

A1 average gains (of the most recent 14 sessions)
B1 average losses (of the most recent 14 sessions)
RS =SUM(A1/B1)

relative strength index (RSI)

A1 RS
B1 =SUM(100-(100/(1+A1)))

return if exercised

A1 sales price of stock
B1 invested capital
C1 option premium received
D1 =SUM(A1-B1)/(B1-C1)

return on book value of capital

A1 net operating profit
B1 taxes

    C1 invested capital
    D1 =SUM(A1-B1)/C1

return on covered calls

    A1 strike of the option
    B1 basis in the stock
    C1 premium received
    D1 =SUM(A1-B1)+C1

return on equity

    A1 profit for a one-year period
    B1 shareholders' equity
    C1 =SUM(A1/B1)

return on invested capital

    A1 sales price
    B1 invested capital
    C1 =SUM(A1-B1)/B1

return on investment net of margin

    A1 current market value
    B1 basis
    C1 interest cost
    D1 cash invested
    E1 =SUM (A1-B1-C1)/D1

return on long options

    A1 closing net sales price
    B1 opening net purchase price
    C1 =SUM(A1-B1)/B1

return on net investment

    A1 sales price
    B1 invested capital
    C1 costs
    D1 =SUM(A1-B1-C1)/B1

return on net investment with net cost basis

A1   sales price
B1   invested capital
C1   costs
D1   =SUM(A1-B1)/(B1+C1)

return on purchase price

A1   sales price
B1   purchase price
C1   =SUM((A1-B1)/B1)*100

return on total capitalization

A1   profit for a one-year period
B1   interest paid on long-term bonds
C1   shareholders' equity
D1   par value of long-term bonds
E1   =SUM(A1+B1)/(C1+D1)

return on uncovered calls

A1   premium received
B1   strike price of call
C1   current market value of stock
D1   =SUM(A1-B1-C1)

rule of 113

A1: =SUM(113/interest rate)

rule of 69

A1: =SUM (69/interest rate)+0.35

rule of 72

A1: =SUM(72/interest rate)

short interest ratio

  A1   short interest
  B1   accumulated daily volume for 30 days
  C1   =SUM(A1/(B1/30))

simple interest

  A1   principal amount
  B1   annual rate
  C1   =SUM(A1*B1)

standard deviation

  A1 ... A20   each session's closing price
  B2 ... B20   each session's net change
  C2 ... C20   =SUM(B2*100) (copy and paste for each cell in 'B')
  D20   =STDEV(C2:C20)
  E20   =SQRT(252)*E20

stochastic oscillator

  %K:
      A1   closing price, current
      B1   lowest low, last 14 periods
      C1   highest high, last 14 periods
      D1   =SUM(A1-B1)/(C1-B1)*100
  % D:
      A2   %K, latest day
      B2   %K, second latest day
      C2   %K, third latest day
      D2   =SUM(A1+B1+C1)/3

straight-line depreciation

  A1   basis of asset
  B1   recovery period
  C1   =SUM(A1/B1)

tangible book value per share

  A1   net worth

B1 preferred stock
C1 intangible assets
D1 average shares of common stock issued and outstanding
E1 =SUM(A1-B1-C1)/D1

taxable income

A1 total income, all sources
B1 adjustments
C1 exemptions
D1 deductions
E1 =SUM(A1-B1-C1-D1)

total return per year

A1: capital gains
B1: total net income
C1: basis
D1: years held
E1: =SUM((A1+B1-C1)/C1/D1)

total return with dividends

A1 sales price
B1 invested capital
C1 costs
D1 dividends earned
E1 =SUM(A1-B1-C1+D1)/B1

weighted average capital, half-months

A1 period 1 (number of months)
B1 value (capital in period 1)
C1 period 2 (number of months)
D1 value (capital in period 2)
E1 period 3 (number of months)
F1 value (capital in period 2)
G1 =SUM((A1*B1)+(C1*D1)+(E1*F1))/24

weighted average capital, half-months

A1 period 1 (number of months)

B1 value (capital in period 1)
C1 period 2 (number of months)
D1 value (capital in period 2)
E1 =SUM((A1*B1)+(C1*D1))/12

weighted average interest rate

A1: investment balance # 1
A2: investment balance # 2
A3: =SUM(A1+A2)
B1: rate, investment # 1 (decimal form)
B2: rate, investment # 2 (decimal form)
C1: =SUM(A1*B1)
C2: =SUM(A2*B2)
C3: =SUM(C1+C2)
D1: =SUM(C3/A3)*100

working capital turnover

A1 one year's revenue
B1 current assets
C1 current liabilities
D1 =SUM(A1/(B1-C1))

Index